Cartographies of Youth Resistance

*The publisher and the University of California Press
Foundation gratefully acknowledge the generous support of the
Ahmanson Foundation Endowment Fund in Humanities.*

Cartographies of Youth Resistance

HIP-HOP, PUNK, AND URBAN
AUTONOMY IN MEXICO

Maurice Rafael Magaña

UNIVERSITY OF CALIFORNIA PRESS

University of California Press
Oakland, California

© 2020 by Maurice Rafael Magaña

Library of Congress Cataloging-in-Publication Data

Names: Magaña, Maurice Rafael, 1979– author.
Title: Cartographies of youth resistance : hip-hop, punk, and urban autonomy
    in Mexico / Maurice Rafael Magaña.
Description: Oakland, California : University of California Press, [2020] |
    Includes bibliographical references and index.
Identifiers: LCCN 2020014436 (print) | LCCN 2020014437 (ebook) |
    ISBN 9780520344617 (cloth) | ISBN 9780520344624 (paperback) |
    ISBN 9780520975583 (epub)
Subjects: LCSH: Youth—Political activity—Mexico—Oaxaca (State)
    | Subculture—Mexico—Oaxaca (State) | Youth—Mexico—Oaxaca
    (State)—Social conditions.
Classification: LCC HQ799.2.P6 M34 2020 (print) |
    LCC HQ799.2.P6 (ebook) | DDC 305.2350972/74—dc23
LC record available at https://lccn.loc.gov/2020014436
LC ebook record available at https://lccn.loc.gov/2020014437

29   28   27   26   25   24   23   22   21   20
10   9   8   7   6   5   4   3   2   1

For Jeff Juris,
whose conviction, brilliance, and humble generosity
inspire me to do and be better.

For Jyri and Bety,
who refused to let others die alone or be forgotten.

For Rafa,
who showed me how to move in between worlds with dignity.
Que en paz descansen.

CONTENTS

ILLUSTRATIONS

MAPS

TABLES

FIGURES

PREFACE

The city of Oaxaca de Juárez, initially named Antequera, was founded in 1529 in a small valley occupied by a group of Zapotec Indians. It is an example of [a] sixteenth-century colonial city and of town planning, given that it retains its [origin] in the form of [a] checkerboard with square blocks and portals on all four sides of the square. To [plot] the Villa de Antequera, Alonso García Bravo chose a point midway between the rivers Jalatlaco, Atoyac and the *Cerro del Fortin*. The [plan] initiated from a central plaza basis of two axes, east-west and north-south, with a slight tilt to compensate for the lighting and sunlight, due to its latitude.

The centre of the city remains the centre of economic, political, social, religious and cultural activities that give dynamism to the city. It retains its iconic architecture and the buildings representative of a cultural tradition of more than four centuries of art and history. A total of 1,200 historic monuments [have] been inventoried and listed. The major religious monuments, the superb patrician townhouses and whole streets lined with other dwellings combine to create a harmonious cityscape, and reconstitute the image of a former colonial city whose monumental aspect has been kept intact. Fine architectural quality also characterizes the nineteenth-century buildings in this city that was the birthplace of Benito Juárez and which, in 1872, adopted the name of Oaxaca de Juárez. Being located in a highly seismic zone, the architecture of the city of Oaxaca is characterized by thick walls and low buildings. The mestizo population keeps alive both traditions and ancestral customs.

—UNESCO WORLD HERITAGE CENTRE

The *zócalo* (main plaza) has been the economic, social, and political center of the provincial city of Oaxaca since colonial times. The zocalo's open square is bordered by the Catedral Metropolitana de Nuestra Señora de la Asunción on the northern end, and by the state capitol building with its stone arches on the southern end. The façade of the cathedral, whose construction began in 1535, is made of the green cantera stone typical of the colonial architecture of the city, and is the reason the city is known as la Verde Antequera. The city center in general, but the zocalo and surrounding few blocks in particular, are the backbone of heritage tourism in the city and the site of frequent ethnic festivals and cultural events. Domestic and international tourists come to Oaxaca to experience Mexico's pre-Hispanic past, Spanish colonial period, and the Indigenous Mexico of today (Wood 2008).

The normal festivities and carefully curated public spaces of the historic city center were nowhere to be found in July 2006, however. Instead of state-sponsored cultural events, that year the zocalo was the site of a massive encampment of tens of thousands of teachers, activists, students, housewives, campesinos, and punks. The encampment completely engulfed the main square and spilled out into the surrounding streets, where a dense network of tents, tarps, plastic sheets, and signs bearing political grievances and slogans unsettled any image of Oaxaca City as an engine of heritage tourism (figure 1). Along with the ethnic festivals and state-sponsored events went the tourists—though they were not the only ones missing from Oaxaca's streets and public spaces that summer. Perhaps even more shocking than the encampments and near complete absence of tourism was the total absence of uniformed police from the streets of Oaxaca, as well as the fact that the governor and much of his cabinet had fled the state for several months. In the governor's place were hundreds of creative depictions of him, in both two and three dimensions. Graffiti, murals, puppets, and dolls portrayed the governor as a pig, rat, devil, and criminal. Instead of uniformed police, the streets were patrolled by a community security force composed of teachers and youth from local anarchist and punk collectives. Decisions were made through popular assembly and consensus, rather than by politicians, in the zocalo and other public spaces of the historic city center.

Despite the weight and high stakes involved in this experiment with radical direct democracy and the looming threat of state and paramilitary repression, Oaxaca City was not void of festivities during those months.

FIGURE I. Zocalo encampment, June 2006. Photo credit: Susy Chávez Herrera.

The social movement that arose as a response to the violent eviction of striking teachers from the zocalo displaced the governor, his cabinet, and police from the city and soon began to organize their own festivals and cultural events. Popular resistance and grassroots power were celebrated widely even in the face of political violence carried out by paramilitaries and eventually by federal police. Although the normally serene blue skies of the Verde Antequera were hidden underneath a cloak of smoke from the burning tires and buses used in a citywide network of self-defense barricades, the city was also animated by thousands of Oaxacans dancing in the streets to the sounds of irreverent songs of government corruption, political rats, and women promising to serve up scrambled *huevos* to their political representatives (figure 2).

OAXACA CITY, MEXICO, JUNE 2009

Three years after the popular takeover of Oaxaca City, picturesque blue skies and the lush green mountains cradling this colonial gem were once

FIGURE 2. Youth activists and artists dancing in *calenda* procession in the streets of Oaxaca in 2010. Photo credit: Susy Chávez Herrera.

again visible. Instead of the social movement encampment, the zocalo was full of families enjoying lazy afternoons together. The metal benches located throughout the square held multiple generations of Oaxacans, including lovestruck teenagers enjoying their time away from the watchful eyes of their parents. Small children chased each other around the plaza and played with colorful and festive balloons and inexpensive Chinese-made toys purchased from street vendors. Many tourists enjoyed the benches as well, while others took in the public square from the half dozen restaurants with outdoor seating that dot the perimeter. Tourists and locals alike were treated to dozens of free cultural events and festivals showcasing the folklore, artisanal goods, and gastronomy of Oaxaca's sixteen Indigenous ethnic groups.

Police once again roamed the streets—though they multiplied both in terms of raw numbers and in terms of the local, state, and federal units they represented. The year 2006 marked not only the extraordinary social movement that took grassroots control of Oaxaca City and several municipalities for six months but also a dramatic increase in the militarization of Mexico under the drug war. The Mexican government has spent billions of dollars to bolster its military presence throughout the country to combat drug trafficking, including over US$2 billion in military aid from the United States.

This massive injection of funding fueled the growth of militarized policing throughout the country, including regular restructuring of police and military forces, which makes keeping track of them very difficult. This uneasy balance between business as usual and militarization is the new normal in parts of Mexico whose economies rely on tourism. This tension is especially stark where social movements threaten the highly unequal, violent, and corrupt status quo, concentrated in the poorer, browner, southern states like Oaxaca.

OAXACA CITY, MEXICO, JUNE 2016

Almost ten years to the day that the violent eviction of striking teachers from the zocalo sparked the popular takeover of Oaxaca City, teachers were again on strike, and the zocalo was again the site of encampments and social movement activity. As had occurred ten years prior, the state's response was not negotiation but repression. The most violent attack came on June 19, 2016, in the Mixtec town of Asunción Nochixtlán, located about an hour outside the capital city of Oaxaca. Federal and state police opened fire on teachers and their allies who were defending their barricades, which blocked the federal highway connecting Oaxaca with Mexico City.

Networks that were created in 2006 mobilized in response to the government aggression. Self-defense barricades were again erected in the capital city, as well as in communities throughout the state, to prevent, or at least impede, security forces from circulating. The zocalo was again housing cultural events in solidarity with the teachers and the town of Nochixtlán, to show the government that the people would not be intimidated into silence. Artists once again painted murals and stencil art denouncing government repression and celebrating resistance throughout the city center. With the major highways taken, private bus lines full of tourists and other people trying to leave the city navigated narrow dirt roads. Drivers placed decals in their windshields urging the government to "find a peaceful compromise to the teachers' just demands." Calls from the national and international community urged the government to stop the attacks and instead sit down at the negotiation table with the teachers' union. The government eventually sat down with the teachers and pulled their security forces back, but only after police murdered eight people, injured 108 more, and arrested twenty-two (Matías Rendón 2016; Pérez Alfonso 2016).

. . .

This book connects the dots between mundane moments of seeming tranquility and acquiescence and extraordinary moments of political and social upheaval. *Cartographies of Youth Resistance* looks for the connective tissue between those times when nothing remarkable seems to be happening, the government's control over the city appears to be complete, and business as usual looks secure and those episodic events that signal popular dissent, when the public sphere is dominated by militant radical action that appears to leave the status quo hanging by a thread. This book is about Mexican civil society during an era characterized by widespread disillusionment in electoral politics. This disillusionment comes from years of unfulfilled promises following the "political opening" signaled by the end to one-party rule in 2000, as well as the economic promises made by the politicians and technocrats who tried to sell the Mexican people on the North American Free Trade Agreement (NAFTA). This era has also been characterized by the nation's bloodiest years since the 1910–20 Revolution, due to the ongoing drug war and militarization of Mexican society.

This is not, however, a story about political apathy or nihilism. This book tells stories of radical hope, imagination, and creation that are being written by Indigenous and migrant youth in southern Mexico. These young people combine horizontal organizing practices and urban autonomy with hip-hop and punk culture to create meaningful channels for social and political participation. They do all of this under the specter of Mexico's bloody drug war and neoliberal abandonment. By listening to their stories and taking their political analysis and knowledge seriously, we get a glimpse into how the most marginalized members of society—in this case, Indigenous, racialized, urban, migrant, poor and working-class youth—often have the clearest view of the more just society that lies on the horizon, in the cracks that exist in the spaces between the extraordinary and mundane.

ACKNOWLEDGMENTS

This book would not exist without the love, care, support, critiques, and labor of so many people. So many that I apologize if I missed you on this list.

First and foremost, this book would not have been possible if not for the courage, conviction, imagination, and love of the hundreds of thousands of Oaxacans who took to the streets in 2006. I am forever humbled and indebted to those who generously shared their experience, knowledge, hopes, and fears with me. Baldomero Robles Menéndez, whose stunning photographs grace the cover and many pages of this book, is as generous as he is talented. Abril, Monica, Chivis, Eric, Tete, Mare, Chiquis, los hermanos Santos, Serckas, Mentes Liberadas, and the rest of the members of VOCAL, CASOTA, Arte Jaguar, Estación Cero, AK Crew, and CESOL were key interlocutors, teachers, and friends. Shout out to Violeta at Librespacio La Jícara for keeping the books coming and always on point with her curation! Demos and the Barrita-Rios family, Conchita, Irma, Diego, Kayla, and Paola all provided friendship and family that keep me connected and grounded in Oaxaca. Alejandra Aquino Moreschi and Fred Decosse are great friends and colleagues who help me stay optimistic about what being an academic can look like. Conchita Nuñez, Margarita Dalton, Gustavo Esteva, and Roberto Olivares were all generous with their time and knowledge of Oaxacan history, society, and politics. Jyri Antero Jaakkola and Alberta "Bety" Cariño came from very different places and experiences, but both dedicated their lives to creating the world they wanted to see by enacting relationships of solidarity and mutual aid. They were killed for doing so. This book is dedicated to them and their families who continue their important work.

At the University of Oregon I was fortunate to have many colleagues and mentors that helped me survive what can be the incredibly isolating experience of graduate school. I owe a tremendous amount of gratitude to Lynn Stephen for her guidance, mentorship, and friendship. She continues to model what engaged and genuinely committed scholarship looks like. The longer I spend in academia, the more thankful I am for the opportunity to have trained under her. The late Sandi Morgen also pushed me to be a more critical thinker and better teacher, as well as helping me believe I was a good ethnographer. Her generosity continues to amaze me. Lamia Karim and Daniel Martinez HoSang also provided key insights and support as I developed my project. Josh Fisher, Jen Erickson, Ernesto Garay, José Mendoza, Angela Montague, André Sirois, Grant Silva, Lidiana Soto, Rupa Pillai, and Cristal Magaña helped keep me human while I navigated graduate school. Carlos Aguirre, Phil Scher, Madonna Moss, Michael Hames-García, Ernesto Martínez, Gabriela Martínez, Ellen Herman, Deana Dartt, and Alaí Reyes-Santos all supported me during my time in Eugene. As an undergraduate at the University of South Florida, committed mentors gave me a skewed view (in a positive sense) of the field I was joining. Jonathan Gayles pushed me to apply to graduate school and helped me navigate the application process. Together with Dr. Gayles, Nancy Romero-Daza, Lorena Madrigal, David Himmelgreen, and Kevin Yelvington all helped me develop as a scholar and think of myself as one— no small feat for a high school "dropout" and community college transfer student.

The research and writing for this book were supported by numerous grants and fellowships. The University of Oregon Department of Anthropology, Graduate School, Center for the Study of Woman in Society, and Center on Diversity and Community all helped make those first few summers of fieldwork possible. Extended periods of dissertation fieldwork were made possible due to the generous support of a Tokyo Foundation Sassakawa Young Leaders Fellowship Fund grant and a dissertation fieldwork grant and community engagement grant from the Wenner-Gren Foundation for Anthropological Research. The time and space necessary to complete the write-up stage of the dissertation was made possible by generous support from a dissertation fellowship from the Ford Foundation and a visiting researcher fellowship from the Center for U.S.-Mexican Studies at the University of California, San Diego. My time in San Diego was as enjoyable as it was productive thanks to Alberto Diaz-Cayeros, Gregg Malinger, and my cohort of visiting scholars: Alexis Salas, Sarah Luna, Danny Zborover, Veronica Pacheco, Michael Lettieri, Karina Cordova, Kathy Kopinak. Others in San Diego who made me feel at home are Ramona Pérez, Nancy

Postero, Maria Lorena Cook, Elena Zilberg, Rosaura Sanchez, Beatrice Pita, and Laura Gutiérrez.

Additional time to write and deepen my thinking was made possible due to an Institute of American Cultures postdoctoral fellowship at University of California, Los Angeles, where I was graciously hosted by the Chicano Studies Research Center and the César Chávez Department of Chicana/o Studies. The Institute for Labor Education and Research and the Labor Center helped me turn that fellowship into three amazing years at UCLA. Ellie Hernández, Maylei Blackwell, Gaspar Rivera-Salgado, Kent Wong, Abel Valenzuela, Juan Herrera, Chon Noriega, Darling Sianez, Connie Heskett, Javier Iribarren, Rebecca Epstein, Elvia Vargas, and Elizabeth Espinoza all deserve particularly deep gratitude for helping me feel at home and helping me grow as a scholar and teacher. During my time at UCLA I also had the pleasure of learning from Victor Narro, Leisy Abrego, Gaye Theresa Johnson, Hannah Appel, Jessica Cattelino, Nancy Guarneros, Mario DeLeon, Cinthia Flores, Carlos Salinas, Hugo Romero, Sharon Luk, and Elena Shih.

I have received great support and *aliento* from the community of scholars at the University of Arizona since I arrived in fall 2016. My colleagues in Mexican American studies have been especially supportive of me since my first day on campus. I owe a great deal of gratitude to Michelle Téllez and her daughter Milagro, who have become like family, and to Patrisia Gonzales, who in addition to being an amazing colleague helped my daughter arrive in this world safely and bravely. Ada Wilkinson-Lee, Lydia Otero, Raquel Rubio-Goldsmith, Anna Ochoa O'Leary, Roberto "Cintli" Rodriguez, Tony Estrada, Anita Huizar-Hernández, Lillian Gorman, Nolan Cabrera, Javier Duran, Collin Deeds, Marcela Vásquez-León, Luis Coronel, J. P. Jones, Andrea Romero, Marla Franco, Leah Stauber, and Brian Silverstein have all helped me and my family make Tucson our home.

My editor at UC Press, Kate Marshall, believed in this project and its potential, perhaps, even before I did. I can't thank her enough for her feedback and guidance throughout the process and for finding reviewers who engaged with the manuscript genuinely and critically. Enrique Ochoa-Kaup helped me navigate the publishing process and get this book to the finish line. My thinking on this project benefited from many conversations, workshops, conferences, and seminars over the years. I would like to thank Nancy Postero and María Josefina Saldaña-Portillo in particular for their careful guidance and input, as well as Jeff Juris, Ana Aparicio, Ed McCaughan,

Arturo Escobar, Karen Brodkin, Aída Hernández Castillo, María Teresa Sierra, Leo Chávez, Carlos Vélez-Ibánez, María L. Cruz-Torres, Gina Perez, Frances Aparicio, Javier Auyero, Joo Ok Kim, Chris Perreira, Lorenzo Perillo, Juli Grigsby, Mohan Ambikaipaker, Mariana Mora, Xóchitl Chávez, Gilberto Rosas, Korinta Maldonado, Pablo Gonzalez, Santiago Guerra, Aimee Villarreal, Tehama López Bunyasi, Luis Sánchez, Brenda Nicolas, Xóchitl Flores-Marcial, Daina Sánchez, Odilia Romero, Annie Fukushima, Patrisia Macías-Rojas, Akimi Nishida, Laurence Ralph, Sameena Mulla, Maria Fernanda Escallón, and Jong Bum Kwon for their support over the years. Each of you in your own way and at the right time helped me get here.

Finally, my deepest and greatest gratitude, debt, and love go to my family. To my partner, best friend, intellectual confidant, and accomplice Susy Chávez Herrera: To say that this book would not be possible without you is as obvious as it is understated. You encourage me to get back up after the rejections and to celebrate the successes. You keep me grounded while also reminding me to always dream big. To our daughter Emma Luna Magaña Chávez, you have given me renewed inspiration and motivation to do work that matters. You also remind me of what matters most and that each day is a blessing. To my mother Miriam Attias, you are my hero. You never cease to amaze me with your resolve, generosity, resilience, and how you never stop challenging yourself and learning new things. All those word-of-the-day lessons we did together when I was a child instilled a love of language in me that helped me imagine myself as a writer. To my late father Rafael Magaña Niebla, you continue to inspire me and give me strength. You overcame so much in life so that your children could become who we wanted to be. Not a day goes by that we don't remember you and miss you. And your jokes still crack me up. To my siblings, Setty and Adrian Magaña, you both teach me about perseverance, hard work, and the importance of having a sense of humor like our *jefe*. To Setty "Tortilla" Attias and Japhlet Bire Attias, many of my fondest memories from childhood and adulthood involve you, your love, and your smiles. My late abuelita Lolita inspired me to be an author. After all, she decided the best way to learn English was to write her own books and become a published author in her sixties. I have so much love and respect for el abuelo Sam, who adopted me after my father passed away. He was always plotting how the oppressed people of the world would come together to overthrow militarism and empire . . . but only after feeding his dozens of adopted animals, taking the "viejitos" to run errands, finding ways to help those making their way to El Norte, and creating solar-powered *naves espaciales*. And thank you to all los Magaña, Niebla, Attias, and Rimblas that I did not name individually, because that would be a book in and of itself, as well as the Hughes family and Joel Wigstadt, who are family by choice and have taught me so much. All of you helped me get here.

ACRONYMS AND ORGANIZATIONS

AAA	Autonomy, *Autogestión*, Self-Determination collective
APCO	Popular Neighborhood Assembly of Oaxaca
APPO	Popular Assembly of the Peoples of Oaxaca
BARL	Autonomous Block of Liberationist Resistance
CACITA	Autonomous Center for the Intercultural Creation of Appropriated Technologies
CACTUS	Center for Community Support Working Together
CASOTA	Autonomous Oaxacan Solidarity House for Self-Managed Work
CDI	National Commission for the Development of Indigenous Peoples
CESOL	Liberationist Social Center
CIPO-RFM	Popular Indigenous Council of Oaxaca Ricardo Flores Magón
CNTE	National Education Workers Coordinating Committee
COCEI	Coalition of Workers, Peasants, and Students of the Isthmus
CU	Ciudad Universitaria (the UABJO campus located in Oaxaca City)
ESMUJ	Multidisciplinary Youth Space
EZLN	Zapatista Army of National Liberation
FMIN	National Independent Teachers Front

FPDT	People's Front in Defense of the Land
FPR	Popular Revolutionary Front
IJO	Institute of Oaxacan Youth
INEGI	National Institute of Geography and Statistics
MULT	Movement for Triqui Unification and Struggle
MULTI	Independent Movement for Triqui Unification and Struggle
NAFTA	North American Free Trade Agreement
OIR	Intercultural Occupation in Resistance
PAN	National Action Party
PFP	Federal Preventative Police
PLM	Mexican Liberal Party
PRD	Party of Democratic Revolution
PRI	Institutional Revolutionary Party
Sección 22 (or Local 22)	Dissident wing of Oaxacan teacher's union
SEP	Secretary of Education
SNTE	National Educational Workers Union
UABJO	Benito Juárez Autonomous University of Oaxaca
UBISORT	Union for the Social Well-Being of the Triqui Region
UNAM	National Autonomous University of Mexico
UNITIERRA	University of the Land
UNOSJO	Union of Organizations of the Sierra Juárez of Oaxaca
URO	Former Governor Ulises Ruiz Ortiz
VOCAL	Oaxacan Voices Constructing Autonomy and Liberty

Introduction

RETHINKING SOCIAL MOVEMENT TEMPORALITY
AND SPATIALITY THROUGH COUNTERSPACE
AND URBAN YOUTH CULTURE

WHEN I ARRIVED IN OAXACA to study the 2006 social movement
described in the preface, I was prepared to study a series of events with a
clear beginning and end. The violent eviction of striking teachers from their
union encampment in the zocalo of the city on June 14, 2006, is generally
understood as the beginning of the social movement that took grassroots
control of the capital city for six months. Upon news of the attack against the
teachers, thousands of Oaxacans rushed to the city center in their defense,
forcing the overwhelmed police to retreat. The people then decided to remain
in the zocalo and surrounding streets and public spaces indefinitely. As we
will see in chapter 1, those spaces taken over by the teachers and their allies
were incubators of what became a broad-based movement that included over
three hundred existing movements and organizations, as well as countless
individuals with no formal political affiliations. As far as the end of the movement, many commentators point to the month-long siege of Oaxaca by the
Federal Preventative Police in October and November of 2006 that allowed
the government to retake physical control of the city as marking the end.

Social movements, however, are rarely—if ever—so tidy as to have clear
start and end dates. Similar to the law of conservation of energy, which states
that energy can be transformed but not created nor destroyed, the energy
that fuels mass mobilizations does not appear out of nowhere, nor does it
disappear. It is shaped by prevailing grievances and harnessed from existing
repertoires of contention (Tilly 1986). After peak mobilizations subside, that
energy transforms into new forms of organizing and sparks new political
imaginations and cultures. This dynamic is partially captured by the idea
of "protest cycles," which argues that the residue left behind by social movements, regardless of "success" or "failure," influences subsequent waves of

protest (Tarrow 1998). Building on this idea, this book shows that it is necessary to reframe social movements themselves in ways that allow us to rethink the boundaries (both geographic and temporal) we assign to them.

Cartographies of Youth Resistance is a book about the life of social movements. This book shows how young people build on existing organizing traditions and experiment with novel political cultures to help sustain social movement energy through the ebbs and flows of peak mobilizations and visible movement activity. *Cartographies of Youth Resistance* does this by examining the transformation of social movement energy through an ethnographic focus on the production of space, youth culture, and radical politics. Looking at social movements through these interrelated processes instead of framing them as discrete objects illuminates their rhizomatic nature, historical antecedents, and long-term impacts. In order to examine these dynamics, I employ Henri Lefebvre's notion of *counterspace* (1991). I define *counterspaces* as spatial projects produced through the political imagination and practice of social movements, as an alternative to the spaces created by the dominant system.[1] This concept allows me to demonstrate how the power generated by social movements is spatialized and helps sustain activism through the ebbs and flows of mass mobilizations.

For example, chapter 1 introduces the reader to a youth-run social center that was opened after the Federal Preventative Police retook the city. At that point, militarization and police surveillance had made maintaining a visible dissident presence, such as through encampments and direct actions, too difficult and dangerous to sustain—especially for groups with little political capital. The increase in under-the-radar and quotidian organizing that happened in counterspaces like the social center was crucial in keeping the momentum from 2006 going, and these spaces also served as bases from which strategic direct actions could be staged when necessary.

The social center and other counterspaces discussed in this book were sites of what James C. Scott (1990) calls *infrapolitics*—the invisible struggles engaged in daily by marginalized groups. In Scott's formulation, marginalized people are fully aware of the imbalance of power, such that the decision to make their resistance invisible is a tactical one. Scott uses the terms *hidden transcripts* to frame the invisible daily practices through which marginalized people resist domination and *public transcripts* to frame the public performance of acquiescence. In this book, I look at what infrapolitics and their transcripts look like in space. I frame counterspaces like the youth-run social center as allowing activists to keep their quotidian organizing out of the public eye (hidden transcript) while giving the appearance that the space around them is under control (public transcript). In other words, surveillance and militarization are "working" at squashing dissent. Focusing on counterspaces like the social center, together with the more spectacular spaces of social movements produced through direct actions and large mobilizations, yields a more complete picture of the life of social movements and of how power and resistance operate. Such a move allows us to heed Lila Abu-Lughod's (1990) call for anthropologists to develop methodologies for the study of resistance as a diagnostic of power and the ever-shifting relations through which power is (re)produced and contested.

Oaxaca provides especially fertile ground for examining these dynamics, in part due to the effects that neoliberal development (including heritage tourism), militarization, and the criminalization of dissent have had on activism and the policing of public space. I refer to this confluence of forces as *neoliberal militarization*, whose intensification since 2006 has made maintaining a visible dissident presence increasingly dangerous. Youth have responded by seizing urban space through a novel repertoire of tactics and strategies, such as networking territorialized activist and artist spaces (e.g., social centers and cultural venues) with the ephemeral spaces constituted through direct actions (e.g., encampments, roadblocks) and public cultural production (e.g., murals, graffiti, stencil art, music). This book provides a cartography of those counterspaces, which are linked together to form constellations of resistance and creation. These activist constellations harness and sustain the energy of social movements, and the politics, cultures, and imaginations that fuel them.

Once we move beyond a view of social movements as discrete units, an important part of the story becomes the layering of histories of activism and, in places like Oaxaca, competing regimes of space making. The UNESCO World Heritage Site that includes Oaxaca City also includes the Zapotec archaeological site of Monte Albán. In present-day Oaxaca, then, the politics of heritage tourism involves histories and artifacts of pre-Hispanic and colonial space making, entangled with deepening geographies of inequality that push Indigenous migrants to the edges of the city—as well as to the edges of the economy, politics, and society. In part because of these histories, Oaxaca has also been the site of organized resistance for centuries—a legacy that the youth featured in this book claim as their inheritance. One way to envision this layering of activism and space is through the metaphor of the *palimpsest*, or the "layered space of movement, epochs, objects, information, and ideas, actual, imposed, and superimposed" (C. A. Smith 2016, 62).[2] The metaphor of the palimpsest is based on the ancient practice of reusing parchment to produce new manuscripts by scraping off previous layers of text. Over time, the underwriting (*scriptio inferior*) would reappear, thus complicating the meaning of the manuscript page.

When applied as an analytic for understanding space and time, the palimpsest illuminates the horizontal and vertical entanglement involved in their production. Each layer and set of meanings is enmeshed in the previous iterations in ways that do not abide by the logics of linear time or Cartesian space (Alexander 2005, 190; C. A. Smith 2016, 63). Politics, after all, consists of multiple nonlinear temporalities (Draper 2018). The concept of the palimpsest allows me to chart how youth carve out space for themselves to be seen and heard in urban space, while not losing sight of the fact that they do so in a terrain shaped by centuries of colonial and state control, violence, and capitalist influence, as well as Indigenous and grassroots organizing and resistance.

OAXACA AS RACIALIZED SPACE OF UNGOVERNABILITY

Oaxaca's Indigenous communities have resisted domination by outside forces for centuries—including incursions by other Indigenous groups like the Aztecs, as well as from Spanish colonizers and the Mexican state (Chassen de López 2004; Stephen 2002). The Ayuukjä'äy (Mixes, in Spanish) are an Indigenous group from the northern highlands of Oaxaca known as *los jamás conquistados* (never conquered). This nickname is said to refer to their successful defense against efforts by the Mexica (Aztecs), Zapotecs, and Mixtecs to absorb them as they spread their empires, as well as the inability of Spanish conquistadores and the Mexican army to exert control over them (Matías Rendón 2015). These histories of anticolonial, anti-imperial Indigenous resistance and the idea of being unconquerable is a source of great pride for many of the youth in this book—whether they are Ayuukjä'äy or not. Oaxaca is one of only two states in Mexico with a majority Indigenous population, according to government statistics.[3] It is home to sixteen Indigenous groups, each with its own language and culture, making it both the most diverse state in Mexico and home to the most Indigenous-language speakers in the country (INEGI 2010). The visibility of the state's Indigenous populations and their histories of resistance are used to fuel outside portrayals of Oaxaca and its people as backward, ungovernable, and the "antithesis of modernity" (Chassen de López 2004, 4).

In 418 of the 571 municipalities in the state, the communal assembly is the official decision-making structure, and Indigenous customary law is constitutionally recognized. This means that governance through political parties and electoral politics takes place in only a minority of municipalities. For some, the absence of electoral politics in these territories reinforces long-held notions of Oaxaca as a racialized space of ungovernability and exposes the porous borders of Mexico's postcolonial racial geographies (Saldaña-Portillo 2016). The formation of the Mexican state has relied on a temporal displacement of the Indigenous to the past, as well as racial geographies that relegate living Indians to rural territories, until or unless those territories are desired for their resources, at which point the Indigenous inhabitants are forced to flee (or migrate) to urban centers throughout Mexico and the United States. María Josefina Saldaña-Portillo reminds us that the settler colonial paradigm in Latin America renders Indigenous people "not properly Indian" when "they do not stay in their proper place," such that land dispossession results in both a spatial displacement and an erasure of identity (2017, 153).

This book examines what happens when members of these Indigenous diasporas challenge the settler colonial paradigm by insisting that they are both urban and Indigenous. Moreover, for youth involved in the 2006 social movement and subsequent political projects, Indigenous governance through communal assembly and Indigenous customary law provide a model of politics otherwise. Indigenous self-governance as practiced in a majority of Oaxacan municipalities powerfully demonstrates the point that anthropologist Audra Simpson highlights in her study of Kahnawà:ke Mohawk politics: there can be "more than one political show in town" (2014, 11), and that can be a dangerous thing for the apparatus of electoral politics.

Although the Mexican state acknowledges the right of Oaxaca's Indigenous communities to exercise customary law, this kind of politics of recognition is limited. Indigenous communities are not free, for example, from incursions and abuses by the Mexican military and police. Nor are they free from the nexus of neoliberal and neocolonial forces that seek to displace them from their land in order to extract valuable natural resources like gold, silver, marble, petroleum, and wind power, in the most recent iteration of the colonial project of extraction, dispossession, and elimination. The implementation of the Mesoamerica Integration and Development Project has given the political economy of extraction new life in the region since 2008. This project connects Mexico, Central America, Colombia, and the Dominican Republic, facilitating neoliberal development based on foreign investment, privatization, and extraction of natural resources. Predictably, this has exacerbated human rights abuses, dispossession of Indigenous peoples' lands, and environmental degradation. [4] Authoritarian governments and paramilitary forces in the region have responded to a groundswell in grassroots organizing against the development project by murdering dozens of Indigenous leaders, among them Bernardo Vásquez in Oaxaca and Berta Cáceres in Honduras (Bacon 2012; Jagger 2017; OAS 2017).

The enormous biological, cultural, and ethnic wealth of the state stand in stark contrast to the socioeconomic reality of most Oaxacans, whose state regularly ranks among the lowest in the nation in the Human Development Index and the highest in rates of infant mortality, maternal mortality, and domestic violence. While the Mexican government has long neglected Oaxaca and the majority of its inhabitants, the national and global shift toward neoliberal economic reforms exacerbated the long-standing social and economic despair in the state. As part of the economic restructuring adopted by the Mexican government in the 1980s and 1990s, the neoliberal state abandoned the countryside, gouging subsidies and other state supports for small- and medium-scale agriculture, while allowing subsidized US crops to flood the market. This shift has been devastating in states like Oaxaca, whose inhabitants have long counted on some combination of subsistence farming and small-scale commercial agriculture (e.g., coffee, corn, beans) (Bacon 2004; Barkin 2002; Fitting 2006; Gálvez 2018).

In addition to opening up communal lands to extractive development, the state and investors have focused on bolstering tourism. The tourist economy in southern Mexico is a product of neoliberal capitalism and relies on a trafficking of ideas around authenticity, indigeneity, cultural distinction, and nostalgia (Babb 2010; Poole 2011). Florence Babb argues that the state has "turned to tourism as both as a development strategy and as a way to refashion nationhood in a time of neoliberalism and globalization" (2010, 3). Tourism in Oaxaca relies heavily on the commodification of the state's cultural and ethnic diversity vis-à-vis the marketing of ethnic festivals, textiles, crafts, and other folklore. Oaxaca is also home to beautiful and undeveloped beaches, important and accessible archaeological ruins, and the picturesque historic city center. These qualities serve as the backbone of marketing campaigns encouraging tourists to visit the UNESCO World Heritage Site. In parallel with an increased reliance on tourism in the state, the neoliberal abandonment of the countryside has fueled rural-to-urban migration and exacerbated neocolonial legacies of generational poverty and historic marginalization. These inequalities have made it difficult for the state and business interests to maintain the carefully crafted public spaces marketed to tourists. The response from the state has largely been to militarize those same spaces in an attempt to cleanse them of "indecent displays of political behavior" (Poole 2009, 199).

The current moment in Oaxaca and Mexico as a whole, which is characterized by the state's embrace of certain neoliberal policies and ideas (such as tourism as development, ending subsidies for small- to medium-scale agriculture, and opening up communal lands for private ownership), coupled with increasing militarization and authoritarianism, leads to a confluence I term neoliberal militarization. Here I am in dialog with anthropologist Shannon Speed's concept of neoliberal multicriminalism (2016). Speed developed this concept to highlight the current breakaway from the promises of neoliberal multiculturalism, such as human rights, democracy, and rule of law (Hale 2005), toward the abandonment of populations—especially Indigenous people—to market forces and illegal economies. With neoliberal multicriminalism, Speed also recognizes the simultaneous move toward higher levels of authoritarian governance and militarization. My use of neoliberal militarization builds on Speed's theorization of the violent shift away from the unfulfilled promises of neoliberal multiculturalism with an explicit emphasis on the spatial manifestations of neoliberalism (displacement, crafting of tourist spaces, etc.) and of militarization (surveillance, policing of bodies and spaces, etc.).

THE UNGOVERNABLE IN AN ERA
OF NEOLIBERAL MILITARIZATION

The initiatives launched by young people who came of political age during the Oaxacan social movement of 2006 shed light on possible paths forward for a generation of working-class, migrant, and racialized Mexican youth, who have few options for exercising citizenship or economic participation that allow them to escape the criminalization and surveillance that neoliberal militarization imposes. While the militarization of Indigenous regions in southern Mexico is nothing new (Stephen 1999), an unbridled militarization has exploded in Mexico under the guise of the drug war (*guerra contra el narcotráfico*) declared by President Felipe Calderón upon taking office in 2006. Since then, the Mexican government has infused billions of dollars to bolster the military presence throughout the country, including over US$1.6 billion in military aid from the United States under the bilateral Mérida Initiative (Ribando Seelke and Finklea 2017). Militarization is framed as the necessary response to drug trafficking and the unprecedented level of violence in Mexico. Moreover, under the Calderon and Peña Nieto administrations, the state declared a "state of exception" (resulting in such laws as the 2008 Penal Reform and 2017 Internal Security Law), which permits the government to suspend the constitutional and human rights of people accused of organized crime (Hernández Castillo and Speed 2012). Far from making citizens safer, the reforms have only fortified the carceral state (Speed 2016).

The exact human toll of the drug war is notoriously difficult to quantify, given its nebulous boundaries and government obstruction of investigations into the violence, but even conservative estimates put the numbers nationwide at over 100,000 deaths during 2006–16 (Lee and Renwick 2017), over 22,000 disappeared during 2006–14 (Tuckman 2015), and 281,418 people displaced during 2011–15 (CMDPDH 2015). Equally disturbing—and criminal—has been the state's documented role in perpetuating the violence through extrajudicial killings, torture, disappearances, and arbitrary arrests (Human Rights Watch 2017). While seemingly indiscriminate and shockingly widespread, state violence touches certain communities more than others.[5] Shannon Speed, among others, argues that Indigenous people are especially vulnerable to state violence under the guise of the drug war:

> The Mexican state perpetrates violence against them [Indigenous people] through its discourses of criminality in the context of its charade of opposing drug trafficking. Agents of the state at all levels both act from and redeploy ideologies of race, class and gender in their acts of violence . . . and they do so comfortably in the context of ideologically generated impunity. (2016, 11)

A national security discourse that equates dissent with crime is layered over a centuries-old script that marks Indigenous bodies as "Other" and a seemingly universal trope that paints racialized youth as threats to public morality and safety. Bodies marked in these ways are deemed "ungovernable" (Reguillo Cruz 2012), which in turn justifies the continued militarization, surveillance, and enforcement of Mexico's racialized geographies (Mora 2017) and the criminalization of the youth who inhabit them.[6] *Cartographies of Youth Resistance* introduces readers to a network of Mexican youth that actively challenge these forces through the construction of insurgent identities, spaces, and politics that were sparked during the extraordinary milieu of the 2006 social movement and that have been nurtured in the counterspaces produced and maintained by youth organizers in the years since then.

Social movements and activists have been criminalized by consecutive authoritarian regimes under the cover of the drug war (Hernández Castillo and Speed 2012). While the Mexican government has long practiced what political scientist Jonathan Fox (1994) calls authoritarian clientelism, where the state employs a parallel strategy of repression and co-optation to control political dissent, the current iteration of Mexican authoritarianism is especially widespread and brutal. National, international, and intergovernmental human rights organizations have denounced political repression as an increasing risk to Mexican democracy and human rights. The position of activists in the country has grown so perilous that the Mexican Commission on Defense and Promotion of Human Rights (La Comisión Mexicana de Defensa y Promoción de los Derechos Humanos) launched a program in 2013 specifically aimed at protecting activists. Oaxaca provides a window into how federal and state governments have used the war on drug trafficking as a pretext for cracking down on dissent. Despite not being a major theater in the official drug war, state violence in Oaxaca is rampant. Human rights reports have documented many such instances, including the 2006 crackdown on the social movement that left twenty-six people dead and hundreds more arrested and tortured (CCIODH 2008), and a 2016 police attack against protesting teachers and their allies in the town of Nochixtlán that left eight dead and dozens injured (Amnesty International 2017). A global report for 2017 listed Mexico as the third most deadly country in the world for human rights activists (Front Line Defenders 2017), with Oaxaca the deadliest state (López Dávila 2018).

The epidemic of violence in Mexico, in all its nefarious forms, disproportionately touches the lives of young people, and its effect is compounded by a wholesale disinvestment in their futures by the state through neoliberal cutbacks. More than 21 percent of Mexico's population between the ages of 15 and 29 is unemployed and not enrolled in school (Rocha 2011). In Oaxaca, an astounding 85.4 percent of the youth who are employed are found in the informal sector, including 67.1 percent of those with a college education (Guerrero 2017). Mexican journalist Ricardo Rocha (2011) calls these employment and education statistics "only the most visible data of the collective crime that this country commits against its youth every day," citing the fact that homicide is the leading cause of death for youth. The murder of Mexican youth has become so widespread that scholars and human rights activists refer to them as *juvenicidios* (Valenzuela Arce 2015). Affronts against the dignity and lives of Mexican youth are even more severe and pervasive for Indigenous, migrant, and racialized youth. This includes unequal access to schooling, safe housing, dignified employment, and health care; the effects that discrimination and surveillance take on the body, mind, and overall well-being (Browne 2015; Fanon [1967] 2005); and more obvious manifestations of violence that result from an uninterrupted colonial logic that constructs Indigenous bodies as legitimate targets for physical attacks (Mora 2017; Stephen 1999). Moreover, the epidemic of gendered violence, and feminicide in particular, that has spread throughout the country has not spared Oaxaca. In fact, Oaxaca is one of the deadliest states for women, and impunity for gendered violence against Indigenous women is particularly rampant (Speed 2016, 6). In these ways and others, physical violence and social death are the specters that loom over the lives of the youth in this book.

The histories and counternarratives of the generation of youth that came of political age during the Oaxacan social movement of 2006, however, shed light on how Mexican youth are constructing alternatives to death and despair for themselves, for each other, and for their communities. *Cartographies of Youth Resistance* frames their collective projects as correctives to narratives of youth apathy that dominate national commentary. Far from apathetic or hopeless, the youth organizers whose stories fill the pages of this book are engaged in the everyday work of creating social change, and through their collective political and social projects they place electoral politics and neoliberal policies on trial for failing to offer meaningful solutions, hopeful futures, and channels for substantive participation for youth.

INSURGENT INDIGENEITY, YOUTH CULTURE, AND SOCIAL MOVEMENT ORGANIZING

This book examines what happens when the forces of neoliberal militarization collide with social movements. This is a story of radical hope, imagination, and creation. The protagonists are Indigenous and migrant youth in Mexico who combine horizontal organizing and urban autonomy practices with hip-hop and punk culture to create meaningful channels for political and social participation. They are largely first- or second-generation migrants to the city from Indigenous communities throughout the state, and some are return migrants from the United States, Mexico City, and other parts of Mexico. Many of them identify as *indígenas urbanos* (urban Indigenous), which is in direct tension with the narrow schema for determining indigeneity set forth by state institutions. Up until the 2012 national census, for example, the National Institute of Geography and Statistics (INEGI) determined indigeneity based purely on language. Other essentialist notions of indigeneity are based on static notions of a people bound to their ancestral lands or use of "traditional" dress.

Cartographies of Youth Resistance highlights the politics of a generation of youth who mobilize around collective Indigenous identities that are tied to political consciousness, social commitments, and family histories. It is these social and political relationships that inform their identities as urban Indigenous, not parameters imposed by the state, anthropologists, or linguists. For these young people, participation in the 2006 social movement was a continuation of the rich history of Indigenous organizing and resistance to domination outlined earlier. For example, a youth collective that emerged from the 2006 social movement called VOCAL (Oaxacan Voices Constructing Autonomy and Liberty) articulates a vision of indigeneity that explicitly connects their collective identity as urban Indigenous to "the insurrection of 2006, [where] in the barricades we happily realized the 500-year war of colonization had not completely torn our Indigenous roots from us. In those nights of struggle . . . the values from our indigenous origins that had apparently been lost powerfully manifested themselves between us" (VOCAL 2007a).[7] VOCAL articulates an insurgent indigeneity that is in many ways specific to the experience of urban youth in the 2006 social movement. Elsewhere they make reference to practices of reciprocity and social obligations between individuals and their communities, which are fundamental to *comunalidad*. This concept was developed by Indigenous Oaxacan intellectuals Jaime Martínez Luna and Floriberto Díaz as a way of theorizing Indigenous communal life, identity, and epistemology (Martínez Luna 2010; Robles Hernández and Cardoso Jiménez 2007).

VOCAL and other urban activists of their generation articulate and mobilize a decidedly decolonial politics. They explicitly frame their activism as resistance to a racialized system of economic, cultural, and political domination that they see as spanning centuries of colonial, liberal, and neoliberal state formation. Their analysis of power is very much in line with Peruvian sociologist Aníbal Quijano's (2000) conceptualization of "the coloniality of power." For Quijano and others such as Walter Mignolo (2000), Nelson Maldonado-Torres (2007), Catherine Walsh (2007), and Ramón Grosfoguel (2007), coloniality of power refers to the ways that colonial structures of power and domination produced a hierarchical system of categorization (e.g., Indian, *mestizo*, *criollo*, male, female) and knowledge production that has persisted to this day. In this theorization, there is nothing "post" or resolved about colonialism. This means that moving beyond the entrenched systems of racism, violence, inequality, dispossession, and environmental destruction born of colonialism means making radical changes in relations of power, knowledge, and culture—a shift also referred to as "the decolonial turn."

Bolivian theorist and historian Silvia Rivera Cusicanqui (2012) is critical of the coloniality of power paradigm and cautions against, among other things, the co-optation of the practice and action of decolonization by scholarship emanating from academic institutions of the Global North. Rivera Cusicanqui argues that generating knowledge through South-South dialog and centering genealogies of decolonization that come from the struggles and epistemologies of oppressed peoples in the Global South must be central to any decolonial project. What I wish to highlight for the purposes of this book is both the usefulness of the coloniality of power paradigm for understanding the continuity of the structures of power and domination that activists in Oaxaca challenge, and also the decolonial practice exercised by activists, which resonates profoundly with that advocated by Rivera Cusicanqui. VOCAL, for example, roots their identity and politics in Indigenous epistemologies like *comunalidad* and Indigenous histories of resistance, and also emphasizes South-South political solidarities and knowledge exchanges. Chapters 2 and 3 will delve deeper into the decolonial politics of youth activists in Oaxaca. Finally, while it is outside the scope of this book, there is also a large body of literature generated by Native scholars, scholars of color, and scholars in the Global South that examines what decolonization implies for research (Harrison 1997; Mora 2017; TallBear 2014; L. T. Smith 1999). These interventions parallel the decolonial politics of the youth in this book, especially in regards to taking seriously the knowledge produced by marginalized communities and social movements.

Whereas the urban Indigenous identity mobilized by social movement youth is grounded in their collective generational experiences, they are also part of a larger movement of urban and diasporic communities in Mexico, the United States, and throughout the Americas that are (re)defining indigeneity from the ground up. These communities include the Oaxacan diaspora who maintain Indigenous identities and *comunalidad* through ongoing participation in the cultural, civic, and political life of their communities across the transborder space theorized as Oaxacalifornia (Blackwell 2017; Rivera-Salgado 1999; Sánchez-López 2017; Stephen 2007). Winnebago/Ojibwe ethnographer Renya Ramirez (2007) explores the ways that Indian communities who live in urban California travel between reservation and city to strengthen community, culture, and identity, expanding notions of citizenship in the process. Scholarship has also examined how urban communities in Mexico link rural and urban space through the reterritorialization of Indigenous identities within cities, as is the case with Maya migrants in Cancún (Castellanos 2010) and Wixárika university students in Tepic, Nayarit (Negrín 2019). Understanding this context of urban indigeneity is important for moving beyond essentialist debates of authenticity and focusing instead on how Indigenous people build community, identity, and politics in ways that disrupt dominant spatial and temporal orders that relegate Indigenous people to the past or in bounded, peripheral territories.[8]

Much as I use indigeneity as a dynamic and relational social formation (de la Cadena and Starn 2007; Faudree 2013) and not a static category rooted in biology, I understand the label *youth* to be a dynamic, relational, and heterogeneous social identity that is culturally and historically constructed (Urteaga 2011). In other words, youth is not a demographic category nor one rooted in biology, and this is not a study about adolescent development, youth deviance, or adulthood's "Other" (Juris and Pleyers 2009). This is a study about how youth construct themselves as political actors in relation to multiple communities across time and space. Youth, in the context of this book, is an overtly political and self-ascribed identity. The politicization of youth identity in Mexico stems in large part from the prominent position that previous youth movements have had in the national consciousness and leftist organizing, with the 1968 student movement representing an especially significant reference point. One result is that students, as opposed to youth, are commonly held up as model activists and the hope for the nation's future. Neoliberal education reforms, however, have set into motion the privatization of the nation's public universities and placed an outsized emphasis on producing professionals in engineering and technology (Solano 2013). Unfortunately, the labor market has not kept pace, which results in many overqualified engineers and tech professionals working as middle management for foreign-owned maquiladoras (Booth 2012). The privatization of education, coupled with few prospects for class mobility, means that postsecondary schooling is increasingly seen as an impractical investment of time and resources for many working-class youth. The current generation of youth are commonly referred to as *Ninis*, which stands for *ni estudian ni trabajan* (they don't study, they don't work), as a way of highlighting their perceived lack of economic and social productivity. Claiming a politicized youth identity is a way of combating the stigma marginalized youth carry, while also critiquing the structural reforms that have made the possibilities of their being students increasingly untenable. Given the significance of shared generational experience of the social, economic, and political impacts of neoliberal restructuring and militarization, and the historic importance that the 2006 social movement has played in their political formation, I refer to the youth in this book collectively as the "2006 Generation."[9]

The 2006 Generation formed the frontlines in the most innovative and directly democratic currents within the social movement. These youth activists and organizers combined insurgent Indigenous identities with a political culture that wove together strands of liberationist,[10] antiauthoritarian, urban autonomist, and horizontalist politics (Magaña 2014).[11] Many of them were also heavily involved in the production of hip-hop and punk cultures, which helped extend movement networks beyond the "politicized." Youth served many functions within the movement, ranging from organizing self-defense brigades to staging artistic interventions in public spaces and spaces created by the movement; documenting the movement's actions as independent researchers, reporters, and artists; and opening social centers for people of all ages to rest, eat, and congregate in the context of an otherwise stressful and dangerous environment marked by police and paramilitary repression. Eventually, after a brutal month-long campaign of repression, the federal government retook control of the city. Attempts to hold the movement together after 2006 proved difficult, as internal fractures were deepened by the government's dual strategy of repression and co-optation.

This book makes the case, however, that the history of the Oaxacan social movement does not end in 2006. Part of the movement's legacy can be found in a unique horizontalist political culture that youth experimented with during the grassroots takeover, and which continued to be practiced and honed post 2006 through subsequent youth political and cultural initiatives.

These include counterspaces opened by movement youth like social centers but also interventions that transform public space, like direct actions, as well as murals and stencil graffiti with oppositional messages. Through these diverse tactics, youth organizers seek to reclaim the egalitarian promise of public space and give visual form to their utopian visions and sensibilities. I refer to these collective practices and sensibilities as *rebel aesthetics*. These rebel aesthetics give form to the social and political imagination of activists and open up space for passersby to imagine alternatives to the dominant spatial and social arrangements. Publicly visible art is an especially important part of the 2006 Generation's cultural politics, given the dangers and challenges in maintaining a dissident presence in the city via traditional organizing practices in the current era of neoliberal militarization.

This book is my attempt at ethnographically grounding Robin D. G. Kelley's argument that the cultural products produced by social movements reveal "the cognitive maps of the future, of the world not yet born" (2003, 10). Work in cultural studies has theorized the importance of youth (sub) culture as a form of resistance to capitalism and other dominant power structures (Hall and Jefferson 2006; Hebdige 1979). Cultural studies has made important contributions to the scholarship on youth culture and politics, moving the researcher's gaze beyond deviance and delinquency and focusing on youth as producers of culture and as political actors. *Cartographies of Youth Resistance* intervenes here by going beyond a focus on youth resistance through consumption patterns and style to focus instead on the intersection of social movement organizing, cultural production, and spatial politics. This book is more concerned with the relationship between artistic sociospatial practices and the production of social and political relationships than with textual analysis or interpretation of art. Nor will the reader find neat definitions and categorizations of genre.

I do want to provide some clarity on how I am using punk, hip-hop, graffiti, and street art in this book. When I speak of punks, punk culture, and/ or the punk movement in Oaxaca, I am referring to a local network composed of anarchist and other radical political collectives, bands, and DIY producers of artifacts including patches, stickers, fanzines, silk-screened shirts, jackets, and so forth.[12] While there is very much a local scene with a day-to-day life, it is deeply connected to global networks and movements. The music that brings punks together in Oaxaca spans multiple genres as framed by the music industry, including anarcho-punk, metal, death metal, hardcore, and *metal prehispánico*. As I will explain in greater detail in chapter 2, my interlocutors refer to their scene as the punk movement or sometimes as the anarcho-punk (*anarcopunk* in Spanish) movement, based largely on the central role that anarchist-infused political organizing plays in their lives. Understanding the politics and genealogies of the Oaxacan punk movement is not only important in terms of the movement's place in local politics, but also for decentering the Global North and whiteness in the history, present, and future of punk.

When I refer to hip-hop culture and the hip-hop community in Oaxaca, I am talking about a network of musicians, visual artists, dancers, and promoters involved in the four elements considered the foundation of hip-hop: emceeing (rapping), deejaying, b-girling/b-boying (breakdancing), and graffiti art.[13] Although much of the scholarly and media attention has focused on the musical aspect of hip-hop, the reality is that the core elements of hip-hop culture interact, overlap, and nurture one another. For many of the pioneers of graffiti in Oaxaca, the punk movement was their first frame of reference in terms of a rebellious subculture, so many identify with punk.[14] This overlap between youth cultures is a useful reminder that hip-hop and punk cultures, like all cultures, are fluid and dynamic and often thrive off cross-fertilization. The genealogies and artistic practices of artists and activists in the Oaxacan punk and hip-hop communities help illuminate what scholar and punk zine author Mimi Thi Nguyen calls "multisubculturalism" (Nguyen 2012, 221), or the traversing of multiple urban youth cultures, movements, and scenes, blurring genres and categorization.[15]

In terms of visual art, most of the artists featured in this book practice multiple forms within what can be generally labeled street art, including graffiti, murals, stencil art, and wheatpaste (posters or other printed materials applied with paste). Even though they tend to be multidisciplinary artists, most of them identify as *grafiteros*, in part because they began with graffiti due to its accessibility and appeal.[16] As described in greater detail in chapter 5, many of the 2006 Generation grafiteros I worked with were first exposed to graffiti and stencils through the anarcho-punk movement. Before the explosion of hip-hop-inspired graffiti (e.g. bombs, wildstyle, tags, etc.) in Oaxaca hit in the mid-1990s, punks were painting anarchist symbols and political slogans on the city's walls, as well as circulating punk zines from places like Mexico City and Ciudad Juárez that depicted punk graffiti. However, it was not until hip-hop-inspired graffiti began to appear in Oaxaca that most 2006 Generation artists began painting the streets. Many of them mixed punk and hip-hop influences and aesthetics to create a unique style that is not easily categorized as either punk graffiti or hip-hop graffiti. To further complicate matters, many of the grafiteros have gone on to further develop their talents and have branched out into studio arts, such as sculpture, painting on canvas, multimedia installations, and engraving and printmaking. Their expansive talents, multisubculturalism, and individual diversity make labeling them or their art accurately quite elusive. For these reasons, the way I describe artists shifts according to context: at times I refer to them as grafiteros (usually when speaking of their formation), street artists (in the context of the 2006 social movement and the immediate years that followed), urban artists and visual artists (in later years once many artists began exhibiting in sanctioned spaces like galleries and universities and not exclusively in the streets), or as 2006 generation artists (when highlighting the politics and aesthetic practices that they share as members of the 2006 Generation).

This book builds on the important insights from cultural studies, anthropology, ethnic studies, and allied fields by offering an in-depth ethnographic study of the role of artists as both producers of culture and as activists within the Oaxacan social movement (Kelley 2003; McCaughan 2012; Redmond 2013; Reed 2005; C.A. Smith 2016; Zolov 1999). The case of 2006 Generation youth artists compels us to move beyond an artist/activist dichotomy in order to fully appreciate the ways that artists' work is often central to social movements, while also recognizing that artists often participate deeply in social movement organizing in ways that go beyond their art. This book highlights the voices of youth artists in asking how they understand their own cultural politics and places it in the broader context of neoliberal militarization, Indigenous organizing, and urbanization.

CHARTING TERRAINS OF RESISTANCE AND CREATION

The organization of this book reflects its emphasis on rethinking social movement temporality, spatiality, and continuity between waves of activism. Chapter 1 provides a historical and ethnographic account of the 2006 social movement and provides the local and national context within which it emerged. Through a focus on the cultural politics of space making within the social movement, I show how young people came together to assert their place as political actors with rights to the public sphere. Some of the more significant spaces I explore are a citywide network of barricades, the visual space created through protest art, and a social center opened in an abandoned police station. While they carved out spaces for themselves as youth, they also made important intergenerational connections that helped legitimize them as political actors within the broader social movement. The horizontal politics and sociality practiced by youth as they produced these counterspaces proved influential for the 2006 Generation's emerging cultural and spatial politics, which are the focus of the remaining four chapters.

Through analysis of two influential youth collectives—CASOTA and VOCAL—chapter 2 excavates the diverse ideological and social movement genealogies that have shaped the politics of the 2006 Generation. In mapping these genealogies of resistance, chapter 2 demonstrates how urban, Indigenous, and migrant youth in Mexico mobilize an antiauthoritarian politics that is horizontal and articulate a gendered critique of the masculine protagonism of movement leadership. In the process, youth create and indigenize political space and also re-vision what it means to be Indigenous and practice Indigenous politics in a globalized, post-NAFTA Mexico. Chapter 3 examines how these two youth collectives spatialized their politics and their experiences from 2006 via the creation of territorialized and networked counterspaces, where they continued to hone the horizontal political cultures they experimented with during the height of grassroots control of the city. Via this examination, this chapter provides evidence for one of the main arguments in *Cartographies of Youth Resistance,* that social movements and the political cultures they produce are more sustainable and impactful if organizers are able to link the more ephemeral spaces of direct actions and protest art with longer-lasting counterspaces like social centers and cultural venues.

Chapter 4 builds on the previous chapter's argument about social movement sustainability and space making by demonstrating through three event-centered analyses how youth organizers include difference and radical politics in the tourist-dominated capital city. In my analysis of the relationship between space and power, I place Lefebvre's concept of counterspace in dialogue with Foucault's understanding of power as capillary to argue that attending to the material and social constitution of power and space allows us to better grasp the complexities of how power and resistance are produced, contested, and negotiated. In doing so, I elaborate the concepts of palimpsestic space and rebel aesthetics to frame the collective practices through which activists and artists give visual form to their utopian visions and sensibilities.

Chapter 5 traces the formation of two pioneering graffiti crews—Arte Jaguar and AK Crew—and anarchist currents of the local punk movement, to further demonstrate the centrality of cultural production in the space-making practices and rebel aesthetic of the 2006 Generation. This chapter offers in-depth analysis of how engaging in cultural production can create the structural mechanisms for collective action, while also helping foster politicized identities, discourses, and political cultures—in this case, radical

horizontalism, urban autonomy, and decolonial anarchism. The case of artists within the youth movement also sheds light on some of the challenges
in sustaining ideals of horizontalism and autonomy over time and across
difference. Various collectives and individual artists, for example, have been
absorbed into local and global markets—including the tourist economy.
Others have retreated to their working-class colonias or rural communities after becoming disenchanted with having to rely financially on selling
their work to tourists in order to sustain their art spaces in the city. I close
the book with this account because the trajectory of artists is in many ways
emblematic of the shared and divergent paths of the 2006 Generation more
broadly, whereby they must navigate the two-pronged approach of repression
and co-optation characteristic of post-Revolution Mexican statecraft, as well
as exclusionary and co-opting market forces. Ultimately, this chapter illuminates how social movement energy transforms and fluctuates across ebbs
and flows of activity, and through the emergence and decline of particular
groups and collectives.

The concluding chapter gives a brief update on where the main collectives
and networks of counterspaces discussed in the book stood as of 2019. This
update offers a window into what the case of the 2006 Generation tells us
about social movement temporality, spatiality, and impact; the challenges
posed by neoliberal militarization; and the limits and potential of horizontalism and youth organizing. Ultimately, we get a sense of how migrant,
urban, and Indigenous youth in Mexico are creating radical possibilities for
a world with greater dignity.

ONE

Building Youth Counterspaces, Horizontal Political Cultures, and Emergent Identities in the Oaxacan Social Movement of 2006

MENTES LIBERADAS had been making regular visits to the teachers' encampment in the zocalo for several weeks before the repression started.[1] He was a longtime member of the local anarcho-punk scene—the punk movement, as members refer to it—and part of the Liberationist Social Center (CESOL). Mentes Liberadas did not spend much time talking directly with the teachers. Instead, he would check in with activists from his collective and other affinity groups from the Oaxacan punk movement who had been keeping a watchful eye on the encampment, given the rumors that had been circulating that the police were going to evict the teachers. The anarcho-punks did not exactly have a close relationship with the teachers' union, in part because the teachers mostly viewed them with suspicion and even disdain. The punk movement also had real issues with the union's leaders (and the fact that there were leaders in the first place). The punks were sympathetic, however, to the cause the union was fighting for—higher salaries for teachers, scholarships for students, and more resources and facilities for schools. Moreover, the punk movement is at its core antiauthoritarian and antifascist, so the threats of police violence against the striking teachers were a bigger concern for them than any issue they had with the powerful teachers' union.

The phone call reached Mentes Liberadas at 5:30 a.m. on June 14, 2006. The police were evicting the teachers and their families from the zocalo. That the eviction was violent did not need to be said, because Mentes Liberadas knew as well as anyone else that the teachers' union would not abandon their encampment simply because the police (or anyone else) told them to. Mentes Liberadas immediately jumped on his bicycle and pedaled the four miles from his working-class neighborhood on the northwestern outskirts of the city. What he found when he arrived was a chaotic scene: somewhere between 870 and 3,000 police officers (Osorno 2007; Martínez Vásquez 2007, respectively) entered the zocalo where the teachers and their families were sleeping between 4:00 and 5:00 a.m. They attacked them with batons and burned their tarps, tents, and possessions, all while officers launched tear gas from a privately owned helicopter directly at the people on the ground. Far from being afraid, however, Mentes Liberadas remembered being excited. Not excited because of the attack, but excited to see that by 7:00 a.m. thousands of Oaxacans had joined them in taking over the downtown streets in defense of the teachers. Overwhelmed by the sheer numbers of protesters, the police returned to their barracks by midday and refused to deploy against the growing movement. According to Mentes Liberadas,

> It lasted several hours; I think it was around eleven o'clock in the morning that we were able to recover the *zócalo*. In my opinion, what motivated the *banda* to go and support the teachers was that we were sick and tired of so much repression.[2] That was the moment for all of us to show them that we were fed up with so much injustice by all pouncing at the same time against the police. They were the ones who were always fucking with us. This way we would show the government that it wasn't cool to keep doing what they were doing anymore.

This chapter provides a history of the social movement that emerged from the events of June 14, 2006. We will gain an appreciation of the crucial role that youth like Mentes Liberadas played in the broad-based social movement that took grassroots control of Oaxaca City and several municipalities throughout the state for six months. The movement brought together an incredibly diverse set of actors with different experiences, organizing norms, political agendas, and visions of social change. This included activists who had been politically formed through their militancy in vertical organizations, such as leftist opposition groups and labor unions, as well as liberationist, anarchist, and autonomist youth who embraced horizontal organizing and vehemently rejected any form of hierarchical organizing.[3] Participating in this diverse movement and in the extraordinary exercise of grassroots control of the capital city deeply marked how youth understood politics and their place in society and in public space, continuing to shape their political subjectivities and identities a decade later.

URBAN SPACE AND THE POLITICAL LANDSCAPE
IN OAXACA AND MEXICO

Before detailing the immediate lead-up to the events of June 14 and the formation of the 2006 social movement, we should understand the cultural, political, economic, and historic significance of urban space in Oaxacan politics. The center of Oaxaca City, especially the zocalo, has been the social and political center of the state for centuries. This is, of course, in line with the role of the plaza in Latin America as the "preeminent public space, a source and symbol of civic power, with a long tradition as the cultural center of the city" (Low 2000, 35). This consolidation of power is evident in the physical layout of the Oaxacan zocalo. Its open square is bordered by the seat of the Roman Catholic Church on the northern end, and by the state capitol building on the southern end. In addition to housing the official structures of state and church power, the zocalo has long been the focus of popular protest, with mobilizations regularly targeting it and the surrounding area.

Another layer to the cultural politics of urban space in Oaxaca came in 1987, when the historic center of the capital city and the nearby archaeological site of Monte Albán were designated a UNESCO World Heritage Site. This site is at the center of a marketing campaign that paints Oaxaca City as a provincial capital where tourists can experience Mexico's pre-Hispanic past, Spanish colonial period, and the Indigenous Mexico of today (Wood 2008). According to the UNESCO website, twelve hundred historic monuments line the streets of Oaxaca to "create a harmonious cityscape, and reconstitute the image of a former colonial city whose monumental aspect has been kept intact."[4] Achieving the desired arrangement and (re)production of Oaxacan history, tradition, and contemporary culture requires the policing of boundaries and bodies so tourists can visit this colonial relic without the hassle and so-called chaos normally associated with Latin American cities. In part, this means relegating Oaxaca's urban poor and working class to the urban periphery, and Oaxaca's Indigenous present to small towns, ethnic markets, cultural festivals, and other sanctioned spaces for tourism.

According to the above logic, Indigenous punk youth and striking laborers, for example, do not belong in the city center. When geographies of power and marginality (Fernandes 2010) in Oaxaca fail to prevent poor, working-class, and migrant bodies from the city center, they must be removed, made invisible, or incorporated into the carefully curated landscape that is the most visible centerpiece of Oaxaca's neoliberal economy.

The control of raced, classed, and gendered bodies in space is of course not new. Speaking of Porfirian Oaxaca City, Mark Overmyer-Velásquez states that "[e]lites, attempting to reinforce their positions of power, conceived of and organized city spaces to reflect their dominant, class-and-race-exclusive form of modernity . . . that confined nonwhite workers to the city's margins" (2006, 40–41). The spatialization of difference and power continues in contemporary Oaxaca and provides the dominant spatial logic and practices against which youth counterspaces and politics are produced. Moreover, the youth organizing explored in this book suggests that in addition to race and class, we must also account for social categories such as gender and youth when considering who has meaningful access to the city.

Lefebvre's theorization of space can help us frame the tension between what the government thinks the city should look like and the lived realities of that space. For Lefebvre (1991), social space is constituted through three interlinked moments. This triad consists of space as perceived, conceived, and lived, which he refers to as spatial practices, representations of space, and representational space, respectively (Lefebvre 1991, 38-40). In contemporary Oaxaca City, major tensions exist between the representations of space as *conceived* by politicians, urban planners, the tourism industry, technocrats, and social engineers, and the way that those they call inhabitants and users *perceive* and *live* that space. In other words, space cannot be planned and controlled unilaterally and disconnected from the people who inhabit, use, and relate to that space. These tensions often play out in the historic city center. State, business, and civil society engage in a constant struggle to control the physical space, as well as the visual narrative told by its architecture, infrastructure, and social space.

Resistance to the exclusionary and top-down space-making practices of the state, urban planners, and business have also long been an important part of the cultural politics of urban Oaxaca. In 2002, for example, the zocalo was the site of a contentious year-long battle over Oaxaca's cultural patrimony and who had the right to alter it. The late painter Francisco Toledo, widely considered the most important Oaxacan artist of his generation, led a creative grassroots campaign against plans to open a McDonald's in the zocalo. Toledo created an organization to spearhead the campaign, the Defense and Conservation Board of the Cultural and Natural Patrimony of the State of Oaxaca (PRO-OAX). In addition to collecting over ten thousand signatures against the fast-food store's opening, PRO-OAX handed out handmade Oaxacan tamales and atole to over five hundred people in front of the proposed locale

(Altamirano 2002). Toledo explained the objective as being to "raise awareness among the people of the importance of eating dishes that are native to Oaxaca's delicious cuisine." Toledo often mobilized the language and logic of cultural patrimony in his campaign, which the state and tourism industry deployed to justify their own control over public space. Toledo declared, "The great response from the citizenry is evidence of the dissent against McDonald's, which the municipal government must take into account in order to preserve the historic city center that UNESCO declared a World Heritage Site" (Altamirano 2002). After a year of protests and debates, the mayor and future governor Gabino Cué announced that the fast-food chain would not be allowed to open its franchise in the zocalo. Many celebrated the decision as a victory for Oaxaca's cultural patrimony and against Yankee imperialism (Poniatowska 2002).

In 2005, Governor Ulises Ruiz Ortiz foreshadowed his heavy-handed approach to governing, making him widely unpopular even before the 2006 uprising. Soon after entering office, Ruiz unilaterally initiated a series of unpopular public works targeting the backbone of the historic city center, including major remodeling of the zocalo and other important plazas and parks. Ruiz's remodel included plans to "modernize" the zocalo by removing the majority of the vegetation and replacing it with cement. This sparked a series of protests stemming from allegations of corruption in the granting of government contracts, concerns over the perceived assault on Oaxaca's cultural patrimony and the environment, and discontent over Ruiz's unilateral decision making. José, a middle-aged Indigenous teacher active in the social movement of 2006, told me that the first barricades of the Ruiz era were raised by people trying to protect an ancient tree in the zocalo from being destroyed as part of the remodel. Although the tree was eventually removed, Jose described the barricades as "a symbol of popular protest against (Ruiz's) authoritarianism and corruption" that would resurface in 2006.

Part of the remodel also included relocating the executive branch from the zocalo to Tlalixtac de Cabrera, a town outside of the city where the new Ciudad Administrativa (Administrative City) currently sits behind large metal fences, walls, and armed guards. Ruiz's reasoning for doing so was clear, yet ultimately unsuccessful—to avoid encampments, rallies, and other political disruptions in the zocalo (Díaz Montes 2009). This move was one of his first attempts to "cleanse" the plaza of "indecent displays of political behavior" so that it "might be rendered a neutral space to be filled with strolling tourists and temporary cultural displays" (Poole 2009, 199). Struggles over who has the right to alter the World Heritage Site, what constitutes beautification versus vandalism, and the proper balance between "modernization" and "conservation" continue to be salient in Oaxaca City. This book is an effort to highlight and understand the role that youth as cultural producers and political actors play in how these contestations over cultural politics become spatialized in the context of the 2006 Oaxacan social movement and in the political life of Oaxaca in the decade that followed.

OAXACA'S TEACHERS' UNION AND NATIONAL POLITICS IN 2006

No discussion of Oaxacan politics and urban space would be complete without including Sección 22 (Local 22), the local dissident wing of the National Educational Workers Union (SNTE). Sección 22 has been one of the most powerful organizing forces in Oaxaca for several decades and was instrumental in the emergence and organizing power of the 2006 social movement. With over seventy thousand members and generations of organizing experience, Sección 22 brought tremendous resources and knowledge to the movement, but they also brought a decidedly more hierarchical (vertical) organizing logic that was not always congruent with the horizontalism (nonhierarchical, antiauthoritarian organizing) mobilized by youth.[5]

The SNTE is the largest and arguably most powerful labor union in Latin America, with 1.5 million members. But neoliberal reforms threaten to weaken the power of public sector workers and the teachers' union in particular (Hernández Navarro 2013). Originally formed in 1943 under the corporatist system of the postrevolutionary Mexican state, the teachers' union was granted a monopoly on representing all of the nation's educational workers in primary and secondary schools, and like other "favored" unions their membership was converted into vast electoral reserves to be tapped during election cycles (Cook 1996). In response to corporatism and corruption, teachers throughout the country, but especially in southern states, waged a decades-long struggle to democratize their union. Teachers in Oaxaca have been at the forefront of this movement, which has cost over one hundred teachers their lives in that state alone (ibid.). Political scientist Jonathan Fox (1994) refers to this strategy of fostering, co-opting and repressing unions in Mexico as part of the Mexican government's system of "authoritarian clientelism". In 1979, the struggle to democratize the union led to the formation of the democratic caucus within the SNTE, the National Education Workers Coordinating Committee (CNTE), which represents roughly 30 percent of the union's membership (Cook 1996, 3).

Sección 22 of the CNTE, Oaxaca's dissident wing of the teachers' union, has mobilized its membership on an annual basis for the past four decades in order to pressure the Oaxacan government to renegotiate their contracts. On May 1, 2006, Sección 22 marched through the center of Oaxaca City and presented the government with a list of demands for a new round of contract negotiations. The list contained seventeen demands, including the restructuring of wages, classrooms or schoolhouses for rural communities where teachers were forced to teach outdoors, scholarships, and uniforms and shoes for low-income students (Martínez Vásquez 2007, 60). That year, however, Governor Ulises Ruiz Ortiz refused to enter into meaningful negotiations with the union, which set in motion the series of events leading to the formation of the 2006 social movement. Ruiz entered office with a hard-line stance against protests, declaring an end to sit-ins and marches in Oaxaca. Instead of negotiating, he launched a media campaign aimed at turning public opinion against the teachers. Union officials also accused the secretary general of the state of fomenting internal divisions within the union. Most notably, union leader Enrique Rueda Pacheco was widely believed to have accepted bribes from the government in an unsuccessful attempt to end the union's mobilizations.

With the governor refusing to negotiate, Sección 22 set up an encampment in the zocalo on May 22, 2006. After another week of stalemate, the teachers mobilized on May 31 to block access to gas stations and main roads in the historic city center. At this point public opinion was divided. Many people seemed to be as tired of the frequent protests by the teachers as they were skeptical of the governor, who entered office amid widespread allegations of fraud. On a national level, attention was largely focused on the highly contested presidential elections to be held on July 2 between ruling-party candidate Felipe Calderón (PAN) and third-party candidate Andrés Manuel López Obrador (PRD).[6] Calderon was eventually declared president-elect by the Federal Electoral Tribunal (TEPJF), although he entered the presidency on very weak political footing amid massive protests and allegations of electoral fraud.

Parallel to the elections, the Zapatistas spearheaded *La Otra Campaña*, a project meant to strengthen connections between communities, groups, and social movements in Mexico as an alternative to the process of political party campaigns. Also in May of that year, San Salvador Atenco, a town near Mexico City, was besieged by state and federal police after residents set up roadblocks in support of flower vendors who had been attacked by police. The government responded to this act of solidarity by sending in police, who according to a 2008 human rights report, killed two youths, arrested over two hundred people and sexually assaulted and tortured forty-seven female detainees (CCIODH 2008, 15). The swiftness and brutality with which the state responded can be partially explained by the fact that Atenco was already a national beacon of hope for social movements and communities in resistance. In 2002, residents of Atenco formed the People's Front in Defense of the Land (Frente del Pueblo en Defensa de la Tierra) and successfully resisted the federal government's attempt to displace them in order to construct a new airport on their land (Arellano Chávez 2010; Gibler 2009). The siege of Atenco in 2006, the contested presidential elections, and the momentum surrounding La Otra Campaña are all significant background for understanding the importance of the social movement that emerged that summer in Oaxaca and the brutal response by the local, state, and federal governments.

THE EMERGENCE OF THE OAXACAN
SOCIAL MOVEMENT OF 2006

It is in this context of ongoing struggle that the 2006 social movement emerged, giving surprising coherence to the grievances of diverse segments of Oaxacan society. The final action that triggered the formation of the movement occurred during the very early morning hours of June 14, 2006, when police forces violently removed sleeping teachers and their families from their encampment. Police used batons, dogs, guns, and tear gas launched from privately owned helicopters on the sleeping teachers and their families. The indiscriminate bombing of the area with tear gas left hundreds of people seeking refuge and medical assistance—including many nonteachers who lived, worked, or had other business in the busy downtown area that morning. One hundred thirteen people registered at local hospitals as a result, with injuries ranging from gunshot wounds to miscarriages and perforated lungs (Martínez Vásquez 2007, 66).

The union had a radio station called Radio Plantón, which served as a parallel public space to that of the encampment. According to communications scholar Margarita Zires, "the radio began to convert itself into an important voice of the Movement, an alternative media public space ... it formed part of the milieu of the encampment in the zócalo" (2009, 164). The radio warned of the possibility of a police action directed at clearing the encampment in the days leading up to June 14. When the time came and the police attacked, they also attacked the teachers' union headquarters and the radio tower, taking the station off the air.

The governor's decision to repress the teachers immediately backfired. In a powerful display of horizontal and spontaneous mobilization, thousands of people joined the teachers in the streets to denounce the use of force against nonviolent protesters—including many people who were not otherwise sympathetic to the teachers' union. The police eventually refused to continue and returned to their barracks. By midday on June 14, 2006, the teachers and their allies—new and old—retook the zocalo and established an even larger encampment (Sotelo Marbán 2008). The coalition that formed that day included a wide range of people and organizations with varied agendas and motivations for participating. For example, Doña Inés, a retired nurse, lent her medical services to those in need at an impromptu medical clinic set up at a nearby church.[7] She made a point of emphasizing that she had always been "apolitical" and not necessarily in agreement with Sección 22's tactics, although she respected the rank-and-file teachers and had family members who were active in the union. Her support on June 14 and in the following months was born of the outrage she shared with many Oaxacans when they learned of the indiscriminate and unprovoked use of force ordered by the governor.

Many youth also came to defense of the teachers following their eviction. There were many reasons for this, but the three that I heard most frequently from youth were (1) their own relationship to teachers, such as having family or friends in the union; (2) self-defense, after being affected by the indiscriminate tear-gassing that morning; and (3) an antagonistic relationship with police that predated the movement. Graffiti artists and punks were most likely to highlight their mistreatment at the hands of police prior to 2006 as part of the reason they were ready and willing to be at the frontlines on June 14, and in the months and years that followed. Mentes Liberadas talked about helping the teachers out of desperation, having been victimized by the police over the years for his participation in the punk movement. University students also played a key role in the early moments of the growing movement. Students at the Benito Juárez Autonomous University of Oaxaca (UABJO), for example, organized the takeover of their university's radio

FIGURE 3. March during June 2006. Photo credit: Susy Chávez Herrera.

station, Radio Universidad. This radio station proved to be as crucial for the emerging movement as Radio Plantón had been for the teachers, helping organize actions and mobilizations. Two days after the police attacks, hundreds of thousands of Oaxacans participated in a massive march demanding the governor's removal (see figure 3).

THE FORMATION OF THE POPULAR ASSEMBLY
OF THE PEOPLES OF OAXACA (APPO)

On June 17, Sección 22 convened a public assembly, inviting over three hundred organizations and movements active in Oaxaca to discuss how best to capitalize on the momentum generated over the past days. The teachers proposed extending the structure of their union's assembly-style decision-making body, the State Assembly of Sección 22 Delegates, to Oaxacan civil society (Martínez Vásquez 2007). They called the new organizing structure the Asamblea Popular de los Pueblos de Oaxaca (Popular Assembly of the Peoples of Oaxaca, or APPO).[8] The assembly as decision-making structure has a long and dynamic history in Oaxaca. The majority of the state's municipalities are governed through *usos y costumbres* (Indigenous customary law and tradition), and in those communities decisions are made through the assembly, not electoral politics.

After the first meeting, the APPO agreed on the resignation of Ruiz as their principal demand, though it would be a mistake to limit the grievances of the APPO to this single goal. The APPO also pushed for a new state constitution that represented the pluralism of the state, and they demanded an end to the repression of political dissent, which was widespread under Ruiz's predecessor José Murat but had grown exponentially with Ruiz's administration (Martínez Vásquez 2007). The APPO, the main organizing structure and civic space of the movement, consisted of over three hundred existing social movements, civic organizations, nonprofits, and political associations and organizations, all with diverse agendas (Esteva 2010). While the APPO was an essential part of the movement, many individuals and collectives who participated in the movement did not necessarily identify as *appistas* (APPO members). For this reason, it is important not to conflate the broader social movement of 2006 with the APPO, as is often done. This distinction is especially pertinent when considering participation of youth who identified as liberationist or anarchist, and others who participated in the more horizontal spaces of the movement, while rejecting the more formal spaces that tended to privilege established organizations, activists, and political styles.

While the APPO was far more inclusive than the existing political institutions of the state, it was largely dominated by organizations that brought preexisting, often vertical, political practices and agendas to the movement. It is also important to recognize that youth, women, and unmarried men are often barred from participating in community assemblies. While such exclusions were not explicit in the assembly, many of the same social forces behind them were replicated in this movement space. Youth, for example, were largely excluded from participating in the assembly, and women were often alienated by the aggressive masculine style of debate that dominated it (Stephen 2013). [9] In the remainder of this chapter, we will explore how youth carved out their own spaces for participation in the movement where they could experiment with alternative political cultures and cultural politics—spaces that, drawing on Henri Lefebvre's work (1991), I refer to as counterspaces. Youth brought their emergent politics into the broader movement, where they sometimes disrupted vertical organizing practices, other times were marginalized by them, and yet other times coalesced with them to create even more hybrid forms. Youth, therefore, played a vital role in strengthening the more horizontal practices of the movement.

Ultimately, through both horizontal and vertical organizing, the broader movement was able to control the capital city of Oaxaca, as well as several municipalities in the state, from June to November of 2006. Elsewhere (Magaña 2010), I analyze the simultaneity of vertical and horizontal organizing logics in the Oaxacan social movement through the framework of what Arturo Escobar (2008), borrowing from Manuel De Landa (1997), calls "meshworks." This concept allows us to follow the parallel power structures operating within the movement in order to appreciate how they act to yield a total effect. Next, I will highlight the role that youth played in establishing and expanding the horizontal spaces within the movement, while not losing sight of the importance of the more vertical currents.

WOMEN AND MOVEMENT RADIO: TRANSMITTING AND PRACTICING HORIZONTALITY ON THE AIR

During the six months of popular control, the movement held cultural events, organized massive mobilizations, and executed state functions such as policing, trash collection, and governance, as well as transmitting original grassroots radio and television programming throughout the state, and internationally, via the internet. Movement-run media were crucial in the development of the movement, in mobilizing diffuse networks of activists and sympathizers, and in providing a space for participation for Oaxacans with little political capital—including youth, women, and Indigenous Oaxacans with varied levels of organizing experience. Radio Plantón of

Sección 22 and Radio Universidad of the UABJO were invaluable organizing and communications tools for the teachers' union and the emerging social movement. The government recognized this fact, targeting the former early during its offensive against the teachers and sabotaging the latter via an infiltrator who poured acid on the transmission equipment.[10]

The reach of movement-run media dramatically expanded on August 1, when several hundred women marched to the main state-run radio and television station, Channel 9 (COR-TV), to request airtime. Thousands of women had marched through the city banging on pots and pans to call attention to women's participation in the movement, in what was called La Marcha de las Cacerolas (the March of the Pots and Pans). A large contingent decided to continue the march to Channel 9 to protest what many felt was biased, pro-government coverage. When they were denied airtime on the public station, they decided to occupy it. A teacher I'll call Maribel explained the situation to me in an interview at a local cantina in 2007:

> Unfortunately, the media always says that nothing is happening in Oaxaca—this is because they are all bribed by the government. This is why we women took Canal 9. We had to tell our side of the story. We had to show that yes, there is something happening in Oaxaca and it is not what the *mal gobierno* or its media say. We Oaxacan women had to take the TV and radio to show that in our state *el pueblo* stood up and said, "Enough, we have had enough of this corruption, of this violence, of these bad politicians."

With support from fellow activists, women maintained control of the station for several weeks, renaming it Radio Cacerola (Saucepan Radio). The radio station was a key public space "occupied by the movement" (Zires 2009, 173) and "the chief means for people to voice their opinions, receive news, and have debates" (Stephen 2013, 152). Radio Cacerola quickly became one of the most important spaces produced by the movement—both in terms of the physical and social space of the radio station itself, as well as the shared sonic space created through radio programming. Speaking of 1940s and '50s Los Angeles, cultural historian Gaye Theresa Johnson (2013) argues that the radio helped produce shared sonic spaces where Mexican American and Black youth could discover mutual identification and prefigure future political affiliations. Similarly, the importance of movement media such as Radio Cacerola goes beyond their logistic utility to include the social and political relations that were fostered through the shared sonic and social space they created.

Radio Cacerola was one of the first movement counterspaces created by people who were marginalized not just in society but even within the larger social movement. The women's takeover of the radio was not ordered by the assembly or union leadership, but instead was an impromptu decision made horizontally by activists in the streets. Many of the women who participated in the takeover and spoke on the air had little or no experience in public speaking or *formal* leadership positions. The space produced by women through their takeover of Radio Cacerola challenged long-standing hierarchies and exclusions within Mexican society based not only on gender but also on race, ethnicity, class, sexuality, and age. Given the uncomfortable reality that such societal exclusions and oppression are often reproduced even within progressive social movements, inclusive counterspaces like the radio are crucial if social movements are to achieve their emancipatory aspirations and radical potential.

Radio Cacerola aired grassroots programming in at least six different Indigenous languages, bringing the long-standing institution of Indigenous radio (Wortham 2013) from Oaxaca's rural communities to the capital city and shared sonic spaces. In this way, the radio bridged Mexico's racial geographies and prefigured the movement's demand that Oaxaca's ethnic diversity be respected and represented. Moreover, Radio Cacerola featured programming linking local events to national and international ones, and to the structural forces behind them. For example, movement broadcasters discussed the epidemic of violence against women and femicides in Oaxaca—topics rarely discussed publicly at the time—in relation to the more well-known case of the mujeres de Juárez; they discussed poverty in Oaxaca in relation to neoliberal structural adjustments; and they connected the heightened authoritarianism of recent years in relation to Plan Puebla Panamá, extractivism, and land dispossession in the region (Dunlap 2017; Gómez-Barris 2017). In sum, Radio Cacerola and other movement media discussed the challenges posed by neoliberal militarization, bridged ethnic and linguistic difference as well as geographic distance, and centered women's narratives and actions.

FROM THE AIRWAVES TO THE BARRICADES: NETWORKING SPACES OF SELF-DEFENSE

Radio also represented an important pillar in the movement's organizing structure and proved crucial in aiding community-based self-defense. After local police refused to leave their barracks to attack the movement, the head of Oaxacan Security and Transportation Aristeo López Martínez assembled a clandestine security force, rumored to include out-of-state paramilitaries.[11] They entered neighborhoods at night in convoys of trucks with highly armed and masked men, made illegal arrests, and fired on movement installations and encampments. Radio Cacerola announced the location of these forces, and when arrests were made, the radio broadcast a description of the vehicle(s) used and encouraged people to find and stop them (Stephen 2013). The radio was also used to mobilize people to reinforce occupied government buildings.

In the middle of the night on August 20, 2006, paramilitary forces opened fire on and destroyed the transmission tower for the station. Activists reacted immediately; by the morning of August 21, they had already taken over the remaining twelve commercial radio stations in the city.[12] On the following night, convoys of up to forty trucks of undercover police and paramilitaries continued their attacks, shooting at movement encampments and murdering Lorenzo Sampablo Cervantes, an unarmed architect who was helping guard one of the radio towers. These takeovers demonstrate the flexibility and adaptability of social movements that combine vertical and horizontal organizing logics (i.e., meshworks). Activists didn't have to wait for decisions to pass through a bureaucratic apparatus before taking action. Instead, when circumstances dictated immediate action be taken, people in the movement made the necessary decisions collectively but independent of the assembly. This flexibility was crucial, given the unpredictability of the paramilitary repression.

In response to the paramilitary attacks, movement networks mobilized to erect a citywide network of approximately fifteen hundred self-defense barricades. They were erected every night, and most were removed at 6 a.m. to allow traffic to circulate, although some were more permanent, depending on security concerns. This was especially true after the Federal Preventative Police (PFP) were sent by the federal government to retake the city and attack the movement in late October. Neighbors gathered rocks, tires, downed trees, and cars, and commandeered buses and semitrailers or whatever objects they could acquire to build the barricades. The construction of barricades began at the grassroots level and was then promoted through the radio and the APPO assembly. This is another example of the flexibility of the movement's parallel power structures. It is also important to recognize that the construction of barricades is part of an existing and rich "repertoire of contention" in Oaxaca (Tilly 1978). Activists drew on previous experiences, such as the construction of barricades in 2005 to contest Governor Ruiz's remodeling of the city center, when mobilizing their efforts. In this way, they built on, and learned from, their predecessors and contemporaries.

The barricades quickly became community spaces where neighbors who may never have spoken before would spend all night drinking coffee, eating, dancing, and talking while reclaiming the streets, their barrios, the historic city center, and their right to be free from violence. Since the street is a basic unit of public life, an everyday public space where people are brought together to interact (Tonkiss 2005), it is not surprising that the reclaiming and reconfiguring of Oaxaca's streets in 2006 proved to be a transformative experience for the countless who participated. The raising and guarding of barricades "turned strangers into comrades" (Dzenovska and Arenas 2012, 646) and transformed residents from Oaxaca's urban *colonias* (neighborhoods) from a population to be governed into participants in an active experiment in radical direct democracy.

The network of barricades, along with the occupied radio and television stations, were crucial in deepening the grassroots power of the movement, which encompassed broad sectors of Oaxacan society, cutting across vast differences and geographies. According to Gustavo Esteva,

> The sudden presence in the movement of groups from the popular neighborhoods . . . was unexpected. It was not known to what extent the communal social fabric also existed in those neighborhoods. The barricades arose spontaneously as a popular response to the governor's attacks on the APPO encampments and rapidly took on a life of their own, to the extent of becoming autonomous focal points for social and political organization. Long sleepless nights provided the opportunity for extensive political discussion, which awakened in many young people a hitherto nonexistent or inchoate social consciousness. (2010, 985)

Esteva highlights the importance of the barricades in fostering the participation of Oaxaca's popular neighborhood residents and youth in particular. Young people in Mexico are among the most vulnerable to the impacts of the recent global economic crisis and the neoliberal assault on social programs and public education. For poor and working-class youth in Oaxaca there were—and continue to be—very few spaces open where they could feel their participation was legitimized by the larger Oaxacan society. It was in this social milieu that youth with diverse levels of political formation and organizing experience found a space for meaningful participation.

David Venegas, an APPO council member who was chosen to represent his neighborhood barricade and a founding member of the youth collective VOCAL (explored in detail in chapter 2), described the impact that the barricades had in decentering the formal spaces of the movement and expanding the more horizontal spaces:

> That's when my participation, along with the participation of hundreds of thousands of others, began to make a more substantial difference. . . . We eventually started discussing agreements and decisions made by the APPO Council and the teachers' union. There were a number of occasions when the barricade chose actions that went against those agreements, which in my view only strengthened our capacity for organized resistance. In this way, the barricades reestablished and modified the social fabric of the neighborhoods. (quoted in Denham and C.A.S.A. Collective 2008, 290–91).

Here David contrasts the horizontal decision making at the barricades with the top-down practice of the "APPO Council and teachers' union." This speaks to some of the tensions within the movement that led youth to form their own spaces built on the more horizontal models experimented with in the barricades. David's analysis echoes Esteva's in terms of the role that the barricades played in expanding the horizontal power of the movement. David grounds the long-term impacts of the barricades in the city's *colonias* vis-á-vis novel and strengthened social relations. Subsequent organizing efforts by movement youth, such as VOCAL, sought to extend these social relations to greater Oaxacan society and political organizing.

During a February 2010 discussion at CASOTA (Autonomous Oaxacan Solidarity House for Self-Managed Work, also described in detail in chapter 2), David again referred to the tensions between the horizontal and vertical structures within the APPO. He described an occasion when the APPO Council entered into negotiations with the government and offered to remove the barricades, even though the government had yet to address any of the movement's demands. David explained:

> People who claimed to speak on behalf of the assembly told us [at the Brenamiel barricade] to let the ADO [private bus company] through, because they had come to an agreement with them. *Ni madres* (fuck that), we told them! We took control of this street and they are not going through here. If you want them to go through, let them through the streets that you have taken.

In November 2006, following one of the more violent battles with federal police, one of the more strategically important barricades (known by the name of the intersection it occupied, Cinco Señores) produced a flyer addressing the issue of ongoing movement negotiations with the state. In it, the authors criticized the APPO Council for offering to remove the barricades without consulting the barricades as collective actors. The flyer acknowledges the need to engage the state, particularly in order to end the repression, but denounces the fact that the Council acted unilaterally without consulting the barricades. This was just one of several moments when the competing logics of vertical and horizontal organizing within the movement proved to be contradictory.

These tense moments were highly significant in the development of horizontalist political cultures that youth have practiced in later projects such as VOCAL and CASOTA. The verticalism practiced (at times) in the more formal organizing spaces, such as the APPO Council, struck many youth as antithetical to their ideals of direct democracy and consensus-based decision making. This incongruity fueled the new generation of organizers to work on and hone practices of horizontalism in the counterspaces they created and participated in. These examples of what youth activists want and don't want serve as important reference points as they continue the difficult project of enacting social relations that do not perpetuate hierarchy and privilege.

YOUTH COUNTERSPACES IN THE 2006 SOCIAL MOVEMENT

Punks and Anarchists as a Popular Security Force

Radical social movements have the potential to offer blueprints of what a more just and inclusive society might look like in the present. The social movement of 2006 provided such clues about Mexican society both in terms of the reimagining of public space and politics, as well as through social relationships that were created and reworked in the context of grassroots control of the city. Here, Victor Turner's work on ritual, liminality, and communitas is instructive. Turner famously theorized the potential significance of rituals for transforming or reinforcing hierarchy and structure in small-scale societies and beyond.[13] Turner argued that the liminality of rites of passage and other rituals presents us with "a moment in and out of time" where hierarchy and social structure temporarily give way to "an essential and generic human bond" (1969, 96–97). Turner highlights the modality of social relationship with the Latin term *communitas,* which he juxtaposes with the hierarchy of structure. Social movement scholars have picked up on Turner's work to describe the extraordinary milieu opened up by egalitarian social movements in terms of communitas (see Juris 2008; Winegar 2016).

The experience of members of the punk movement vis-à-vis the teachers' union and community elders in the context of the 2006 social movement offers insights into the liminal yet meaningful impacts that living the communitas of social movements can have for marginalized members of society. As mentioned in this chapter's opening, prior to the 2006 social movement anarcho-punks were mostly viewed negatively by the teachers' union and many members of Oaxacan society. When asked to reflect on 2006, Mentes Liberadas spent a lot of time focusing on the way society at large treated and viewed punks. He described nonpunks in his community viewing him and his friends with suspicion and disdain, though he went on to explain that in the early days of the social movement the social stigma began to erode and give way to a certain level of status elevation (Turner 1969). Shortly after helping the teachers retake the zocalo on June 14, his organization (CESOL) and allied collectives of punk, anarchist, liberationist, and autonomist activists built their own encampment in the zocalo, alongside Sección 22 and other organizations. Mentes Liberadas recalled:

> All of the teachers in the state were there, all seventy thousand of them, so we talked to them and explained to them what our movement was about, what we were doing, and why we were there. We did this in part because they would stare at us at first, asking themselves "What's up with those *vándalos?*" And before the movement everyone looked at us like, *"¿Que onda con esos bueyes?* [What's up with those fools?]" But since the battles with police in 2006 they saw that the ones who didn't think twice about jumping into the confrontations were the youth. . . . After that it was like we earned some respect. The movement earned the respect of the teachers and the people that were there, from the organizations. They thanked us for having helped them. And once we had our encampment they would come around and ask us if they could come to us if something happened, if we could support them with that part, with security.

The youth who participated in the initial battle with police earned a new-found respect among their elders by being viewed as a popular security force. Being accepted and validated by teachers is particularly significant for youth, given the social role that educators play in regulating youth behavior and as gatekeepers of societal norms (Flores 2016; Rios 2017; Sojoyner 2016). Even though many of the youth organizers I worked with in this study were of high school or college age, only a small handful had studied (or planned to study) beyond high school. They were not used to having their nonconformity and rebellious spirits validated by teachers and other elders in their communities, though they were accustomed to being criminalized by the police and by society in general due to these very aspects of their identities. Although many were only teenagers in 2006, they had already been on the receiving end of police violence due to their appearance and cultural practices, such as distributing fanzines, graffiti writing, or holding/attending concerts.

The punks and other liberationist and anarchist youth groups formed a collective in 2006 to give coherence to their participation in the growing social movement. They called their collective Bloque Autónomo de Resistencia Libertaria (Autonomous Block of Liberationist Resistance), hereafter Autonomous Block or BARL. The newly organized Autonomous Block collective formed part of the larger encampment's security unit, and they were given official teachers' union ID badges identifying them as security. This facilitated their movement to and from the encampment, as well as their participation in regular rounds of security checks of the barricades throughout the city, as well as the main movement radio station at the time, Radio Universidad, located on the UABJO campus. Several punks from the collective beamed when they spoke of receiving "official credentials" from Sección 22 that read "Encampment Security Force."

While potentially transformative and impactful, the social validation of youth that stemmed from their role as a popular security force could also be seen as problematic and limited. The validation that punk youth, graffiti artists and other young people from the margins of Oaxacan society earned through their defensive labor in battles with police and paramilitary forces was rooted in an uneven relationship to state violence and risk. Not only were many of the youth victimized by police before the social movement, but in the context of 2006 and subsequent campaigns of repression and arrests, many of these young people did not have access to the same resources as union members and other professionals within the movement. Here the distinction between *appistas* and social movement activists who did not identify with the APPO is crucial. Mentes Liberadas raised precisely this issue:

> The legal arm of the APPO would visit the *compañeros* that were arrested. They would ask them, "What's your name? What organization are you from?

So are you from the APPO?" And if the compañeros replied "No, I'm not from the APPO, I am from the *pueblo*," then the lawyers would say, "Well, then we can't get you out." They left them alone in jail and they had to figure things out on their own. It was basically up to their families to get them out.

Even though the social order and hierarchy became unsettled during those six months of grassroots control in 2006, the scenario that Mentes Liberadas paints here speaks to a reproduction of the pre-2006 order. Those who were active in the movement but tended not to identify as *appistas* were often punk youth, graffiti artists, and other people at the margins of society. Their reluctance to identify with the APPO was rooted in a distrust of the perceived political culture, practices, and ambitions of organizers operating in the formal spaces of the movement (APPO), and often stemmed from their previous relationships (or lack thereof) with the types of people who often take up the most space in these arenas—opposition militants, union leadership, and other hypermasculine authority figures. Without access to movement resources, like lawyers, non-*appista* movement activists were left in vulnerable positions vis-à-vis government repression that mirrored their pre-2006 social locations. A "liminality of status elevation" (Turner 1969) occurred in the extraordinary social milieu fostered by grassroots control of the city. Although Autonomous Block activists received social validation and even official union ID badges for their defensive labor, their newfound status in relation to the union was not only temporary but ultimately ended up reinforcing the "structural principle"—in this case social hierarchy—through its temporary inversion (Turner 1969). It was, after all, union leadership, teachers, professionals, and elders who, even in this scenario, were the gatekeepers of social validation for youth and decided who deserved legal help.

Moreover, the validation of youth for their defensive labor reinforced a form of masculinity within the movement that values youth in general, but young men in particular, for their willingness to place their bodies in violent situations (figures 4 and 5). This should not gloss over the reality that young women also put their bodies on the front lines in confrontations with police, only that their defensive labor is seldom recognized as such. Maylei Blackwell (2011) and Dionne Espinoza (2001) have conducted important research on the role of women in the Chicano movement that highlights how social movement labor is often gendered in ways that reproduce gender norms and roles, minimize the importance of labor deemed women's work, and fail to recognize women's labor that challenges the gendered division of

FIGURES 4 & 5. Anarcho-punk security force. Photo credit: Baldomero Robles Menéndez.

labor, much like the efforts of the young women who defended the streets of Oaxaca in 2006.

The role of youth as popular security force within the movement leaves us with the following contradiction: On the one hand, marginalized youth receive a problematic message about the dangerous and often gendered channels available to them for social movement participation. On the other hand, one cannot ignore the pride with which youth like Mentes Liberadas shared their stories of earning the respect of teachers and other elders, which has certainly had a transformative impact on how they understand their collective agency as urban youth. Moreover, many of these relationships between young people and elders from their communities that were fostered or strengthened in 2006 remain intact today.

Youth and Movement Radio

The Autonomous Block's new status as card-carrying members of the security team allowed them greater mobility and access to movement spaces beyond the encampment and barricades. Mentes Liberadas recalled that once his collective had ID badges, they gained access to the movement radio station, Radio Universidad at the time, which had been previously denied to them. In July 2006 members of the Autonomous Block asked those running the station for airtime and were given two hours a day for their own radio program. They used their new platform to introduce the punk movement to the broader Oaxacan social movement and to all listening over the airwaves and the internet. Another member of the punk movement recalled how older people would call in to request certain punk songs Autonomous Block had played, because the social and political lyrics resonated with them. In addition to the music, youth used their airtime to tell listeners about fanzines, both as a genre and regarding the content of the texts the Autonomous Block collective produced, which included social issues like discrimination against punks, racism, and women's rights.

Mentes Liberadas said they received a lot of calls from people who wanted to discuss these issues, as well as people calling to offer the youth words of support:

> The people from the *colonias* would call us. Most of the time they called to offer their support for what we were doing. Some would say that we were very brave, because they also had kids and knew how dangerous the situation was. They would tell us that we needed to take care of ourselves. More than anything they were words of encouragement, and that is what motivated us to keep going. And at the same time, we opened those spaces, the radio in this case, to the people so that they could check it out and come into the radio booth. Before that, it was very difficult to get access to commercial radio. People would say, "Wow, so this is how radio works! Before this I had

no idea about radio" or "Thank you for opening this space to us. For giving us the chance to learn about radio."

The physical and social space of the movement radio stations, together with the sonic space occupied by the airwaves, constituted important counterspaces produced by the social movement. Much like the barricades, the radio brought together previously disparate sectors of Oaxacan society, such as punk youth, professionals, and rural farmworkers, and thus challenged existing geographies of power and marginality (Fernandes 2010).

Rosalía, a funny yet stern young woman from the Isthmus of Tehuantepec, was active in the social movement and later in the collective VOCAL. Rosalía juggled being a single mother, a dental student at the public university (UABJO), a migrant to the city, and a tireless activist. She explained what it was like for youth to participate in the radio station and the barricades:

> I didn't know how to do too many things at the time . . . I mean it was difficult, I was only sixteen. But there were a lot of us young people that had been guarding the barricades, many of us came from being *grafiteros* [graffiti artists], from being skaters, others were street kids. We ended up saying "We need to ask for a space on the radio and tell them what the situation is like for the youth, since we are also supporting the movement by being at the barricade." And because we were part of the university barricade, they gave us the space.

Rosalía explained that at first, she felt intimidated by the political rhetoric and knowledge of older activists, but she and her friends found confidence and a sense of belonging within the larger social movement through their contributions as barricader@s, which some of them parlayed into participation in other aspects of the movement, such as radio broadcasts.[14]

Along with their radio show, punk youth organized a concert on the university campus where they collected a cover charge of one kilo of food. After the show, they took the food to the zocalo and donated it to a delegation of teachers from one of the more remote and marginalized areas in the state, the Sierra Mixe. Mentes Liberadas explained:

> So we went, we gave them the food, we explained what organization we were with and how we had collected all the food. They thanked us, but it also gave us a connection with them. Committees would come from their communities and bring them five hundred tamales, they would come in a truck and say "Here are five hundred tamales from Ayutla. Here are two boxes of bananas from such and such a place." They would send them various things and

then they [members of the town's encampment] would say "Go send twenty tamales to the *muchachos* [youngsters] from the collective"; "Send them some fruit." So, it was like a connection, a relationship we developed with them.

Through these new relationships that bridged the urban-rural divide, youth participated in a collective remapping of Oaxacan society that challenged the existing racial geography. Although some of the relationships across difference proved to be temporary, others have endured. For example, 2006 Generation collectives continue to connect with rural Indigenous communities that they mobilized with in 2006 by offering workshops ranging from art for youth, how to launch a community radio station, and how to make bicycle-powered machines.

Barricades as Laboratories for the Radical Imagination

The dense network of horizontally organized barricades provided the physical space for many young people and others with little or no previous organizing experience to foster a sense of ownership in the movement. For those who lived in an urban or peri-urban neighborhood, the barricades provided a space of participation in the growing movement without the activists having to leave their neighborhood. This was especially important for those the political rhetoric or aggressive style of the established opposition groups that dominated the more formal spaces of the movement did not resonate with. In her ethnography of the 2006 social movement, Lynn Stephen documents that the "sometimes nasty debate [found in the APPO assembly] discouraged people who came from rural and indigenous communities" (2013, 249). Moreover, many young activists vehemently rejected any political culture that could be interpreted as authoritarian. This was especially true for punks, anarchists, and liberationists, who were heavily involved in the movement but tended to seek out and create spaces built through horizontalism. The barricades were often such spaces, where families, neighborhoods, anarchist youth collectives, and graffiti crews served as the main organizing forces, *not* opposition parties, unions, or NGOs (Esteva 2010; Magaña 2015).

Given the context outlined above, the barricades also served as an entrée into the movement and organizing more generally. Silvia, a young woman who was active in the social movement and in 2006 Generation projects, explained her involvement:

Many of us met for the first time in the barricades in 2006 . . . the barricades became part of my daily life but they were also part of a greater strategy. That was how we protected ourselves and the radio, but also how we showed, through our civil disobedience, that the government could not govern the city.

Silvia migrated to Oaxaca City from a town in the Costa region of the state, and she was studying sociology at UABJO in 2006. Her involvement with the movement began as a researcher, but because one of the most important barricades in the city, Cinco Señores, blocked the entrance to her neighborhood, she passed through it every day. As she began spending more time there with her neighbors, her role soon changed from researcher to *barricadera*. In many ways, the barricades offered urban migrants and youth the social space within which to create and strengthen social and political relationships that are not easy to make in urban cities. Silvia went on to become an active and dedicated organizer beyond 2006, thanks in large part to the experiences and relationship forged in the barricades.

In the quote above, Silvia makes the important point that beyond the practical strategy of self-defense and defense of territory, the barricades were a symbol of popular control of the city. The barricades acted as hubs for local grassroots control of territory, and the social space they fostered provided a laboratory for experimenting with the alternative, nonhierarchical social relations that are integral to practices of horizontality. These spaces were extended in subsequent youth projects, which Silvia alludes to above when she states that "many of *us* met for the first time in the barricades." The word *us* represents the 2006 Generation youth who went on to form the network of collectives discussed in the rest of this book. These collectives provided organizing spaces for young activists to hone the praxis of horizontalism that emerged in the barricades.

Graffiti artist and rapper Serckas Fontseka is from the town of Zaachila but participated in various Oaxaca city barricades in 2006. He explained the experience of guarding the barricades:

On the one hand it was hanging out with the rest of the *banda* [crew], you tried to be cool during tense moments. On the other hand, it's being with people in an unconventional way. People became great friends immediately, because you shared in the struggle. Also you become aware that there are all kinds of people, with different goals. And also [people] that you would have never come into contact with otherwise. For example, you would see *rukos* [older people] that in other times didn't even come out of their homes, and now they were out defending, and socializing with you.

Serckas' account of the barricades as a point of encounter and interaction for otherwise disparate sectors of society speaks to the creation of novel social relations fostered by the emergent social space the barricades produced. The barricades represent a radical grassroots space produced "from below" by thousands of Oaxacans through collective struggle and resistance—or counterspace. The social relations produced in these emergent counterspaces formed a vital part of the social movement network of 2006 and provided a sense of collective identity for participants, especially those who did not belong to a formal organization (Esteva 2010; Zires 2009).

The artwork of graffiti artists in the barricades also played an important role in the movement, serving to demarcate territory, visually articulate a collective identity based on their shared barrio/barricade, and disseminate news. An artist from the nearby *colonia* of Pueblo Nuevo remembered painting a piece at his neighborhood barricade:

> I was at the barricade the first day of the *desmadre* [PFP repression]. I painted a semitrailer for the people of my barrio because they asked me, since they knew that I painted, "Why don't you paint something over here, in the barrio?" I said "Of course!" [It read] *¡Viva Pueblo Nuevo! Oaxaca, México . . .* I remember vividly, it had a woman with her fist raised, and the fucking phrase took up the whole trailer.

Many grafiteros were active in the social movement as artists, barricader@s, and in confrontations with the police. The social space of the barricade, where community elders validated youth participation, was vital in fostering a sense of ownership among urban youth of the movement, their neighborhoods, and the city as a whole. This status elevation is similar to what we saw with the punk movement, though as we will see in later chapters, the durability of this phenomenon for street artists was quite different than it was with the punks. Moreover, the sense of belonging within the broader movement for marginalized youth proved to be key for the expansion of the social movement beyond the more formal spaces of the teachers' union and the APPO.

For many youth from popular neighborhoods, the sense of social belonging created through the barricades was rare. The current generation of youth in Mexico carry with them the stigma of being referred to as the *nini* generation: *"ni estudian, ni trabajan"* (they don't study, they don't work). Labeling youth *ninis* implies that the marginalization of Mexican youth is a result of their own laziness and complacency, not the effect of global economic restructuring and neoliberal policies. For poor and working-class youth in Oaxaca, there were (and continue to be) very few spaces open to them where they could feel their participation was legitimized by the larger Oaxacan society. In this social milieu, people began to identify with their local barricades. Among youth we see the emergence of an identity as barricader@s, or participants in the barricades, which continues to carry significant social capital. A 2006 Generation activist named Monika, remembered the horizontal power produced in the barricades as one of the more important legacies of the social movement:

> I think that all of us that are in the movement, that are still in the movement, were and are barricader@s. That is where we come from. That is where we learned so many things . . . things that I had never done before nor could have imagined doing. That is where the people came together and when it was time to act, and if we all felt it was correct, we would do it. Even if, for example, [former Sección 22 leader Enrique] Rueda Pacheco tried to stop us.

The grassroots power produced in these moments, when the barricader@s chose actions that challenged the leadership class, strengthened horizontal relations created in the barricades. These kinds of alternative, counterhegemonic relations are much more difficult to produce from within established organizations and movements, where existing social inequalities tend to become entrenched and reproduced, despite the most sincere of revolutionary intentions.

Punks Take Over a Police Station

Shortly after the appearance of the citywide network of barricades, a diverse group of youth who participated in various collectives and barricades took over an abandoned police station near the zocalo and created a youth-run social center (figure 6). The space served as a parallel yet autonomous space to the encampment in the zocalo and gave youth a more stable place to experiment with the politics and modes of socialization that were emerging in the barricades. This space proved to be a prototype for collectives and spaces opened in Oaxaca after 2006, both in terms of the spatial layout and use of space, as well as in terms of the political culture with which they were experimenting. The Autonomous Block and other punk, anarchist, and liberationist groups and individuals were prominent protagonists in the creation and maintenance of this new space.

FIGURE 6. Detail of Okupa courtyard. Photo credit: Baldomero Robles Menéndez.

According to a statement released by the new group, the objective of their new space was to "create an alternative, cultural, autonomous, self-organized space" for youth. They called their new collective Ocupación Intercultural en Resistencia (OIR, which also means to listen), and they called their new space the Okupa, thus positioning their project in the global context of the Okupa movement, which is what the squatting movement is called in Spain and Latin America. The desire among Oaxacan youth for spaces such as the Okupa stemmed in large part from their experiences of marginalization and criminalization. In their 2006 manifesto, they explained their choice to occupy the police station:

> We chose an abandoned building that for many years served as the municipal police station. Arrested in the streets, in raids on music concerts, only because of our manner of dress, for our age, and for our rebelliousness, many of us were arrested and beaten by the municipal police who were stationed here in this space.

As with youth participation in the barricades and during confrontations with police, we see the strong impact that being harassed by police can have in shaping the political subjectivities of young people. The fact that they were able to reclaim and redefine the very space where many of them had been beaten and humiliated by police into a space of hope and possibility in the context of the broader social movement emboldened these youth to believe in their collective agency.

Once the decision was made to occupy the old police station, the newly formed collective, OIR, distributed flyers and announcements on the radio informing the rest of the movement of their intentions to abandon their encampment in the zocalo and focus on the new space (figure 7). They had a lot of work to do, cleaning and hauling away the rubble that had accumulated from years of abandonment. They also had to restore electricity and plumbing in order to make the space welcoming for elders and families. Mentes Liberadas is a master electrician, so he was able to train some of his fellow *okupas* to help him with the electricity, and other members of OIR contributed plumbing skills. Mentes Liberadas, Pati, and Baldomero all spoke with great pride about the collective sweat and selflessness that it took to transform the police station from a space of repression into a space of hope, where their collective imaginations and dreams could be cultivated.

The work of historian Robin D. G. Kelley is instructive when thinking about the importance of the Okupa as a counterspace for youth in the context of the 2006 social movement. In his theorization of the Black radical imagination, Kelley speaks of the significance of "freedom space" as "the product of a collective imagination, shaped and reshaped by the very process of turning rubble and memory into the seeds of a new society" (2003, 197). I believe Kelley's "freedom space" captures the power and essence of the counterspaces I examine in this book. Spaces like the Okupa and the barricades were the product of a collective reimagining of mundane and even repressive spaces (city streets and the police station, respectively) into spaces where a more just and inclusive society could be incubated.

Soon after taking over the building, OIR held an assembly to discuss what each room and space was going to be used for. Mentes Liberadas and his collective CESOL set up a popular library, mostly containing anarchist texts and fanzines. A group of punks set up a silk-screening workshop, where they produced stickers, patches, posters, and flyers (figure 8). They also set up a popular food kitchen where anyone could eat for free. Youth would collect donations from vendors at the local markets, usually bruised or overripe produce that could still be cooked. The central patio was used for holding flea markets, where people would barter items and sell crafts made by political prisoners. The patio was also used for concerts. Artisans set up a workshop where they made Oaxacan folk art figurines called *alebrijes* out of recycled

OKUPA

ESTE ES NUESTRO ESPACIO, TU ESPACIO!!!

RESISTE

La okupación, es el nombre con el que se conoce la acción de apropiarse de un edificio o lugar abandonado con la intención de utilizarlo como vivienda o lugar de reunión, dando a este hecho además un carácter público y reivindicativo. La palabra se aplica a veces al propio edificio, una vez *okupado* o *invadido*, y a las personas que lo utilizan se les suele conocer como *ocupas*

FIGURE 7. Front cover of flyer distributed during 2006 to introduce the Okupa space. Photo credit: Baldomero Robles Menéndez.

FIGURE 8. Stickers printed in the Okupa silk-screening workshop in 2006.
Photo credit: Baldomero Robles Menéndez.

materials. There was a sound room for recording music or other audio for
alternative media projects, and part of the space could be used as a dormitory for people visiting from rural communities, the homeless, or anyone else
seeking shelter.

Once it was functional, an event was organized to introduce people from
the surrounding barricades and encampments to the new space. The event
was a *calenda,* a traditional Oaxacan procession with music, dancing, and
fireworks that usually leads people through local streets to the site of a party.
Mentes Liberadas recalled:

FIGURE 9. Federal Preventative Police (PFP) entering Oaxaca City from the south in 2006. Photo credit: Baldomero Robles Menéndez.

> At that time we already had the popular kitchen running, so as a way to introduce everyone to it, we organized a dinner for all of the *raza* [the people]. . . . So the *calenda* arrives to the space, we feed everyone, including people from the *colonias*, from organizations, from the encampment, teachers. . . . We gave them a tour of the space. We said, "Look, here is the workshop where the artisans will make *alebrijes* out of wire," and days beforehand the artisans had made two or three things to show the people what we were going to do. . . . Other folks had set up a garden, and they had already sowed two or three plants so there was something to show the people, to show them, "here are the fruits [of our labor]." To show them that we were working *toward* something.

Local children began showing up the very next day for the free workshops. Mentes Liberadas recalled that seeing the kids participate in the new space was the moment when they realized that the space was functioning. His pride when he spoke about showing the fruits of their labor to community members during the tour was palpable, as was the joy of having children involved through art workshops. Even after other aspects of the social hierarchy returned after 2006, experiences such as these endure. This is the power of communitas and of freedom space.

Ultimately, the large-scale deployment of the Federal Police in late October (figure 9) forced youth to abandon the Okupa in favor of reinforcing the barricades guarding the university radio station, which were essential logistics installations. While relatively short lived, the experience of running the Okupa proved to be a formative one, as participants went on to form several autonomous cultural and political projects, in addition to strengthening already existing projects like CESOL. The popular library that was set up would be expanded in subsequent years and reopened as a bookstore in the city center called Mompracem Libros—one of the few places that inexpensive and used books are available in the city. Other participants went on to create or join prominent youth collectives that were still around a decade later. One of those was CASOTA, which housed projects like those established through the Okupa, such as an urban garden, silk-screening workshop, sound room, and popular kitchen. Still others went on to open a communal house for self-described anarcho-punks.

CONCLUSIONS: SOCIAL MOVEMENT TEMPORALITY AND SPATIALITY

Women and youth played a fundamental role in the creation of some of the most directly democratic movement spaces, such as the barricades, radio, and encampment. These space were key to the movement's growth and ability to control the state capital for six months. By focusing on the creation of these spaces, we are able to begin to appreciate the importance of space making in the 2006 Generation's politics and for social movements overall. In addition to the physical spaces they created, youth also created political space within the broader movement to critique masculinist protagonism and hierarchical organizing, as well as to challenge the criminalization of youth within the broader Mexican society. Thanks in large part to their role in creating horizontal intergenerational spaces, youth were finally recognized by authority figures (movement leaders, teachers, elders, etc.) as legitimate social and political actors. Movement youth also capitalized on the extraordinary milieu of 2006 to inscribe and spatialize their difference (political, racial, class, subcultural) within the movement and the city.

The social movement that emerged in Oaxaca in 2006 underwent many fractures, mutations, and revivals in the years that followed. A combination of brutal repression, co-optation, and internal divisions left participants with very different interpretations of the movement's impact and legacy. Some participants remain disillusioned that key figures and organizations sold out the movement for personal gain, and they feel that the opportunity to create real change was lost when they lost physical control of city. Others are convinced that the movement never died, that it is alive in the collective conscience of all who were touched by the extraordinary events of 2006, and that when the time is right, people will again take to the streets to continue what they started. Through a focus on urban youth collectives since 2006, subsequent chapters outline how the movement has altered Oaxaca's spatial and racial politics. Silvia, David, Monika, Rosalía, and other barricader@s went on to form youth collectives and spaces like VOCAL and CASOTA, where they continued to experiment with the horizontal political cultures that were forged within the barricades and other 2006 counterspaces. Chapter 2 explores the genealogies and contours of the radical politics, imaginations, and subjectivities that fuel those political cultures. Chapter 3 examines how the 2006 Generation spatialized those political cultures through initiatives like CASOTA.

TWO

Urban Autonomy, Indigenous Anarchisms, and Other Political Genealogies for the 2006 Generation

IN THE EARLY MORNING HOURS of June 14, 2006, in the Zapotec town of Guelatao de Juárez in the Sierra Norte region of Oaxaca, sixteen-year-old La Bruja Zapoteka ("the Zapotec Witch," henceforth La Bruja) woke up and turned on the radio like she always did. La Bruja had a slight frame with almond-shaped eyes, and she combined a punk and *darketo* ("goth" in a *loose* translation) aesthetic. She often wore black clothes and black boots to go along with several facial piercings, tattoos, and hair that was often colored green, red, or purple. As she dressed for school that morning, she was alarmed by the news she heard: the community radio station was announcing the police attack against the teachers in the capital city.[1] Her family had been fearing such news for days. Her father was a secondary school teacher and was serving his turn at the union encampment that morning. Since she was the oldest of three siblings, La Bruja went to Oaxaca City to search for her father. The teenager from the small highland town roamed the unfamiliar capital city, which was full of fire, smoke, and police. Although she was scared, she refused to turn back until she had found her father. She eventually found him unharmed and returned home the next morning.

Once back in Guelatao, La Bruja joined her neighbors, who immediately began organizing solidarity actions with the emerging movement in Oaxaca City. This included taking over the community radio station in order to counter what townspeople felt was biased pro-government coverage, and collecting and delivering donations to the movement encampment. La Bruja participated in the 2006 social movement both from her Zapotec town and through regular visits to the city, where she began to connect with other young activists. She eventually moved to Oaxaca City to join the growing constellation of 2006 Generation collectives, including the youth-run social center CASOTA (Autonomous Oaxacan Solidarity House for Self-Managed Work). Although her activism began with the 2006 social movement, she drew on deep wells of political and social influences in constructing her politics, as did many of her 2006 Generation peers.

In addition to her father's militancy in Local 22 of the teachers' union, members of her family and community had been politically active for generations. Her father and uncle were part of the 1968 student movement in Mexico City and survived both the Tlatelolco massacre of 1968 and El Halconazo in 1971.[2] Though she stopped short of implicating either of membership in our interview, she mentioned that she grew up around members of the urban guerrilla organization, the 23 of September Communist League.[3] It was clear that she carried these generational experiences of resistance and repression with her as she organized for social change. At the community level, La Bruja's hometown carries an outsized influence in regional and national politics for a town of under six hundred people. In addition to being the birthplace of Mexico's first and only Indigenous president, Benito Juárez, Guelatao is an important site in the struggle for Indigenous autonomy and has been since at least the 1970s, including through the work of the Union of Organizations of the Sierra Juárez of Oaxaca (UNOSJO) and Fundación Comunalidad A.C.

Due to the importance of Indigenous autonomy movements in Oaxaca, several leaders from the state, including those from the aforementioned organizations, served as advisors to the Zapatistas (in the Zapatista Army of National Liberation, EZLN) in Chiapas. The cross-fertilization between the Sierra's Indigenous autonomy movements and the Zapatista insurgency greatly influenced La Bruja's politics—her sense of what is possible, what is worth fighting for, and how to engage in collective struggle. La Bruja's earliest memory of politics came when she was eight years old and participated in a children's march to welcome a Zapatista caravan that passed through Guelatao on their way to Mexico City. She learned her first political slogan in that march, "Zapata Vive!" Although the specifics vary, many 2006 Generation activists and collectives draw on influences similar to those of La Bruja, including the Zapatistas, Indigenous and popular movements from throughout Oaxaca, histories of anticolonial resistance, the 1968 student movement, and the guerrilla movements of the 1970s. They combine these generational influences with their own collective experience of coming of age during an era of neoliberal abandonment and of youth participation in the 2006 social movement, including the brutal police and paramilitary violence unleashed on thousands of people.

In this chapter I excavate the diverse genealogies that inform the 2006 Generation's politics, with an emphasis on how Indigenous epistemologies and organizing traditions mix with global youth subcultures as they travel to the city via regional and transnational migration routes.

Through histories of migration and activism, we see how young people in Oaxaca create political space for Indigenous people and ways of doing politics in the city, and how they create a new kind of urban space in the process. Youth histories from 2006, which are interwoven throughout, highlight how space making can serve as a catalyst for the emergence of new politics and subjectivities. Moreover, the case of 2006 Generation organizers, their political and cultural initiatives, and the unique political cultures and ideologies that fuel them provide a unique window into "understanding how concrete local experiences and histories combine with more distant versions of history and national symbols to produce a hybrid political ideology . . . with multiple levels of meaning" (Stephen 2002, 105). Appreciating the diverse influences on youth organizing in Oaxaca pushes us toward heeding M. Jacqui Alexander's call to make our analytic frameworks of time palimpsestic—that is, to acknowledge the ways that the "new" is structured through the "old" (2005, 191). In this case, that means recognizing the multilayered, entangled histories of both organized resistance and the coercive technologies of the state that partially shape resistance.

The chapter begins by discussing how the most recent layer in the palimpsest of 2006 Generation organizing—youth participation in the Oaxacan social movement and production of counterspaces—incubated a radical politics that continued to be experimented with and honed after 2006. I briefly describe how some of my interlocutors went from being a diffuse collection of activists to founders and organizers of two important 2006 Generation collectives—VOCAL and CASOTA. The chapter then focuses on VOCAL to show how youth organizers wove together various strands of autonomy, anarchist, liberationist, and antiauthoritarian politics with lessons learned from their participation in the 2006 social movement and membership in urban youth subcultures like punk. The sections that follow describe these key influences and locate them in their local, national, and regional context.

To be clear, 2006 Generation organizing is neither uniform nor easily categorized. Instead, it is a bricolage of traditions and practices given coherence largely through the horizontalism through which they are mobilized (Magaña 2014). Horizontalism is neither an ideology nor a singular way of doing politics or creating social change. It is the name activists and theorists have given to a diverse array of organizing processes and ways of relating that experiment with flattening social and political relationships (Sitrin 2006, 2014). As this chapter demonstrates, understanding the 2006 Generation's politics means thinking beyond binary distinctions such as new/old, local/global, urban/rural, Indigenous/non-Indigenous. Instead, we will see how youth build on local organizing traditions that have always been connected to broader networks and histories, while also drawing on politics whose diffuse circulation defies attempts to situate them geographically. For example, one of the political visions that unites 2006 Generation collectives is their praxis of autonomy, which places great emphasis on nurturing horizontal connections between communities in resistance. This means that while they practice urban autonomy from their current location in Oaxaca City, they actively work at linking their struggles with those of other communities. As we will see in the remainder of this book, these exchanges cross multiple scales and borders (regional, state, national, global). Many build on face-to-face connections made during the social movement of 2006, while other connections have been made possible because of digital technologies.

In addition to urban autonomy, segments of the 2006 Generation practice hallmarks of anarchism like mutual aid, antiauthoritarianism, and direct democracy, and many members identify with anarchism or liberationism. Instead of pointing to European philosophers, however, 2006 Generation activists trace their influence *primarily* to organizing practices, norms, and epistemologies associated with what Indigenous Oaxacan intellectuals have theorized as *comunalidad*, roughly translated as Indigenous communal life.[4] The fact that youth point to comunalidad as the main inspiration for their anarchist politics invites us to excavate genealogies of anarchism that decenter whiteness and the West, which are frequently portrayed as the dominant actors and geographies of anarchist politics. Following the lead of the youth in this study and their conversations with community elders, I suggest that we frame their anarchist politics as *decolonial anarchism*.[5]

YOUTH POLITICS AND ORGANIZING POST 2006

The 2006 Generation's commitment to organizing outside the reach of political parties and electoral politics deepened after 2006. In the months following the PFP siege of Oaxaca City and the extended campaign of repression against (presumed and actual) movement activists, various sectors within the movement convened to assess possible paths forward. Notable among these was a statewide APPO assembly held at the local public university (UABJO) on February 10–11, 2007. Discussions centered on four main themes, ranging from how to address rampant human rights abuses to perhaps the most contentious issue—whether to boycott the upcoming local elections, support opposition candidates, or field movement candidates under a separate APPO party. The topic of the upcoming elections was particularly fraught, since the APPO had been launched only months prior explicitly as a nonelectoral, nonpartisan movement. There were concerns shared by movement youth (and others) that some of the more visible and vocal proponents of entering into the elections were opportunists with their own political ambitions. After heated debate, the assembly ultimately decided against participating in the elections. Organizations and individuals were free to participate, but were not allowed to use the name of the APPO in their campaigns or endorsements. Although the outcome was precisely what the youth were calling for, young people remained uneasy about the "opportunism" they saw within the movement and the lack of voice they had in the assembly.

Parallel to the state assembly, youth held a series of meetings to discuss their role in the movement's future, how to hold the movement true to its principles, and how to keep the hope and energy generated during the six months of popular rule alive. These talks were held at Universidad de la Tierra (UNITIERRA), a Zapatista-inspired practice-based learning space in the city. One of the initiatives that emerged from these meetings was VOCAL, which was one of the most visible and active youth collectives in Oaxaca during my 2007–13 fieldwork. Youth like Silvia and David, who met in the streets of Oaxaca while guarding the barricades, were among the founding members of VOCAL. Another tangible result of this process came one year later, when movement youth opened the collectively run social center CASOTA, which gave them a physical space in the center of Oaxaca City from which to continue to hone and ground their politics. VOCAL and CASOTA were part of a dense network of collectives and spaces that emerged out of the social movement, with youth playing a key role in many of them.

Rosalía, who was quoted in chapter 1 about her participation in the barricades and movement-run radio, was a high school student in 2006. In 2010 she shared her memories of the formation of VOCAL and the role that the assembly discussions about elections played in youth deciding to create their own political projects:

In 2006 I met a lot of *banda*, many, many of them at the barricades, and we became great *compisimas* [friends]. Later, in 2007, we got together again and asked, So is this what they are going to do after the social movement, enter into the elections? The APPO, well one group from the APPO, wanted to enter the upcoming elections. In February of 2007, we reaffirmed that we didn't want to enter into the elections. So many people weren't murdered, so many political prisoners, so many disappeared, just so we could enter into elections! We decided that we had to form something; we needed to do something *with* ourselves, and *do* it ourselves. That is when and how we formed VOCAL, and we began to connect with even *more* people.

Rosalía highlights the important role that the creation of counterspaces in 2006, like the barricades, played in bringing people together, especially those without formal political or organizational affiliations. They provided the physical space for regular people to congregate, the social space to discuss the extraordinary events they were living, and the opportunity to participate in the growing movement at the neighborhood and grassroots levels (Magaña 2015). The long nights of drinking coffee, dancing, playing music, and partaking in political discussions while guarding the barricades fostered new forms of sociality, political and social imagining, and horizontal political cultures.

During the first year and a half of their existence, VOCAL and allied youth did not have a physical space of their own from which to grow their new collective and horizontal politics. Instead, they relied on affinity groups like the Popular Indigenous Council of Oaxaca Ricardo Flores Magón (CIPO-RFM) and UNITIERRA, who opened their doors to them. Seeing how these more established organizations benefited from having stable spaces from which to organize and convene reminded movement youth of their own experiences in 2006 of the transformative power involved in the production of counterspaces, which only strengthened their desire to have a space of their own.

CASOTA eventually became such a space for 2006 Generation youth, when four young people associated with the social movement opened the communally rented house in the city center in 2008.[6] While closely allied with the larger collective VOCAL, which had about thirty core members at the time, CASOTA actually began as a separate and smaller project with a less pronounced political agenda, though it evolved and articulated a more explicit political vision, which chapter 3 explores more deeply.

Youth who participated in the 2006 social movement represented a diverse array of political ideologies at the time and in the years that followed. Some of the more significant groups outside the scope of this book are Marxist-Leninists and social democrats. I chose not to focus on these groups, because they tended to mobilize and participate through already established institutions entrenched in the landscape of opposition politics in Oaxaca and Mexico, like the Party of Democratic Revolution (PRD) and the Popular Revolutionary Front (FPR). Instead I focus on emergent political cultures, their limits and possibilities, and how their contours are shaped by previous social and cultural movements. Such a focus is necessary for understanding contemporary and future opposition politics, given the fact that revolutionary Left parties are fading in importance in the radical political imaginary of youth globally, who are instead experimenting with horizontalism (Sitrin 2014).[7]

Autonomy is another concept that has been central to 2006 Generation politics, as well as for contemporary Latin American social movements more generally (González Castillo and Martin 2015, 53). Any study of contemporary movements for autonomy in Latin America must position those struggles in relation to the surge in Indigenous and Afro-descendant social movements that started in the late 1980s and 1990s. For the majority of these movements, autonomy has meant communal territorial autonomy by way of "self-determination within the juridical and political limits of the existing state" (González 2015, 11). Such a framework of autonomy is based on the state recognizing and conceding a combination of individual and collective rights to be exercised in a given territory and through Indigenous institutions (Díaz-Polanco and Sánchez 2002, 42; Sieder 2002, 3). Such efforts have had mixed results, in large part due to the lack of political will to bridge "the implementation gap" between the norms and the practice of state-recognized autonomy (González 2015, 12).

In part because of these shortcomings, social movements and communities fighting for autonomy in Mexico have chosen to carve out paths toward autonomy that do not rely on state recognition and implementation. This is perhaps most clearly illustrated by the Juntas de Buen Gobierno (Good Governance Councils), which are the bodies that oversee the implementation of autonomy in Zapatista territories. They were created after negotiations between the EZLN and the Mexican government failed, as a way of putting autonomy into practice without asking the state for permission or support.[8] Taking a cue from social movements on the ground, scholars have shifted their focus from the juridical-political realm to the everyday practices of autonomy exercised by Indigenous communities and social movements throughout Mexico. Examples come from ethnographic studies of education, health care, the economy, and various levels of governance in autonomous Zapatista communities (Baronnet, Mora Bayo, and Stahler-Sholk 2011), as well as community governance and policing in Sonora and Guerrero, and the struggle for autonomy in San Juan Copala, Oaxaca (Gasparello and Quintana Guerrero 2009). Taking a cue from these ethnographic studies of autonomy, this chapter looks at how 2006 Generation activists and collectives understand autonomy and provide a genealogy of their use of it.

VOCAL articulated its political proposal and political genealogy explicitly in their March 2007 manifesto. In the following excerpt, the collective identifies itself as the product of a rich diversity of political and ideological thought, and positions itself vis-à-vis the APPO and political parties:

> Those of us who currently make up this space are autonomous *individu@s* [individuals], liberationist collectives, self-organized spaces, antiauthoritarian people, Magonista organizations, Zapatista collectives, anarchist groups, barricaderos and barricaderas, and members of the APPO and *algun@s* [some] members of La Otra Campaña. *Tod@s* [All] are activists from the current social movement in Oaxaca.
>
> This space is created as a means of bringing together the autonomous efforts of the mobilized *pueblo* of Oaxaca, those of us who actively participate in the social movement, both as a part of, and apart from, organizing structures such as the popular assembly of the peoples of Oaxaca (APPO) and those of us who find it important to keep our social movement faithful to its principles, autonomous and independent of political parties, and reclaiming the assembly form as the most just and harmonious means by which to come to understand ourselves, to self-organize and to self-govern, where the people's accords are not based on the competition of majorities against minorities, nor in other forms of imposition commonly exerted by those in power, but rather, in a relationship of mutual respect among all parts of *el pueblo*. (VOCAL 2007b)

Much like the OIR Okupa manifesto before it, VOCAL's manifesto and subsequent texts make use of the gender inclusive @ instead of the masculine *o* in nouns and pronouns, thus challenging gender designations in the

Spanish language that assume a universal male subject. This signals—at least discursively—that patriarchy is one of the many forms of domination and oppression that 2006 Generation collectives attempted to dismantle through horizontal organizing and relationship building. Chapters 4 and 5 examine what this process looked like ethnographically, including moments when these ideals came into conflict with a culture of *protagonismo* (individualism, opportunism) prevalent within social movement organizing.[9] Protagonismo is not unique to Mexico, and it is inseparable from patriarchy and neoliberalism in its emphasis on the individual heteronormative cis-gendered man as the legitimate political actor, while silencing other voices and making invisible other bodies, especially those of women, gender nonconforming, queer, and youth actors. It would be naive to argue that these forms of oppression were completely absent from the 2006 Generation's politics—they were not. These collectives did, however, consciously seek to eliminate them through horizontal organizing, and they made space to hold one another accountable internally when they fell short.

Explicit in the manifesto is the collective's insistence on remaining autonomous from political parties and an outright rejection of electoral politics. Also important is that they position themselves as both part of the APPO and apart from it. Unlike some other youth currents within the movement that never identified with the APPO, like the punk movement, VOCAL claims their place within the APPO, while simultaneously critiquing and challenging the formal decision-making structures and actors within the assembly. Moreover, they emphasize their collective's desire to "reclaim[e] the assembly"—a reference to the governing model of *usos y costumbres* (Indigenous customary law and traditions) practiced in 418 of the 570 municipalities in Oaxaca, where the communal assembly is the central decision-making structure and public offices are filled not by career politicians but by community members who fill the posts as a way of satisfying communal obligations and service (i.e., they are not paid, and they serve at the will of the assembly, who can remove them at any time).

The fact that the vast majority of municipalities in the state govern themselves through structures and norms that are meaningful to their members and outside of the channels of electoral politics and political parties is tremendously important. Communities governed through Indigenous customary law in Mexico exist "within and apart from settler governance" and call into question the sturdiness of the system of electoral politics (Simpson 2014, 11). However, the conditions imposed on these communities under neoliberal militarization force us to be cautious in overstating how much autonomy they enjoy, especially given the pervasiveness of state violence, land dispossession, and coercion within their territories. Nonetheless, self-governing Indigenous communities provide the 2006 Generation with an autochthonous model of politics otherwise, which is a significant force in fueling their political imaginations, their ways of organizing, and how they build relationships.

The struggle for Indigenous autonomy in Oaxaca has had an influence on the 2006 Generation's politics that goes beyond the communal assembly to include a cultural politics of autonomy based on horizontal and expanding social relations. The struggle is also a way of life nurtured in Oaxaca's Indigenous communities that Zapotec intellectual and Guelatao native Jaime Martínez Luna and Ayuujk intellectual Floriberto Díaz have conceptualized as comunalidad (Hernández Robles and Cardoso Jiménez 2007; Martínez Luna 2010). Comunalidad is based primarily on the four pillars of communal life in Indigenous Oaxacan communities: (1) communal authority via the communal assembly and the system of religious and civil *cargos*, (2) communal territory, (3) communal enjoyment via traditional fiestas, and (4) work via *tequio* (collective labor). We will see later in this chapter how 2006 Generation activists explicitly reference and mobilize comunalidad in their urban autonomy projects.

SOCIAL MOVEMENT SPILLOVER, ZAPATISMO, AND AUTONOMY

Zapatismo remains a highly significant reference point for social movements throughout Mexico, the Mexican diaspora and for other global social movements (Gómez 2016; P. Gonzalez 2011; Khasnabish 2008). Many 2006 Generation organizers' first memories of social movement activism are connected to the EZLN, such as their caravan arriving in La Bruja's town when she was eight years old. The Zapatistas also looked to their neighbors in Oaxaca for counsel as they developed their movement, aware of the rich history of Indigenous autonomy struggles in Oaxaca (Stephen 2002). Several prominent Indigenous activists from Oaxaca, such as Jaime Martínez Luna (from Guelatao) and Joel Aquino (from Yalalag in the Sierra Norte), as well as Oaxaca-based intellectual Gustavo Esteva of UNITIERRA (himself from Mexico City) were advisors to the Zapatistas.

The notion of social movement *spillover* (Meyer and Whittier 1994), or the way that movements influence and carry over to other movements, helps capture the ways that local movements for Indigenous autonomy in Oaxaca influenced Zapatista constructions of autonomy, as well as how the Zapatistas influenced both Indigenous autonomy efforts in Oaxaca and the 2006 Generation's urban autonomy initiatives. At the time of the 2006 uprising, many social movement youth were already adherents to La Otra Campaña, a project spearheaded by the Zapatistas in early 2006 meant to strengthen connections between communities, groups, and social movements in Mexico as an alternative to political party campaigns.[10] La Otra predated the Oaxacan social movement by several months. Identifying as adherents to La Otra united youth who met in the streets and counterspaces of 2006. After early encounters with the EZLN, 2006 Generation organizers and collectives including VOCAL and CASOTA continued to connect with the EZLN—both hosting caravans from Chiapas and visiting the autonomous communities in Zapatista territory. Moreover, the model of Indigenous autonomy practiced in Zapatista base communities in Chiapas, where they unilaterally established their own governing structures independent of the Mexican government, provided a model of politics otherwise (Simpson 2014) for youth collectives experimenting with urban autonomy. Similarly, movements for Indigenous autonomy in Oaxaca significantly influenced the 2006 Generation's politics and organizing—both in providing models for what their own autonomous projects might look like in terms of structure (e.g. a communal assembly) and through a guiding epistemology (comunalidad).

VOCAL's manifesto offers a clear vision of how they viewed autonomy, as well as their framing of the collective itself as a space—in the sociopolitical sense—from which to build autonomy:

> In this space, we struggle for the construction, strengthening, and connection of diverse autonomies, in that we consider the autonomy of the *pueblos*, groups, collectives, individuals, organizations and others, to be a true alternative challenge to the current authoritarian system of government. Autonomy, as a process of building alternative realities, shows that there are other ways of changing things from the root, where the *pueblos* decide their own forms and ways of life and not from the institutions of power that merely reform the oppressive and repressive spaces, such as political parties that produce *tiran@s* (tyrants), caciques, and authoritarianism in the people that assume them through positions of power. It is for this reason that the work of this space is not confined to the electoral calendar, since with or without elections,

autonomy advances through the organization and creation of proposals for an alternative society.

VOCAL emphasizes the plurality of autonomies and the processual nature of struggles for autonomy. They make clear that there is no single way to challenge the current system, but connecting autonomous struggles is a way to create and expand alternatives in the present. Part of this alternative present is freedom from the repressive and co-opting apparatus of the Mexican state. The VOCAL manifesto, together with La Bruja's framing of her own activism as couched in the histories of her father's generation of student activists and guerrilla movements, remind us that the contours of the 2006 Generation's politics are shaped, in part, by intimate knowledge of the state's repressive technologies of governing as manifest in decades of authoritarian clientelism (Fox 1994) and more recent practices characteristic of neoliberal militarization.

Importantly, for members of the 2006 Generation, autonomy refers to more than being independent of political parties and is definitely not autonomy in the liberal sense of the self-reliant individual. Autonomy for them is about the capacity for self-determination, the right to difference, the right to collective or communal governance of territory (including urban space), and it is also about social relationships and solidarity between communities. Their understanding and practice of autonomy centers on networks of mutual aid and solidarity, and therefore they do not view autonomy as an isolating project, where communities close themselves off to the outside world. This idea of autonomy as self-isolation is a common misconception. For example, in 2009 I interviewed a middle-age media activist from an alternative media collective that played an important role in the 2006 social movement.[11] We were discussing the role of youth in the movement when he lamented that the current generation of youth were cynical and did not believe in society-wide change. His interpretation of their politics was that they focused on creating utopias at the level of the individual or maybe the collective or even community, but that they had no "macro-level proposal." This caricature of youth's politics of autonomy greatly misinterprets the scale of change Mexican autonomists are working through and toward. Instead of creating islands, the 2006 Generation's vision of autonomy places great emphasis on nurturing horizontal connections between communities in resistance. In this way, they follow the path set forth by Indigenous autonomy networks in Mexico that have been organizing regionally, nationally, and internationally for decades, including forming the National Indigenous Congress, which is an organization that emerged out of the Zapatista uprising, as well as participating in continental summits like the Continental Conference on Five Hundred Years of Indigenous Resistance in 1990 and the more recent International Comunalidad Conferences held in Puebla in 2015 and Oaxaca in 2018.

CONNECTING AUTONOMIES
AND INDIGENOUS RESISTANCE

Despite the misconception, particularly by older generations of activists like the alternative media activist referenced above, the 2006 Generation's urban autonomy praxis is not focused on creating utopian islands. In fact, one of the aspects of VOCAL and CASOTA's organizing models that has been particularly effective has been establishing strong connections with other communities in struggle, such as rural communities in Oaxaca, Zapatista communities in neighboring Chiapas, and the Frente de Pueblos en Defensa de la Tierra (FPDT, People's Front in Defense of the Land) in the state of Mexico, as well as collaborations with autonomous groups, movements, and communities in countries across the Americas, Africa, and Europe. Through these connections, 2006 Generation collectives are part of global autonomy networks that seek to first organize strong local autonomist projects, and then scale up or expand those initiatives through horizontal articulation with affinity projects, emphasizing solidarity, mutual aid, and exchange.

In January 2008, activists organized the Encuentro de Jóvenes del Movimiento Social Oaxaqueño (Conference of Youth from the Oaxacan Social Movement) in the town of Villa de Zaachila, located about 15 kilometers south of Oaxaca City. Dozens of collectives, including VOCAL, participated in the conference, which was organized around five themes: (1) assessment of the role of youth in Oaxacan social movements, (2) the role of alternative and commercial media in the social movement, (3) autonomy and grassroots power (*poder popular*), (4) youth in the face of state repression, and (5) youth and Indigenous issues. Serckas Fontseka, a barricadero, member of a street art crew, and native of Zaachila participated in the conference. He remembered it as being meant "to create dialog between the elders and the youth, to talk about the situation that we experienced in 2006, to establish new links for self-defense, and to use culture for social and political critique."

One proposal of how to establish these links and strengthen already existing connections was to organize a caravan to visit remote communities throughout the state that were involved in some form of organized struggle and who had participated in some way in the social movement of 2006. The idea was to accompany these communities in their struggles by documenting human rights abuses, disseminating news via alternative media, facilitating the connection of disparate communities with one another, and offering workshops on such topics as how to create community radio stations, silk-screening, video and audio documentation, computer skills, how to create products out of recycled goods, and other skills that youth brought to their own organizing spaces, many of which were practiced in the Okupa during 2006.

What was originally planned as a major caravan with participation from various sectors of the social movement materialized in May 2008, but on a smaller scale. Members of VOCAL, CASOTA, and affinity project CACITA (Autonomous Center for the Intercultural Creation of Appropriated Technologies) managed to organize a "caravan" of one bus, which they called El Sendero del Jaguar por la Regeneración de Nuestra Memoria (The Path of the Jaguar for the Regeneration of Our Memory).[12] Rosalía of VOCAL recalled, "we didn't want it to have any affiliation with any political party, but we definitely wanted it to represent La Otra Campaña." The youth caravan followed the model of the Zapatista's La Otra Campaña in trying to make connections between seemingly disparate struggles in an attempt to strengthen them. The Caravana del Jaguar, as it is often remembered, was instrumental in strengthening and extending connections that were forged in the context of the 2006 social movement between urban youth activists and Indigenous communities throughout the state.

The model proved so impactful and successful that youth organized several more caravans in years that followed, picking up participants from other collectives and connecting with communities throughout Oaxaca and Central America. These efforts continue to expand and fortify horizontal linkages within regional autonomy networks, but also come with great risk, given the vested interest that the state and capitalist actors driving neoliberal militarization have in keeping these communities isolated. Chapter 4 addresses the vulnerabilities autonomous groups and communities face at the hands of these forces.

Some of the youth who participated in the Caravana del Jaguar were migrants to the city from rural Indigenous communities, like La Bruja.

Others were second- or third-generation urban residents. For example, organizers Daniel (VOCAL) and Erick (CASOTA) were both raised in working-class *colonias* outside of Mexico City, and both of their families were migrants from the Mixteca region of Oaxaca. Daniel maintained connections and regularly visited with kin networks in the communities, while Erick did not. The caravan provided youth like Erick unique perspectives into the struggles faced by these communities and allowed youth like Daniel and La Bruja to deepen their knowledge of and connections with other communities. Erick appreciated the opportunity to see firsthand what "problems and struggles people had outside of the city." The principal issues he highlighted revolved around land and territory—violent land disputes within and between communities, and land dispossession tied to extractivism and militarization. Indeed, these are the same circumstances that forced many of the 2006 Generation's parents or grandparents from their land in the first place.

Daniel also highlighted the urgency of social movements bridging Oaxaca's rugged geography and social fragmentation in the context of neoliberal militarization:

> The movement continues in many forms, but right now there is a lot of danger due to these megaprojects by the transnationals. I think this will be a decisive moment in the struggle of the *pueblos*, and in fact one where their very existence is at play. Those projects don't come to negotiate. They come to disappear entire communities. They come to exterminate languages, traditions, ways of life. I think it is very important to shine a light on what is happening right now in Oaxaca.

A nexus of neoliberal and neocolonial forces are displacing Indigenous and campesino communities throughout Mexico and the rest of Latin America from their land in order to extract valuable natural resources like precious metals and energy (Dunlap 2017). The implementation of the Mesoamerica Integration and Development Project in 2008 accelerated this most recent iteration of the colonial project of extraction, dispossession, and elimination in the region. This project, which connects Mexico, Central American, Colombia, and the Dominican Republic, facilitates neoliberal development based on foreign investment, privatization, and extraction of natural resources, which has exacerbated human rights abuses, Indigenous dispossession, and environmental degradation. Authoritarian governments and paramilitary forces in the region have responded to a groundswell in grassroots organizing against the development project by murdering dozens of Indigenous leaders like Bernardo Vásquez in Oaxaca and Berta Cáceres in Honduras (Bacon 2012; Jagger 2017; OAS 2017). In response to these threats, the 2006 Generation prioritized strengthening relationships and solidarity between affected communities and bridging urban and rural movements.

URBAN INDIGENEITY, AUTONOMY, AND COMUNALIDAD IN 2006 GENERATION POLITICS

Many youth in 2006 Generation collectives share an intimate experience, and critical analysis of, the interrelated processes of dispossession, displacement, cultural genocide, and national discourses of *mestizaje* and indigeneity that place some of them outside of recognized parameters for indigeneity in Mexico. These exclusions or negations are often based on some combination of their language usage (e.g., being monolingual in Spanish), residence (urban migrants), or dress (punk or other urban youth aesthetic). Up until the 2012 national census, for example, the National Institute of Geography and Statistics (INEGI) determined indigeneity based purely on language use. Other essentialist notions of indigeneity are based on static notions of a people bound to their ancestral lands or use of "traditional" dress. These collectives recognize that these schemas are based on colonial logics, are part of an ongoing project of elimination, and perpetuate a calculus of cultural genocide that strips Indigenous people of their identity after dispossessing them of their land.

Part of the cultural politics of the 2006 Generation is mobilizing as *indí-genas urbanos* (urban Indigenous). This is a collective, insurgent, and urban indigeneity that has coalitional potential. This identity is not based on an essentialist or racial logic but rather is tied to political consciousness, social commitments and obligations, and kin networks. The cultural politics of urban indigeneity in the context of neocolonial dispossession and elimination reclaims an Indigenous presence in visible and audible spaces of the Mexican nation. In mobilizing as urban Indigenous, collectives like VOCAL place themselves as Indigenous actors in the center of the political and social life of the city. Such a politics challenges the postcolonial racial geographies of Mexico (Saldaña-Portillo 2016), by transgressing the boundaries placed on Indigenous people in Mexico—that they exist only in the past, in remote communities, or in sanctioned spaces for tourism. In doing so, they put into practice a politics of refusal as theorized by Audra Simpson (2014)—a refusal to be eliminated, absorbed, or made invisible. Not all 2006 Generation collectives or organizers claim this identity, though VOCAL does. VOCAL articulated its understanding of urban indigeneity in the following speech given to the APPO statewide assembly in 2009:

> We come from below, from the streets of the rebel city, from the barricades, the *pueblos originarios* (first nations/peoples), from the migrants, from those who are discriminated against for being different. . . . We, the *indígenas urbanos* (urban Indigenous), are in the city, where instead of working the soil for our families, we work machines for bosses and governments. Where capitalist values like individualism, egoism, consumerism, and the cult of "development" and "progress" attempt to permeate our minds and hearts. In the year of the insurrection of 2006, in the barricades we happily realized five hundred years of colonial war had not completely torn our Indigenous roots from us. In those nights of struggle, of unpunished murders, of caravans of death, the values from our Indigenous origins that had apparently been lost, powerfully manifested themselves between us.
>
> Fraternity, solidarity, mutual aid, *tequio*, and *guelaguetza* came down from our *pueblos originarios* and settled once again between us, the urban Indigenous.

The insurgent indigeneity articulated by VOCAL is clearly the product of a confluence of influences and experiences, some of them unique to the 2006 Generation. They explicitly point to the 2006 social movement as a point of rupture where their political consciousness as Indigenous people manifests through their collective experience of struggle. Moreover, when they reference *tequio* and *guelaguetza* (reciprocal exchange of goods) they are referring to practices fundamental to comunalidad—the concept developed by Jaime Martínez Luna and Floriberto Díaz as a way of theorizing Indigenous communal life, identity, and epistemology. Comunalidad as a concept emerges in the Sierra Norte of Oaxaca and is inseparable from the long history of organized resistance of Indigenous communities there, who have been at the center of organized resistance around struggles in defense of territory, communal self-determination, and the affirmation of Indigenous language, culture, and communal organizing (Aquino-Moreschi and Contreras-Pastrana 2016). In their work with Ayuujk and Zapotec youth, anthropologists Alejandra Aquino-Moreschi and Isis Contreras-Pastrana argue that comunalidad is "one of the most important strands of decolonial thought by *pueblos originarios* (first nations) . . . and has impacted the newer generations in multiple ways" (2016, 464).

The mobilization of a collective urban indigeneity by members of the 2006 Generation is part of a decolonial praxis that subverts the colonial calculus of race and indigeneity. For VOCAL, indigeneity is explicitly connected to histories of struggle and communal self-governing, which is in direct opposition to racialized tropes that paint Indigenous people as childlike, passive, and existing to serve mestizos and whites (Mora 2017). When refracted through the lens of palimpsestic time, VOCAL's seemingly disparate claims and references offer a complex and sophisticated critique of capitalism and "the cult of development" as neocolonial projects. Indeed, it is no mistake that they articulate these critiques together with invocations of "the five hundred years of colonial war." They offer an understanding of the temporalities of organized resistance that is nonlinear, multiple, and entangled when they reference Indigenous resistance to colonialism together with "the year of the insurrection of 2006." Moreover, they offer a palimpsestic reading of the spatialities of resistance in southern Mexico by connecting urban and rural manifestations of resistance to (neo)colonialism. It would be a mistake to read this as simply a romanticizing of the past or an ahistorical understanding of Indigenous politics by urban youth.

Also significant when considering VOCAL's discourse of indigeneity is who they are speaking *to*, who they are *not* speaking to, who they are speaking *with*, and to what ends. The speech I quoted above was delivered by VOCAL to the seven hundred attendees at the second statewide assembly of the APPO in 2009. They used their speech to offer an internal critique of the APPO and to share their vision of the movement's future. They did so from the position of self-identified APPO activists, barricader@s, migrants, victims of discrimination, and as urban Indigenous people. Juxtapose this with a recent analysis of how social movements in Oaxaca have "used indigeneity" as a matter of political expediency, for "lobbying" or "seeking redress" from the state, or "international bodies of support and funding," including what the author calls the "gringoscape" (Norget 2010). While the author rightfully echoes Jean Jackson and Kay Warren's (2005) warning about the limits of dichotomous ways of thinking that categorize people as Indigenous and not, the analysis follows a predictable anti-essentialist reading of the politics of recognition. Native American scholars have poignantly critiqued such readings for failing to take into account the power-laden and conceptually diverse contexts where discourses of indigeneity are produced and circulate (Coulthard 2014; Goeman 2013). Such criticism is instructive in in the case of VOCAL and other 2006 Generation collectives, since they mobilize an insurgent Indigenous identity as a part of their collective politics of refusal (Simpson 2014), not a politics of recognition.

Aquino-Moreschi and Contreras-Pastrana (2016) demonstrate how Zapotec and Ayuujk youth create new subjectivities, which may be more useful for understanding the 2006 Generation's mobilization of urban indigeneity:

> The youth are indeed the heirs of their predecessors' struggles, but they are also proposing other ways of being youth, of being Ayuujk or Zapotecos and of being in the community, which destabilize the subjectivities and practices internal to their *pueblos*. The main tensions they experience have to do with the body, identities, the individual and collective lifeworlds. The youth are questioned for viewing a new way of life in migration; for the way they dress, and for their sexuality; for identifying with urban youth cultures which inspire them to affirm their identity as Ayuuk and their communal belonging, but this also pushes them to create new youth identities previously unknown in their pueblos. (473; translation my own)

The authors argue that youth draw on individual and community experiences of migration within Mexico and to the United States, the influence of urban youth culture, discourses of autonomy and comunalidad, and their communities' histories of struggle to redefine what it means to be a member of their communities. Understanding emergent indigeneities (Fortun, Fortun, and Rubenstein 2010) is important for moving beyond essentialist debates of authenticity and anti-essentialist critiques to focus instead on how Indigenous people build community, identity, and politics in ways that disrupt colonial spatial and temporal orders that relegate Indigenous people to the past, to bounded peripheral territories, and other static notions of what it means to be Indigenous. As the 2006 Generation makes clear, this is especially urgent in the current context of neoliberal militarization, which dispossesses Indigenous people of their land and displaces Indigenous communities. Rosalía (VOCAL) explained the connection between autonomy, Indigenous communal practices, and urban migration through her own experience as a migrant to the city from a Zapotec town in the Isthmus of Tehuantepec:

> When talking about autonomy, I should begin from the perspective of my small city or town. In my town in the Isthmus I haven't experienced autonomy in the way the Zapatista *compas* talk about it or how they live it. In my family, in my *colonia*, in my town, it has been different. We participate,

like most people, in the town fiestas, we dress in regional attire, we attend the town meetings, we participate in *tequio*. My family is very involved in organizing in our *colonia*. There is pleasure in *convivencia* [communal living]. For example, when my grandfather passed, within an hour the neighbors were making coffee and bread for everyone to share in our house as we mourned together. For me, this goes beyond solidarity. There exists an obligation in the community. My family will do the same thing for the people who helped us when they have a fiesta or wake in their home. Reciprocity is something the Isthmus culture takes very seriously. It's not just in the fiestas either. It's also during times of mourning and in the basic needs of the *colonia*, block, family, community. At the same time, however, we no longer work the land, and the PRI governs the town. Yet we also have maintained our maternal tongue, which is Zapotec.

I tell you all of this because from my point of view, my idea of autonomy is also that which I lived in my town, even though the government doesn't yet belong to us. That part is more difficult, as is reconciling the differences among us, among the different groups—the rich, although those are very few—and the poor people like us, and of course those in power. So with this being my vision of autonomy, this is what I sought out when I came to the city to study. I desired to keep my language, my way of dressing, my family, my *colonia*, all close to me. So that is what I was looking for when I came to the city, and I noticed that many other people were also looking for their own version of this too. Not exactly the same as me, of course, but they sought what they experienced in their town or city. So coming here to Oaxaca City there is a confluence of many ideas and many different ways of resisting. Part of this is saying I am from the Isthmus, or from the Coast, or from another region.[13]

So we began to look for a certain autonomy in this chaos of the city, which is what we could call urban autonomy. The great majority of the *colonias* of Oaxaca are inhabited by people who are not from the capital. They are from other regions of Oaxaca, and they organize their fiestas, wakes, *convivencias* [social gatherings] and they do them like they do in their pueblos. So this variety in ways of being, of doing things, this is for me, part of urban autonomy. This is probably quite different from what many people think of when they talk about urban autonomy—maybe they think of the youth movement in terms of graffiti, punks, and that type of thing. That is *part of* it, but not all of it. They (youth) are not the only ones looking for urban autonomy. It's also their parents, their family, and they are also part of the resistance, they also express this need for something different. We as VOCAL are sometimes in danger of making this same mistake of focusing too much on youth and the city and not making the connections necessary. For example, in CASOTA we sometimes made the mistake of becoming too insular, like happens sometimes with European activists with their *ocupas* (squats) where they don't let other people in. We can't forget about the people in the *colonias* who also think that politicians are corrupt and that electoral politics is garbage and who practice politics in their everyday lives. For me this is autonomy, whether urban or in a rural community—it is about defending a different way of living and of relating.

Rosalía's idea of urban autonomy serves as a kind of middle ground between essentialist notions of indigeneity and the view her collective (VOCAL) articulates in their discourse of urban indigeneity.

Rosalía's experience of autonomy is defined by the extent to which her town practiced key aspects of comunalidad—she mentions *tequio*, fiestas, and while she does not say *guelaguetza* explicitly, she implies it when she speaks of social reciprocity. She says the one piece that is missing is the governing structure of the communal assembly instead of political parties, which also represent a major hurdle for projects of urban autonomy such as that practiced by her collective VOCAL.[14] It is the social relationships and obligations, however, that represent the most fundamental aspects of comunalidad. According to Benjamín Maldonado:

> One can lose the language, abandon the traditional dress, have migrated to a city . . . but the person who continues to participate in the community can continue to feel *indio* and continue being recognized as a member of an Indian collectivity by their *paisanos* [fellow community members]. On the contrary, when someone becomes individualistic, their attitude belies being part of the community, so the community rejects that person. (2000, 11; translation my own)

MAGONISMO, DECOLONIAL ANARCHISM, AND LIBERATIONIST POLITICS

A final, yet important strand of political thought and practice that informs 2006 Generation politics can be loosely described as anarchist and liberationist. Members of the punk movement, like Mentes Liberadas and his collective CESOL, most directly align themselves with liberationist or anarchist philosophies and movements. This political affinity is common among punks in Mexico, where the dissemination and growth of punk has been linked to antiauthoritarian and anarchist practices and values since its emergence in the 1980s (Poma and Gravante 2016). Hence Oaxacan punks' identification with the global anarcho-punk movement. Many 2006 Generation collectives and activists like those in VOCAL and CASOTA, however, identify more specifically with Magonismo, the brand of anarchism proposed by Oaxacan son Ricardo Flores Magón in the early 1900s. In fact, CASOTA's logo features the profile of Ricardo Flores Magón with a punk haircut and anarchist symbol (figure 10). Angel J. Cappelletti's classic and recently translated history of anarchism in Latin America (2017) frames anarchism as a European import that arrived to Mexico and Latin America in the mid-1800s. Magonismo, however, complicates efforts to categorize anarchist politics in Mexico using such a neat time line or unidirectional flow of culture, ideas, and practices.

Magonismo itself combines European anarchist thought with many of the practices found in Indigenous communities in Mexico that we would now associate with comunalidad; namely, communal land tenure, governance through communal assembly, and mutual aid (Maldonado 2000). Magón, Magonismo, and the Mexican Liberal Party (PLM) he helped establish drew on multiple influences in developing their brand of anarchism and have themselves influenced the politics of a diverse array of social movements—from the original Zapatistas of the Mexican Revolution to the Chicano movement, EZLN, and the 2006 Generation (Beas and Ballesteros 2010; Bufe and Verter 2005; Gómez 2016).[15]

Instead of framing 2006 Generation anarchism as Magonismo or even neo-Magonismo, however, I find it more useful to frame their anarchist politics as "decolonial anarchism." Such a framing invites us to excavate genealogies of anarchism that consider the diversity and multiplicity of entanglements involved in the continued transformation and circulation of anarchist politics. This implies that we decenter whiteness and the West, which are frequently portrayed as the dominant actors and geographies of anarchist politics. Such a move becomes necessary if we are to attend to youth's own understanding of their politics, which point to comunalidad—or at least their understanding of comunalidad—as fundamental to the development of their emergent horizontal politics. They are inspired by Ricardo Flores Magón, inasmuch as they find elements of comunalidad central to his political proposal. Consider Rosalía's response when I asked her if she identified as anarchist:

> The Indigenous *pueblos* of Mexico are not anarchists because of Kropotkin, or Malatesta, or even because of Ricardo Flores Magón. Rather, they are anarchists because of their own forms of living, because of their own forms of relating to one another, their ways of organizing. I believe this to be true because it is actually our practice that makes concepts real. For example, in languages like Zapotec and Mixtec, I don't think concepts like autonomy

FIGURE 10. CASOTA logo, "Magón Punk." Photo credit: the author.

or anarchism even exist. Not in those languages, there are other words, it's different. It's our actions, our practice that matter more than the labels we attach to them.

Rosalía's understanding of anarchism and Indigenous politics developed through conversations with Zapotec intellectual and activist Jaime Martínez Luna, whom she met through her participation in community radio as a high school student. Through dialog and exchanges with their elders, youth like Rosalía have developed a decolonial understanding of their radical politics. They do not look to Western ideologies for revolutionary prescriptions or messiahs as previous generations of activists in Mexico and throughout Latin America did. The political genealogies articulated by VOCAL and Rosalía reaffirm that a true understanding of 2006 Generation politics requires a palimpsestic analysis that belies dichotomized or linear thinking.

Daniel of VOCAL also offered a window into the palimpsestic political imagination of the 2006 Generation:

> I don't self-identify with a particular name or ideology or philosophy or way of thinking. Nevertheless, I do coincide in many ways with liberationist ideas. It can be Magón, Zapata, the proposals that were made during the most recent revolution [the Mexican Revolution of 1910–20]. I coincide with that, but also with a long history of struggle by Indigenous peoples [*pueblos indios*] that goes back hundreds of years, as well as the many attempts at nonviolent uprisings throughout Latin America over the past century. I think there is agreement, more than anything in the practice of struggle.
>
> As far as philosophies, I do coincide with the struggle for autonomy. And that is based more than anything in the life practices, the way of life of Indigenous peoples and communities. These are the values or principles that I fight for. And I think that the diversity that we represent as a movement is also part of those values. I don't think of the struggle for autonomy as a hegemonic struggle that rejects other worldviews. Likewise, I don't think that autonomy needs to be suppressed by other ways of explaining the situation that we are living. Along those lines, there is fraternal dialog with Marxist *compañeros* [comrades] who agree with the principles of the movement. We acknowledge that we don't coincide in our political stances, but we have practically the same motives of [seeking] social transformation. So that doesn't mean that we distance ourselves from them.

Daniel's reluctance to subscribe to one metanarrative or totalizing worldview is shared by many of his peers and is the source of considerable intergenerational frustration and misunderstanding. For example, remember the middle-age media activist who characterized the 2006 Generation's politics as being focused on building utopian islands and lacking substantive proposals for social change. Such a misinterpretation is not uncommon among older generations of activists, who do not always recognize what they see and hear in the 2006 Generation's politics. This disconnect helps explain the need for youth to create their own physical and social spaces from which to continue to develop and practice their horizontal politics. Given that the politics of more established opposition groups in the city did not resonate with many in the 2006 Generation, they sought to create their own counterspaces like CASOTA (see chapter 3), which helped foster the radical politics, imaginations, and subjectivities described in this chapter.

CONCLUSION

This chapter examined some of the transformations that indigeneity, Indigenous politics, and radical politics are undergoing in Mexico, in part due to decades of urban and transnational migration. With displacement and dispossession of Indigenous communities rampant throughout the hemisphere, the case of the 2006 Generation offers important ethnographic insights into how young people are reimagining and redefining what it means to be Indigenous through their politics and urban organizing. In the process, they are also remaking and indigenizing urban space. Though not all of the activists in the 2006 Generation identify as Indigenous, key collectives like VOCAL explicitly articulate a collective identity as urban Indigenous. Of my interlocutors who self-identified ethnically or racially, all did so either as pan-Indigenous or a specific Indigenous group like Zapotec or Mixtec. From their location in urban Oaxaca, organizers draw on Indigenous histories of struggle, popular understandings of Indigenous governance, and Indigenous epistemologies like comunalidad, and they make political space for their enactment and transformation in the city. Through activists' migration histories, we saw how these traditions and visions travel to the city of Oaxaca, where they mix with other influences such as what I call decolonial anarchism, Zapatismo, and, for some, their membership in the punk movement.

The 2006 Generation's politics were also heavily informed by their experience creating counterspace during the height of the 2006 social movement. Participating in the barricades was a particularly meaningful experience for movement youth, where they created intergenerational space, physically took control of city streets, forged strong relationships, and carved out political space for their brand of horizontal politics. Through these actions, youth not only honed their emergent politics, they also brought their unique form of urban Indigenous politics into the wider social movement. Through their post-2006 organizing, such as the formation of VOCAL, youth breathed life into the social movement, helping sustain and transform the energy from the popular takeover into a new cycle of movement activity. Chapter 3 examines how this unique political culture and vision was spatialized through post-2006 counterspaces, with a focus on the social center CASOTA. This will allow us to continue to track the transformation of the social movement and how the 2006 Generation has altered Oaxaca's racial and spatial politics.

THREE

Urban Youth Collectives as Laboratories for Constructing and Spatializing Horizontal Politics in Post-2006 Oaxaca

> Unless we have the space to imagine and a vision of what it means fully to realize our humanity, all the protests and demonstrations in the world won't bring about our liberation.
>
> —ROBIN D. G. KELLEY, *FREEDOM DREAMS* (2002, 198)

IT WAS EARLY EVENING on a brisk and clear November day in 2010 when I arrived at the social center, CASOTA, for my first *Geopolítica* (Geopolitics) research meeting. I was invited by members of VOCAL earlier in the week to participate in this research group, which was made up of various collectives, academics, and NGOs that were aligned with the 2006 movement and who shared concerns over the impacts of extractive development projects in Oaxaca. On this day, members of the group were scheduled to meet to discuss a request for help from community leaders in the Zapotec municipality of San José del Progreso. Like many rural communities in southern Mexico, San José was in the crosshairs of foreign companies seeking to expand their control over the region's resources—benevolently referred to as Foreign Direct Investment by economists and bureaucrats. Concerned about a Canadian mining company's plans to expand their activities in San José, community leaders reached out to members of the activist research group. After several conversations, the research group agreed to issue a report and public presentation on the effects of mining on local communities, including a breakdown of who had financial or political interests tied to mining in the region and an overview of local resistance efforts.

On this evening, as was often the case when I arrived for meetings in Oaxaca, I showed up "early"—another way to say that I showed up at the hour previously agreed upon, which apparently no one else took literally. Rosalía and I waited under a large guava tree that provided partial cover for the open-air courtyard in the middle of CASOTA's house. As we waited, with a larger-than-life mural of Mexican revolutionary and Oaxacan anarchist Ricardo Flores Magón watching over us from across the courtyard, I asked Rosalía about her recent trip to Sweden. Earlier that year, VOCAL had hosted a group of students from a Swedish "free-school" project who were in Oaxaca to learn about the 2006 movement and the rich history of Indigenous resistance in the state. Rosalía gave them a series of urban agriculture workshops at CASOTA, after which they invited her to spend a month in Sweden to participate in what they called a "cultural exchange" (activist knowledge and skills exchange) with Tanzanian farmers and Swedish activists. She felt a deep sense of mutual identification with the African farmers, who were involved in struggles to defend their communal lands from land grabs by the state and foreign capital, similar to what communities like San José del Progreso were facing in Oaxaca and throughout Latin America. Several members of VOCAL had traveled to Europe and throughout the Americas as representatives of the collective for similar exchanges in the years following the popular uprising. The host groups were often connected to Mexico through Zapatista solidarity networks, anarchist-inspired collectives, or groups involved in politically oriented punk, hip-hop, or visual art interested in fostering dialog between social movements.

During its nearly four years of existence from 2008 to 2011, CASOTA served as a hub for such exchanges in Oaxaca. It was both a collective formed by social movement youth and the name of the physical space they opened to house their social and political projects. As a venue, CASOTA usually reflected its membership, primarily youth from the city's *colonias*— but that had changed in recent weeks. Two small children kicked rocks in the courtyard, while two others chased each other around in wild cat-and-mouse games, while a fifth child sat mesmerized on the floor, tracing over the floor tiles with a stick as if it were his paintbrush and the tiles his canvas. Near this child, a young woman in a long red huipil swept the floor, another nursed an infant, and three others sat in plastic chairs chatting in their native Triqui.

The woman and children were part of the Encampment of Displaced Women and Children of San Juan Copala, who had been occupying a corner of the Oaxacan zocalo for several months. They were protesting the paramilitary siege of their municipality, which had declared itself autonomous from the Mexican government in January 2007.[1] The women and children of the encampment began a hunger strike in September but were later evicted by local government in the ritual "cleansing" of the zocalo that occurs ahead of important celebrations (Poole 2009). In this case, the catalyst was Día de los Muertos, which brings national and international tourists to see altars for the dead, sugar skulls, and folklore, not the uncomfortable nonconformity of protesters who are honoring their dead through collective action. CASOTA offered refuge to the women and children of San Juan Copala for several weeks while they negotiated their encampment's relocation to the historic church of Santo Domingo.

This chapter focuses on the creation of CASOTA as a youth-run counterspace through which the radical horizontal politics outlined in the previous chapter were spatialized and grounded. I turn my ethnographic lens to the everyday grassroots practices that produce and maintain counterspace during the ebbs and flows of social movement activity, including the way that social and political relations are spatialized as organizers experiment with the construction of radical political cultures, emancipatory freedom dreams (Kelley 2002), and insurgent subjectivities (Holston 2008). CASOTA, as a counterspace in the center of Oaxaca City, provided a slice of urban territory for youth to enact the relationships central to their politics, such as mutual aid and solidarity with communities in resistance, especially Indigenous communities. The youth of CASOTA rented this small parcel of urban land and the house that sat on it, which is of course a very different situation from having communally owned and governed territory. Although renting the house proved a precarious arrangement, CASOTA provided youth and others associated with the Oaxacan social movement a base in the center of the city, resulting in a powerful and generative experience (figure 11).

This chapter's epigraph, which comes from historian Robin D. G. Kelley's hallmark exploration of Black radicalism, speaks to one of this book's main arguments— that social movements and the political cultures they produce are more sustainable and impactful if organizers are able to link the more ephemeral spaces of direct action, like protests and demonstrations, with longer-lasting counterspaces like social centers and cultural venues. This chapter builds on the previous two by showing how the counterspaces built during that period of extraordinary mobilizations and popular control of the city are connected to the quotidian political and physical spaces that emerged post 2006. These spaces emphasize urban, migrant, and Indigenous youth as creators of social and political life. Counterspaces like CASOTA disrupt the

FIGURE 11. Ricardo Flores Magón and Emiliano Zapata portraits inside CASOTA. Photo credit: the author.

dominant spatial order in Heritage Oaxaca, as well as the hegemony of traditional opposition political groups within the social movement and popular politics. Subsequent chapters supplement these insights into social movement temporality and spatiality by showing how these counterspaces are linked to the ephemeral spaces of direct action and cultural production since 2006.

One of the more powerful aspects for movement participants in 2006 was their reclaiming of space and making themselves visible in the material, social, economic, political, and symbolic center of the city (Magaña 2015). In the months immediately following the violent repression of the Oaxacan social movement in late 2006, youth regrouped and launched initiatives like VOCAL in an attempt to maintain the social and political momentum generated during the grassroots takeover of the city. After about a year of organizing without a space of their own, VOCAL joined another horizontalist collective in their recently opened space, CASOTA.

CASOTA initially began as a small project meant to provide an autonomous centrally located space for different currents within the social movement to come together and regroup after the government's sustained campaign of repression. CASOTA quickly turned into a larger political project, however, when members of VOCAL were invited to open a silk-screening workshop, and later an office, in the house they were renting. Once the political nature of the project became apparent, members decided they needed to come up with a clear political proposal for their collective space. The first step, they decided, was picking a name. They agreed to call the space CASOTA, for Casa Autónoma Solidaria Oaxaqueña de Trabajo Autogestivo (Autonomous Oaxacan Solidarity House for Self-Managed Work), which in addition to being an acronym is also a play on words.[2] *Casota* means big house and is also a reference to a local affinity project named CACITA, for Centro Autónoma para la Creación Intercultural de Tecnologías Apropiadas (Autonomous Center for the Intercultural Creation of Appropriated Technologies). CACITA, which is pronounced *casita* (small house), focuses on the "appropriation of technologies" such as creating bicycle-operated appliances.

Erick, one of the founders of CASOTA, explained that he and his fellow organizers made the conscious decision to look for a space in the historic center of the city despite the higher rents and increased surveillance:

> It was important for us to find a space downtown, we searched and searched before we found the right one. It was important because people are not used to seeing *banda* downtown. This way we make our presence visible. It was also important because a lot of *banda* find it central, as opposed to if we would have opened it in the outskirts of the city. This way *banda* have a space in the city.

Erick makes two critical points here: First, he highlights the collective's conscious effort to counter the social and physical exclusion and invisibility of working-class people, especially young people, from the material and symbolic center of the city. Second, his explanation underscores the logistic importance of having a centrally located space for congregation, encounter, and organizing, connecting youth who inhabit an otherwise fragmented urban landscape.

Sociologist Sujatha Fernandes outlines efforts by barrio residents in Caracas, Venezuela, to challenge similar "geographies of power and marginality," whereby "intensified rural immigration to the cities, growing poverty and segregation, and rising insecurity have led to the criminalization of poorer sectors, which are seen to disrupt the order and health of the city" (2010, 17). CASOTA, as a counterspace opened by movement youth in the center of the city, challenged similar patterns of urban segregation and criminalization of working-class residents.

As we saw in previous chapters, 2006 Generation cultural and spatial politics also subvert the racial geographies of Mexico by bridging urban/rural, periphery/center, and Indigenous/non-Indigenous divides. CASOTA activists searched for a location downtown in spite of various obstacles, including higher rents and regular police surveillance, because not only were they conscious of the benefits that a central location would bring, but they also wanted to challenge social and economic forces keeping *banda* from the city center.

Moreover, it is important to remember that the historic city center of Oaxaca forms part of a UNESCO World Heritage Site and forms the backbone of a major tourism marketing campaign. Achieving the desired arrangement and (re)production of Oaxacan history, tradition, and contemporary culture to greet tourists requires the policing of Mexico's racialized geographies and the bodies that inhabit them so tourists can visit this "colonial relic" without the hassle and chaos normally associated with Latin American cities. In part, this means relegating Oaxaca's urban poor and working class to the urban periphery, and Oaxaca's Indigenous present to small towns, ethnic markets, cultural festivals, and other sanctioned spaces for tourism.

Many of the youth who formed CASOTA, VOCAL, and other counterspaces in this network lived in peripheral neighborhoods, and many were migrants to the city. These areas often lacked basic services, accountable political representation and access to meaningful public spaces like parks or plazas. Anthropologist James Holston's work in São Paulo found that the hardships that come with living in the peripheries of cities in the Global South become "both the context and substance of a new urban citizenship,"which he refers to as *insurgent citizenship* (2008, 4). Within this formulation of citizenship, the experience of urban life—with all of its inequality, fragmentation, and possibility—becomes the basis for demanding rights and belonging in society. For Holston, "insurgent citizen movements" composed of residents from the urban peripheries represent the primary working-class challenge to regimes of inegalitarian citizenship in the Global South, as opposed to the struggles over labor, which took center stage in the past. Holston's insurgent citizenship is also useful for understanding contemporary urban movements in Oaxaca. For instance, while the teachers' union SNTE formed the backbone of the APPO, the 2006 movement was much more than a labor struggle. With access to unionized jobs and higher education under constant attack in neoliberal Mexico, the experience of precarious living in underserved, underrepresented, and over-policed urban peripheries greatly informs the insurgent citizenship mobilized by 2006 Generation organizers. The experience of the urban periphery for 2006 Generation youth, of course, cannot be separated from the experience of physical and cultural displacement from ancestral homelands that informs the insurgent indigeneity mobilized by this generation. Instead, they must be understood as being deeply entangled and mutually constituted elements of their politics and identities. Moreover, even though there are organizers in these networks who do not share these experiences or identities, the collective politics and initiatives they participate in are steeped in insurgent indigeneity and citizenship.

When I asked Mare, a Zapotec rapper and feminist activist who was heavily involved in the social movement and later with VOCAL and CASOTA, about her political involvement, she began by telling me about the Oaxaca City neighborhood she grew up in. She moved there with her mother and sister from their village in the Sierra Juárez after their father was murdered—an innocent victim caught in the middle of a land dispute. Mare described the context that eventually led her to mobilize her own insurgent citizenship as follows: "I lived in a new *colonia* where there weren't even the basic services like water and electricity, the roads weren't paved, there was no transportation, there was no health care in the community." She went on to connect her politicization and her career as a rapper with her love of poetry, which was sparked when a classmate recited a poem in school that was highly critical of the Mexican government and the conditions in which most people were forced to live in. "So that poem was telling my reality. It told my story. . . .

This poem contextualized a México in crisis, and it changed my life." Mare explained that the poem directly challenged the nationalism being promoted in Mexico surrounding the passage of NAFTA in the mid-1990s, focusing instead on the displacement of farmers and the precarity of urban life that migrants and working-class residents faced in Mexican cities.

Youth's experiences of the urban peripheries contrasted sharply with the possibility, congregation, and inclusion they experienced in the movement counterspaces they helped produce in 2006. The Federal Preventative Police, however, destroyed these spaces during their siege of the city in October and November, so youth sought to re-create spaces for collective imagining and action. Their political projects sought to appropriate and produce liberatory space in the city, and were animated by their new sense of ownership or "right to the city" (Lefebvre 1968). Daniel, a member of VOCAL who lived and organized in CASOTA, explained some of the motivations and benefits of having a counterspace in the center of the city:

> I wasn't here for the creation of the house, but at first the proposal for the space wasn't what it is now. It was seen more as a question of housing. Little by little the *compañeros* that were here realized that they had to take advantage of the opportunity and that having a space for the movement was also necessary, especially here in the historic center of Oaxaca. This project has been taking shape little by little. In some ways, we have been able to fulfill aspects of the project, but in others we still lack the necessary efforts, commitment, and work. However, we have been able to create a space that is open to a lot of people, and in difficult times of repression it has served as a safe space for many. Aside from that, we have been able to organize events and activities; allies from different parts of the country and even from other countries have come to share in the struggle. On top of that, the issue of culture and art also counts a lot within the movement, and here youth have a space where they are free to express themselves.

Daniel recognizes the importance of having physical, social, and cultural spaces for organizing. He identifies having a "safe space" where activists can seek refuge from repression as being a key function of CASOTA, but he also emphasizes the importance of having a space where youth can express themselves politically and culturally. Counterspaces like CASOTA have been spaces for youth to exercise cultural citizenship—or their "right to be different with respect to the norms of dominant national community . . . [including] the broad range of activities of everyday life through which people claim space in society, define their communities, and claim rights"

(Rosaldo and Flores 1997, 57). Such spaces are especially crucial in the case of the 2006 Generation, whose alternative politics and cultural practices are criminalized and stigmatized in broader society. Remember that many of the youth who participated in the 2006 movement were already accustomed to being targeted by police due to their cultural practices, such as holding grassroots punk and hip-hop concerts and graffiti writing, and even profiling based on their appearance. CASOTA, much like Okupa before it, provided these same young people spaces in the center of the city to express themselves culturally and politically without fear of being excluded or harassed for their difference.

I hesitate to label such spaces as "safe spaces," however, given the level of police surveillance I observed during my fieldwork. Organizers also reported that CASOTA was ambushed by state police shortly after the space was founded, with police allegedly firing live ammunition and casting tear gas and bricks into the house after a failed attempt to arrest two activists on the street (CASOTA et al. 2008). On another occasion, a VOCAL organizer was stabbed by two men who called him a "fucking *appo*" (a derogatory way of referring to members of the APPO) one block away from CASOTA. Miraculously he was not seriously injured in the attack, but nor was anyone charged for the crime. The lesson in both cases was pretty clear: creating such visible activist spaces without the political capital of a traditional opposition group, like the teachers' union or leftist political party, leaves activists vulnerable to state and paramilitary retribution.

SPATIALIZING HORIZONTALISM, URBAN AUTONOMY, AND LIBERATIONIST DREAMS

Erick, one of the original members of CASOTA, had long hair, a full beard, stocky build, pierced ears, and a serious but mischievous smile. His life experiences obscured the fact that he was only twenty-six years old when we first met in late 2009. The night we first met, Erick was serving food at an event at CASOTA, Jueves de Café y Trova, an evening with live music in the Latin American tradition of *trova* protest music, which is also referred to as *canción nueva* (Zolov 1999; Morris 2014). These events served as fundraisers to help the collective pay rent for the house and keep serving their commitment to nurturing a space for congregation and conviviality for *banda* in the city center. Erick and I stayed in touch after that night. A couple months later, in

February 2010, Erick sent me a text message asking me to lend him a hand with his *tequio* (communal labor) for the house. CASOTA incorporated practices inspired by the system of usos y costumbres that are central to comunalidad, such as the assembly as decision making structure, *guelaguetza* (reciprocity), and *tequio*.

Among Erick's tasks that week was turning the compost for CASOTA's rooftop farm, which was a heavy job for one person. Although I quietly hoped we would get an early start in order to beat the relentless Oaxacan sun, I soon learned that early mornings were not Erick's forte. Instead, we waited until midday to uncover the twelve-by-twelve-foot tarp. With not a cloud in the sky and the sun at full strength, we grabbed our shovels, stood at opposite ends of the enormous pile of mostly organic waste, and began turning it. As we picked out chicken bones and bottle caps from the compost, Erick told me about his decision to migrate to the United States after high school in search of work, his experience crossing the US-Mexico border without papers at the age of eighteen, finding out that the construction contractor he worked for in the US northeast illegally underpaid him and his coworkers, and how this experience led him to join the immigrant rights movement. In addition to the fact that he was born and raised in Greater Mexico City, Erick's experience was different from that of his fellow 2006 Generation organizers in that he did not participate in the social movement of 2006—well, at least not the one in Oaxaca. During the spring of 2006, Erick participated in what were at the time the largest mobilizations in US history, when five million people marched in over one hundred US cities in support of immigrant rights (Narro et al. 2007). A few months later, he was detained at an immigration checkpoint and deported.

Soon after his involuntary return to Mexico, Erick traveled to Oaxaca to visit his extended family, who were split between their ancestral Mixtec village and the outskirts of Oaxaca City. Erick's participation in the Oaxacan movement began during this trip. More specifically, it began on July 16, 2007, when the teachers' union, the APPO, and others associated with the social movement organized the second annual *Guelaguetza Popular*. The Guelaguetza is an important cultural festival that celebrates the traditions, music, and dance of Oaxaca's diverse ethnic groups (J. Quijano 2006), celebrated in communities throughout Oaxaca and the Oaxacan diaspora. The festival has been a key and contested terrain in the ongoing process of constructing a uniquely Oaxacan identity rooted in ethnic diversity. Far from being a celebration primarily for Oaxacan audiences, however, the contemporary state-sponsored Guelaguetza is one of the main folkloric spectacles "through which the Oaxacan state produces its national and international reputation as 'a cradle of multicultural diversity'" (Poole 2011). Indeed, the state-sponsored Guelaguetza is one of the main draws for tourism in the state and is marketed by the government as "the maximum cultural expression of Oaxacans *for the world*."[3] The state government constructed a large auditorium to host the official event in 1974 and began charging admission to the event (Stephen 2013, 66). The state-sponsored event is now financially out of reach for the majority of Oaxacans, with tickets selling on Ticketmaster for the equivalent of one week's wages.

The social movement successfully blocked the official festival from taking place in 2006 and held their own free event in its place known as the Guelaguetza Popular. In 2007, movement organizers announced that the second annual Guelaguetza Popular would be held at the Cerro del Fortín, which is where various incarnations of the festival have been held since precolonial times but also where the government's auditorium was built. In days leading up to the Guelaguetza Popular in 2007, the governor made clear that the dissident festival would not be allowed to take place at the highly symbolic Cerro. The decision of where to hold the Guelaguetza Popular caused friction within the movement between those who thought it wiser to hold the festival in an alternate venue to avoid the physical confrontation that seemed inevitable and those who thought it worthwhile to risk confrontation in order to reclaim the Cerro.

Ultimately, the Guelaguetza Popular was held on July 16, 2007, in the much smaller venue of the *Plaza de la Danza*. Those determined to hold the event at the Cerro held a parallel march toward the venue. Before reaching their destination, however, they were met by hundreds of police. Erick was among the marchers that day, though he likely had no idea what he was getting into. An excerpt from my fieldnotes describes that day's events:

Fieldnotes, July 16, 2007

Today was the Guelaguetza Popular at la Plaza de la Danza, which I attended. ... In the morning, two groups left the *zócalo*. One went to the Plaza to organize the Guelaguetza, and the second group marched to el Cerro del Fortín to try and take over the auditorium so that the Gueleguetza Popular could be held there—the Plaza is far too small a venue for all the people who turned out. Hundreds of police met the ten thousand or so marchers before they could arrive at the Cerro. They tear-gased, beat, and arrested people. At the

FIGURE 12. Youth holding the front line against police during march on July 16, 2007. Photo credit: Baldomero Robles Menéndez.

Plaza, our two MCs gave eerie updates over the microphone of the repression occurring nearby as we enjoyed the festivities. At one point the woman MC alerted us to the clouds of smoke overhead as a sign of what was going on. According to early reports, 40 people were injured (15 of them police and a handful of reporters as well), and 60 people were arrested. Buses were burned, again—the government blames protesters, and the APPO says the government had the buses burned as a pretext for police violence and arrests (figure 12). There were pictures in the newspapers *La Jornada* and *Noticias* of police blindfolding and cutting the hair of barefoot men who were bloodied from the beatings they endured, their shoes, belts, and hair piled on the floor. Not only does the government respond to protests with violence, they humiliate protesters. Further, *La Jornada* reported plainclothesmen in trucks and motorcycles with no plates making "arrests" as well.

For Erick, the experience of mobilizing with thousands of Oaxacans and witnessing the widespread repression firsthand reinforced for him the need to join the social movement in a more formal way. The repression and chaotic dispersal of protesters afterward also demonstrated to him, and reminded others, of the need for a centrally located space where activists could organize, convene, and seek refuge when necessary. This event also marked the beginning of an important shift in my research from focusing on the teachers' union and their allies to better understanding the role of youth in the movement. When I saw the initial list of those arrested that day, it was clear that youth were a significant part of actions and particularly vulnerable to arrest, yet their place in the movement was rarely acknowledged in the narratives of the movement that were circulating at the time. Regeneración Radio, a student-run radio station and website launched as part of the National Autonomous University of Mexico (UNAM) student strike of 1999, which Daniel of VOCAL participated in, released a preliminary list of forty protesters arrested that day. Of the thirty-seven with an age listed, twenty-six were between the ages of 15 and 32—including Silvia of VOCAL, who was 24 at the time. This disconnect between youth participation, vulnerability to repression, and absence from official accounts of the movement was reinforced a year later by a comment a teacher named Abril made to me:

> I would rather fight alongside these *chavos* [kids] than many of my fellow teachers who denounce them. They tell the youth that they don't want them in the movement, they tell them to take off their bandannas, to show their faces and go home. But I tell them that I'd rather stand behind these kids than next to them [fellow teachers] because the kids are the ones who get their heads cracked open by the police. They are the ones who defend us teachers and older people. They tell us, "Teachers, go get out of here. We will hold them off." And they do, they launch rocks at the police with slingshots. These kids are amazing with those slingshots. And I would rather have them next to me than many of my fellow teachers, who are only at the marches because of union obligations.

When Abril offered this critique of the contradictions inherent in a vertical organization pressuring its members to participate in direct actions, it resonated with the unresolved questions I had about the flip side of that critique. What was the role of youth who came to the movement from the margins of Oaxacan popular politics, with no organizational obligations and in many cases no formal political affiliations? I soon discovered that collectives like VOCAL and CASOTA created space for exactly those youth and their allies to participate in a more coherent and organized way.

CASOTA: THE ARCHITECTURE OF
URBAN AUTONOMY IN OAXACA

The spatial layout of CASOTA reflected the collective's political, social, and cultural proposal, as well as the unique blend of influences that inspire them. Many of the workspaces in the house accommodated projects of urban autonomy, *autogestión* (self-sufficiency, self-management, self-organization), and horizontal exchange. These included what the collective called their "dignified trades": bookbinding, printing, publishing, silk-screening, and the production of goods made entirely out of recycled material. Some of these projects were continuations of those housed in the Okupa, while others demonstrated the evolution of 2006 Generation politics.

One of the first initiatives CASOTA launched was the "November 25th Silk-Screening Workshop," which was named to commemorate the worst day of repression in 2006.[4] Artists working out of the workshop raised funds for CASOTA, VOCAL, and other solidarity efforts by selling stickers, shirts, and bags produced on site. Members of CASOTA and VOCAL also sold and bartered other goods they produced at local flea markets (*tianguis*). CASOTA also housed the "Lorenzo Sampablo Cervantes Community Store," named after one of the movement's first martyrs.[5] The store operated around the principle of *comercio horizontal* (horizontal trade), where prices are set at use value, not market value. In addition to selling merchandise produced in house, they prioritized goods made in Oaxaca and featured products made by political prisoners and communities in resistance.[6]

CASOTA also operated a rooftop farm, which is where I helped Erick with his *tequio*. They grew food for consumption and trade, and also hosted urban agriculture workshops. The rooftop farm was part of a larger push by movement networks to foster urban agriculture and food sovereignty (*soberanía alimentaria*), which is connected to their desire to practice and live comunalidad in the city. One of the four pillars of comunalidad is communal land tenure. Given the lack of access to land for most migrants and working-class urban residents, collective urban agriculture is one way some try to re-create a direct relationship with the land, food, and the collective labor of harvesting it. The experiential knowledge that the 2006 Generation gained from the six months of grassroots control of the city also heavily informed their politics around food. Rosalía became involved in the food sovereignty movement in the years after 2006 and helped out with the rooftop farm. When I asked her what made her start thinking about the politics of food, she answered:

> First, I was working with *medios libres* [alternative media], and there you learn a lot, you have a lot of information at your fingertips. You also have

the opportunity to meet a lot of people, to visit them and see how they are living. One thing that always stood out to me, that we all share, is the necessity of food. Every year we get ten million tons of corn from the United States. We used to eat what we produced and that was it. We got everything we needed from the countryside. That is no longer the case, and it's not because the soil is infertile or because the farmer no longer wants to cultivate. It's because we are being led to believe that we need to consume things that are not from our country. So I guess that was what moved me to ask: We all eat, but if the revolution is successful, who will feed us? In our process of building autonomy, is the United States going to continue to feed us? Is Cargill going to keep sending their corn? And Monsanto their seeds?

So that is what it's about, right? Very few *banda* know what's going on with that, with what we eat, the coffee we drink. That in the coffee-growing communities here in Oaxaca, they sell a kilo of coffee for eighty cents and then on average you pay ten pesos for a cup of coffee. So you ask yourself, how is it possible that the farmer who is breaking their back is only getting eighty cents? It's illogical. It's absurd, actually. So it's this reality that influenced me to say: We need a change but not just a change in politics. We need a change that starts from the soil, from that which keeps us alive. If we don't begin there, then how? I've always said, we are what we consume . . . so that's really what inspired me to shift my focus. Now I use the media to tell people about what's happening in the countryside and what they can do about it. That's what really impacted me. It's not so much about saying, oh, we need to have everything green and ecological around here and we want to be healthy. No, we *need* to be healthy. We *need* to work the earth without exploiting her. So that necessity is what it's all about.

Rosalía was not alone in connecting the politics of food to the collective process of building and expanding autonomy. Indeed, the importance of being able to secure food and goods outside of the dominant market economy—especially in the urban context where most people buy their food—was a significant lesson activists took away from 2006. As part of the government's strategy to retake the city, police and military erected checkpoints on all major highways and routes into the city. In addition to restricting the mobility of activists and potential movement sympathizers, the checkpoints were meant to cause attrition by restricting food and supplies entering the movement-controlled capital city. With limited food coming into the city markets and many businesses closing, activists learned the importance of strengthening direct relationships with farmers from surrounding agricultural communities and of growing their own food in the city. In this way,

CASOTA served as a space from which organizers practiced autonomy every day through their rooftop farm.

CASOTA also housed an impressive collection of books for sale, including those donated by scholars and authors who visited the space and presented their books there, such as Mexican scholar Carlos Aguirre Rojas and Uruguayan journalist and theorist Raúl Zibechi, who both write about Latin American social movements. Some book sales raised funds for the collective, while others were designated for allied causes like supporting political prisoners and the families of those murdered in 2006.[7] CASOTA also printed other titles in house under Creative Commons licenses or through direct arrangements with solidarity publishing houses. An alternative media collective in the state of Michoacán donated the printing press. The "Ricardo Flores Magón Library" offered a small space next to the store for folks to read and borrow books for free. The books they sold through the store and lent through the library largely focused on histories of resistance, political theory, and what could be considered liberatory or progressive literature. Facilitating the distribution of such books was part of the collective's efforts to recuperate knowledge for the working-class and rural communities they came from and worked most closely with.[8]

CASOTA also housed a soup kitchen where they offered free meals. They also sold food at events like the Noches de Café y Trova. In addition, they had a free health clinic, where a holistic doctor offered free consultations for a few hours every week. The "June 14th Communal Dormitories" offered a space where activists and students from rural communities or other parts of Mexico could stay for free and tourists in-the-know could rent for a relatively small fee.[9] Many of the projects, such as the health clinic, printing press, and bunk beds in the dormitory, were made possible through the donation of services and used materials. According to a flyer produced by CASOTA, they also hosted various workshops that "emphasize the strengthening of a social consciousness and personal learning through art and culture." These workshops were often held in the "Estela Ríos 'Comandanta Cacerola' Multipurpose Hall," which was named after one of the more active and visible participants in the women's takeover of the state-run TV and radio in 2006.[10] (See figures 13 and 14 for interior shots of CASOTA and figure 15 for the façade.) These workshops were usually free of charge or cost only a nominal fee for materials. The instructors donated their time and were often from other 2006 Generation collectives. Examples of workshops given at CASOTA during my fieldwork were those on painting, graffiti, silk-screening, engraving,

FIGURE 13. B-boys warm up in "Salón de Usos Multiples Estela Ríos" at CASOTA, with large mural of Ricardo Flores Magón and Emiliano Zapata (not visible) watching over them. This is *not* a mural of Joseph Stalin, as one audience member insisted after a talk I gave in 2015. The absurdity of a liberationist collective paying homage to an authoritarian leader aside, this mural is an homage to Oaxacan anarchist Magón. Photo credit: the author.

FIGURE 14. Posters facing courtyard of CASOTA, ranging in themes from political prisoners to solidarity with Palestine. Photo credit: Susy Chávez Herrera.

FIGURE 15. Wheatpaste of Emiliano Zapata on façade of CASOTA. Photo credit: Susy Chávez Herrera.

poster design, film screenings and discussions, popular education workshops and conferences, pirate radio and internet workshops, photography, and stencil making. Workshops are one way that collectives support each other through mutual aid and help recuperate knowledge.

SOCIAL MEDIA, ALTERNATIVE MEDIA, AND SOCIAL MOVEMENT KNOWLEDGE PRODUCTION

VOCAL and CASOTA understood social movement knowledge production and dissemination to be part of the process of building and expanding autonomy. Daniel highlighted this when I asked him to define *autonomy*, which he grounded in a deep faith "that within ourselves exists the capacity to analyze, reflect, debate, and decide what needs to be done." The 2006 Generation sought to empower themselves by analyzing their own activism and to use this capacity to help other communities engaged in struggle. VOCAL, together with other activists and researchers, created a research project named Campaña de Difusión y Movilización en Defensa de la Tierra y el Territorio en Oaxaca, México (Campaign for Dissemination and Mobilization in Defense of the Land and Territory in Oaxaca, Mexico). The *Geopolítica* research team I contributed to by investigating transnational mining firms operating in Oaxaca was a working group within this larger militant research campaign. According to the proposal drafted for the project, its main objective was to:

> Collect and systematize information regarding the exploitation of natural resources in the state of Oaxaca, as well as analyze and document the geopolitical dynamics involved in this process, which generates local resistances due to contradictory conceptions and diverse visions related to the territory.

Organizing the grassroots research team was yet another way 2006 Generation collectives enacted their politics of autonomy, solidarity, and mutual aid with communities resisting extractivism and neoliberal militarization more broadly. While extractivism is not the only source of conflict over lands in Oaxaca, efforts like the Campaña reflect 2006 Generation activists' analysis that extractivism represents the greatest threat to Indigenous territories throughout Mexico and Latin America today. Their multipronged approach to analyzing and resisting extractivism are part and parcel of the 2006 Generation's ethic of defending and practicing comunalidad and autonomy from their location and positionality as urban Indigenous youth.[11] It bears remembering that displacement has directly impacted the 2006 Generation. Activists like Erick and Mare, for example, come from families that have been displaced from ancestral towns. The Campaña as a form of militant research and knowledge production represented part of broader efforts to stop more families and communities from being similarly displaced, especially those in Indigenous territories.

While few, if any, of the organizers from VOCAL or CASOTA have college degrees, several have taken classes at the university level, and many more have participated in popular education workshops. In an attempt to further cultivate their own research skills, organizers from VOCAL and CASOTA started a collaborative project called the Diplomado de Investigadores Descalzos (Barefoot Researchers Course) together with other 2006 Generation groups, including a collective of sociology students from the public state university (UABJO) called Autonomía, Autogestión, Autodeterminación (Autonomy, Autogestión, Self-Determination). The name of the group is a reference to the Zapatistas, who frequently make mention of walking through their journey barefoot and connected to the earth. The mission of the Diplomado, as stated on their blog and again echoing the Zapatistas, was "to learn while teaching, to ask questions while walking, to listen when speaking."

As a part of the Diplomado, they invited activists and scholars to exchange their experiences and knowledge of social movements. Some guests included Uruguayan journalist and political theorist Raúl Zibechi, COCEI (Coalition of Workers, Peasants, and Students of the Isthmus) activist Isabel Nuñez, Mexican anthropologist Benjamín Maldonado, Chicano activist Simón Sedillo, Mexican "deprofessionalized intellectual" Gustavo Esteva, Marxist historian Carlos Aguirre Rojas, Indigenous leader Palemón Vargas Hernández, and Local 22 activists Omar Olivera, Genaro Rojas, and Félix García. Themes and topics of discussion included autonomy, comunalidad, state strategies of repression and co-optation, neoliberalism and development, and experiences from the teacher's movement and the COCEI. These intergenerational—and in the case of Zibechi and Sedillo, international—dialogs represented youth organizers' respect for their activist elders as well as a deep desire to strengthen connections with them and learn from previous generations of social movements and activists in other countries. Many of the organizations and movements that participated in these knowledge exchanges emerged from the rich genealogy of struggle outlined in the previous chapter.

Larger Diplomado discussions were held in the "November 2nd Central Patio," which was the main courtyard in the middle of the house. It was named to commemorate one of the greatest victories of the popular movement, when they successfully repelled thousands of federal police from taking over key installations during the monthlong siege of the city. CASOTA also held a series of film documentaries organized around topics such as autonomy, defense of territory, and the role of art in social movements. The Diplomado made most of these sessions available free to stream or download online through their blog (http://idescalzos.blogspot.com/). VOCAL and CASOTA also had their own websites and blogs through which they kept local and international followers abreast of recent developments, cultural events, and causes they felt were important. For example, CASOTA and VOCAL both published a series of essays and communiqués regarding the crisis in the Autonomous Municipality of San Juan Copala. CASOTA housed the "Iván Illich Center for Documentation," which was named after the Austrian philosopher and Catholic priest who is known for his work on "deschooling" and self-directed learning. CASOTA opened the documentation center to various alternative media collectives with whom they collaborated to produce media. Equipment for these projects was repaired on site in CASOTA's electronics workshop.

Youth proved to be extremely savvy with digital media technologies during 2006, with communiqués, video footage, radio programming, and analysis instantly streamed and uploaded to the internet via independent media websites, YouTube, and blogs. Youth participated in alternative media collectives, who produced documentaries chronicling the movement and video footage capturing graphic scenes of government repression. This grassroots media provided powerful counternarratives to the Mexican mainstream media's pro-government coverage and the lack of coverage outside the country. In the United States, grassroots media coverage, such as videos uploaded online and physical DVDs circulated by members of transborder Oaxacan communities, were instrumental in helping mobilize solidarity efforts in places like Los Angeles.[12] Solidarity media collectives, such as Barcelona-based Kaos en la Red, Madrid-based anarchist site Rojo y Negro, global Indymedia collectives, and Mexico-based Noticias de la Rebelión, also supported the movement by publishing communiqués from the barricades and OIR.

In the post-2006 movement landscape, organizers engage with an even more complex ecology of alternative, activist, and social media. When surveillance and security are of primary concern, 2006 Generation organizers and collectives use the autonomous movement infrastructures of alternative and activist media. The drawback of such media, however, is that they have a relatively limited reach. When widespread diffusion is paramount, organizers and collectives use social media, which is far less secure but has much broader reach (Juris 2012; Milan 2015). For example, calls for mobilizations and denouncements of repression are often shared via Facebook, and media collectives share news via Twitter.[13] Youth also used these social media platforms to learn about and connect with other communities and social movements globally. Importantly, the 2006 Generation's use of these media defies the dichotomy of "hashtag activism" versus "real activism" that critics of contemporary movements like Black Lives Matter (BLM) often try to manufacture (Bonilla and Rosa 2015). 2006 Generation organizers, much like BLM organizers, know that they do not need to choose between mobilizing in the streets or online.

CONCLUSION

Feeling that they were not being represented in the formal spaces of the social movement post-2006, youth decided to create their own spaces where they could continue to hone their emerging politics. These counterspaces provide laboratories for nurturing the kinds of relationships that are central to the 2006 Generation's practice of building urban autonomy and connecting with other struggles for autonomy. For activists in CASOTA and VOCAL, claiming urban indigeneity is not merely about an ethnic or racial identity, and fighting for autonomy is not only about local self-determination. Part of being urban Indigenous for them is about maintaining social relations and obligations with communities of origin and establishing connections of mutual aid and solidarity with other Indigenous communities. Autonomy is about organizing locally but also supporting other struggles for self-determination so that autonomies can grow. CASOTA provided 2006 Generation organizers a space from which to enact and strengthen these political and social relationships. Moreover, by establishing a centrally located base for urban and migrant youth, CASOTA also provided a place of face-to-face exchange and text study for them to deepen the connections to Indigenous epistemologies and comunalidad that are central to decolonial anarchism and urban autonomy.

Spaces like CASOTA, and Okupa before it, are just the kinds of spaces that Kelley (2002) argues are needed for movements to imagine and develop their visions of liberation. Although CASOTA eventually closed its doors, it provided a more stable and longer-lived counterspace from which to envision and practice a decolonial liberatory politics that the counterspaces of 2006 experimented with. Chapter 4 examines how these counterspaces articulated with and helped produce the more ephemeral spaces of direct actions and street art to form dynamic and networked constellations of resistance. This fluidity, coupled with the horizontalist logic structuring the constellations and the deep connections among the different counterspaces, allowed youth to sustain a dissident presence in Oaxaca despite heavy militarization and criminalization of dissent. By following these constellations ethnographically, we gain a much more nuanced and agile understanding of social movements and their fluidity.

FOUR

Networking Counterspaces,
Constellations of Resistance,
and the Politics of Rebel Aesthetics

The police says that there is nothing to see on a road, that there is nothing to do but move along. It asserts that the space of circulating is nothing other than the space of circulation. Politics, in contrast, consists in transforming this space of "moving-along" into a space for the appearance of a subject; i.e., the people, the workers, the citizens: It consists in refiguring the space, of what there is to do there, what is to be seen or named therein. It is the established litigation of the perceptible. . . ."

—JACQUES RANCIÈRE, *TEN THESES ON POLITICS* (2001)

THIS CHAPTER WEAVES together three ethnographic vignettes that focus on different kinds of ephemeral counterspace being constructed. The first two describe direct actions that emerged in response to political crisis. The second describes the kind of space made by visually occupying and altering urban space through artistic practice. Together the three vignettes give us a sense of the quotidian realities and tensions of practicing horizontal decolonial politics in a highly hierarchical and often times violent world— in the case of Oaxaca City, it is a world structured by the priorities and logics of neoliberal militarism. Having seen how the politics of the 2006 Generation emerged, was articulated, and was spatialized in the laboratories created by youth, we now get a glimpse into the generative friction of how these politics are enacted side by side with more hierarchical forms of organizing. We will also see how people mobilize the everyday organizing that happened in spaces like CASOTA to combat state and paramilitary violence at the level of rapid response direct actions—as opposed to the massive mobilizations of 2006.

During the waking hours of February 15, 2011, two planes full of military-trained federal police landed in Oaxaca City, where they were joined by local police forces, Mexican army soldiers and semitrailers full of metal barricades. The soldiers and police blocked off large sections of the city's historic downtown area ahead of then President Felipe Calderón's scheduled visit with newly elected Governor Gabino Cué. Despite the military presence, the teachers' union mobilized its base and held an open-air meeting outside their headquarters located one block east of the zocalo. Police forces violently prevented the teachers from entering the plaza to protest Calderón's visit. Police eventually began firing tear gas and rubber bullets indiscriminately into the crowd, injuring over a dozen protesters and reporters, with a handful of people left in critical condition. There were also fourteen reported arrests (*Noticias Voz e Imagen*, February 16, 2011). Almost five years after the 2006 social movement took and maintained grassroots control of the capital city for six months, the federal and state governments were making a statement that they controlled the streets of Oaxaca, that political dissent would not be tolerated, and that another popular takeover would be crushed before it began.

Although militarization and surveillance have colonized the norms of everyday life in Oaxaca—to the point that trucks full of heavily armed police with ski masks circulating around the city has become normal—this show of force against protesters did not go unchallenged. News of the police repression spread quickly through mobile communication, social media, and face-to-face encounters. Messages on Facebook read: "The Uprising was never over! This has just begun! Everyone to downtown!" Various 2006 Generation collectives that initially refused the teachers' call to protest took to the streets and helped drive the heavily armed police and military out of the area by throwing rocks and their own gas canisters back at them. The loose network of reinforcements quickly erected their own makeshift barricades throughout the downtown area to keep the police and military from returning.

Calls went out that evening to social movement networks through text messages, social media, and independent media sources, announcing plans for mass mobilizations the next morning to protest Governor Cué's compliance in repressing the teachers. Calls also urged people to erect more barricades throughout the city in preparation for the continued government repression that many anticipated. Instead, the federal police followed the president back to Mexico City that night, and the governor, fearing another popular takeover of the city, was forced to issue a public apology to protesters. In the apology he issued the morning after the attack, Cué stated that his administration would investigate and punish "those whose actions affected the teachers, members of the media, and other individuals." He added that the events of that day, "in no way change the will of my government to attend to the legitimate demands of the Oaxacan teachers with respect and diligence" (*Noticias Voz e Imagen*, February 16, 2011).

Years after the 2006 social movement was violently crushed by federal police and paramilitaries, youth and teachers' union activists drew on their shared experiences of mobilizing and self-defense to condemn government authoritarianism and exercise their own claims to the streets and public spaces of Oaxaca, as well as their right to nonviolent protest. The event brings into focus the ways in which the energy harnessed by the social movement in 2006 was effectively mobilized again when needed. The networks the networks and relationships forged through the social movement were still alive and viable in early 2011, which defies some of the narratives that circulated at the time, including that the social movement had failed, since it was unable to achieve its main goal of forcing the former governor from office; that the movement ended in 2010 when the ruling PRI (Institutional Revolutionary Party) was finally voted out of the governor's office; or that the movement was no longer relevant, since it no longer had the ability to mobilize the hundreds of thousands of people it did in 2006.

This book has demonstrated how the energy from the social movement of 2006 (and other movements) was sustained through the formation of a network of youth collectives, including VOCAL and CASOTA. With these histories in mind, we can appreciate that the events of February 2011 did not arise out of thin air. Through analysis of this and the other two vignettes, this chapter illuminates how those more durable counterspaces like CASOTA articulated with the ephemeral counterspaces of direct action and visual street art to form constellations of resistance that collectively remapped the city. These constellations built on and transformed previous geographies of power and resistance, allowing activists to maintain an organized presence in the city after 2006, even with the dangers and limitations posed by increased militarization, surveillance, and criminalization of dissent in Mexico.

In analyzing the diverse ways that youth seek to create social change, it is important to recognize that even those marginalized sectors of society that do not benefit from the promises of "formal" or "full" citizenship still regularly engage in political relationships with the state, with other sectors of society, and with each other (Chatterjee 2004). Focusing on the social production of space and power, and the spatiality of power itself—what Doreen Massey (1994) calls dynamic simultaneity—allows us to better understand the political relationships exercised by marginalized sectors of society and the terrains where they are enacted. The importance of mapping these terrains for our understanding of politics is clear if we consider Foucault's understanding of power, which recognizes that power operates as a social relation diffused through all space, not only within official state structures: "Power is everywhere; not because it embraces everything, but because it comes from everywhere. . . . Power is not an institution, and not a structure; neither is it a strength we are endowed with; it is the name one attributes to a complex strategical situation in a particular society" (1990, 93).

One of the central arguments in this book is that social movements and the political cultures they help create are far more sustainable if movements are able to produce and network diverse kinds of counterspaces. In Oaxaca, such spaces openly challenge the political and capitalist classes' ownership and control of the city's public spaces and public life by permitting congregation and organizing, where a capitalist logic would demand spaces of consumption. Counterspaces do not exist completely outside of dominant space, however. Rather, counterspace is a project, a continual process of contestation that is never complete. Much as hegemony is a dominant project that is always contested and negotiated, dominant space is never complete. Its incomplete nature is exposed and expanded through projects of counterspace, which exist in direct opposition to the strategies and power relations operating in dominant space. Counterspaces, then, become projects that seek to reclaim the egalitarian promise of public space.

Although the Federal Preventative Police (PFP) violently regained physical control over Oaxaca City in late November of 2006, and internal divisions took their toll on social movement unity and coherence, the event described in the first ethnographic vignette is evidence that the shift in Oaxacan politics and the transformation of Oaxaca's streets and public spaces were not erased. In order to illustrate how the power generated by the social movement was incubated, transformed, and mobilized following 2006, I turn to the constellation of counterspaces forged by the 2006 Generation and the role those spaces played in linking youth with each other, the city center, and a constellation of already existing counterspaces.

CASOTA was one of dozens of cultural and political spaces created by social movement youth in the post-2006 years. Returning to the metaphor of the palimpsest is useful for envisioning the way that these counterspaces were layered over, and entangled with, an already existing and rich cartography of resistance, which included spaces such as the zocalo, Cerro del Fortín, and the surrounding downtown streets that had long constituted both sites and objects of struggle in Oaxaca. Creating such counterspaces is one way that 2006 Generation organizers insert themselves front and center into Oaxacan popular politics, inscribe themselves into the region's long history of organized struggle, and directly challenge the invisibility that the dominant neoliberal spatial project prescribes for them and that the militarized state attempts to enforce. In chapter 3, Erick explained that opening CASOTA downtown was a conscious effort to challenge the social and physical exclusion and invisibility of working-class people—*banda*, as he put it—from the material and symbolic center of the city (map 1). The mere existence of a counterspace like CASOTA, full of working-class, migrant, Indigenous, punk, grafitero, and hip-hop youth in the historic city center disrupted the exclusionary logic of the neoliberal city. This is politics in the Rancièrean sense, *par excellence*.[1] For Rancière, the essence of politics is not about groups with competing interests reaching consensus. Instead, much like the spatial disruption caused by CASOTA and other 2006 Generation counterspaces, politics is about defying the status quo and the dominant spatial and political distribution of bodies and objects (Rancière 2010).

Networking Counterspaces: February 15, 2011

During the ebbs and flows of post-2006 political activity, youth counterspaces were incubators for the everyday maintenance and growth of activist political cultures and social networks, as well as serving as launching points for direct actions and places of refuge from repression. Chapter 3 documented what this process looked like on the ground vis-à-vis the spatialization of the horizontalist, liberationist, and autonomist politics of the 2006 Generation. The events on February 15, 2011, described in the first vignette help illuminate the relationship between more territorialized counterspaces like CASOTA and

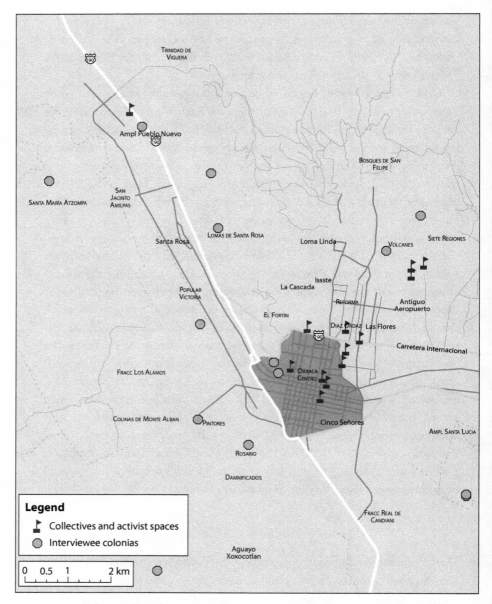

TRINIDAD DE
VIGUERA

Ampl Pueblo Nuevo

BOSQUES DE SAN
FELIPE

SANTA MARÍA ATZOMPA

SAN
JACINTO
AMILPAS

LOMAS DE SANTA ROSA

Santa Rosa

Loma Linda

VOLCANES

SIETE REGIONES

Issste
La Cascada

POPULAR
VICTORIA

REFORMA

Antiguo
Aeropuerto

EL FORTIN

DIAZ ORDAZ Las Flores

Carretera Internacional

FRACC LOS ALAMOS

OAXACA
CENTRO

COLINAS DE MONTE ALBAN

PINTORES

Cinco Señores

AMPL SANTA LUCIA

ROSARIO

DAMNIFICADOS

Legend

⚑ Collectives and activist spaces

◯ Interviewee colonias

FRACC REAL DE
CANDIANI

0   0.5   1   2 km

Aguayo
Xoxocotlan

MAP 1. Colonias where the majority of interviewees lived and spaces opened by youth or affiliated groups in relation to the historic city center, which is marked "Centro." Thanks to the Center for U.S.-Mexico Studies at the University of California, San Diego, and Justin Levitt for their help creating this map. Map credit: the author.

episodic counterspaces of direct action. Organizers convened at CASOTA throughout the day and night on February 15 to share news of the unfolding events, check online sources for news coverage, strategize subsequent actions, and recover from the confrontations with security forces. From the relative safety of CASOTA, activists received and sent updates via text message about the positioning of police and military, as well as the clandestine movement of paramilitaries and plainclothes officers circulating around the city on unmarked motorcycles and pickup trucks.

The network of counterspaces opened by youth post 2006 also included art spaces. Shortly after the attack on protesters began on February 15, I received a mass text message from a graffiti artist from the prominent street art crew, Arte Jaguar. His text called for people to mobilize toward the city center to drive the police out of the area. Even though he lived in a *colonia* about thirty minutes from the city center, he was able to respond immediately to the repression of protesters, because he was in a meeting with other artists at an art space called Estación Cero when he learned of the attacks. Estacíon Cero was located only four blocks from the zocalo. His ability to respond so quickly had he been in his neighborhood is uncertain, especially considering that the vast majority of the youth I interviewed did not own motor vehicles and public transportation becomes highly interrupted during protests and high-profile visits such as Calderón's.

Estación Cero was centrally located and open free of charge, which made it a regular location for youth from disparate colonias to come together. I regularly observed middle school and high school students stopping by after school to seek artistic advice, buy spray paint, or simply hang out. The space also served as a hub for more established artists to come together, as was the case of the meeting being held on February 15. Estación Cero was one of dozens of art spaces opened by graffiti crews, street art collectives, printmakers, and individual artists in the years following the emergence of the social movement. Artists capitalized on the momentum and visibility they received as a result of the national and international circulation of images of the social movement in which their art, especially stencil art, featured prominently. These spaces were important sites of congregation for young people, including those that shared many of the same experiences of marginalization as activists but did not identify with the overtly political agenda of other spaces.

On the afternoon of February 15, I met up with an artist from Arte Jaguar who offered free and low-cost workshops at Estación Cero. He was among those who rushed to the zocalo to challenge the government's attack against teachers that day. He was also active in 2006 and was a regular participant in movement events and actions after 2006. He was giving a workshop at Estación Cero that morning, accompanied by four high school students and aspiring street artists. I had never seen these youth at political events or spaces before, and I wondered if they would have participated in the self-defense action that day had it not been for Estación Cero and the example set forth by their teacher. Indeed, counterspaces like Estación Cero and CASOTA were movement institutions where pedagogies of resistance were practiced and handed down.

Not all of the art spaces that capitalized on the rebel aesthetic that came to be associated with the movement (elaborate stencil art and spray-painted murals with political and social commentary) belonged to collectives and artists that participated in the 2006 social movement. Even among those that were, not all identified with the horizontalist and liberationist politics that emerged from the barricades, Okupa, and other movement spaces.[2] Estación Cero, however, was very much part of this network. Art spaces full of politically committed artists, like those of Estación Cero, demonstrate the power of culture and art to render politics legible and meaningful to a wider audience than overtly political rhetoric. In so doing, they can bring potential activists and organizers into movement networks that might otherwise not engage them. Moreover, the constellation of resistance and creation that included CASOTA and Estación Cero connected barrio youth and gave them access to the city center in ways they likely would not enjoy otherwise.

VIGNETTE II: CINCO SEÑORES ROADBLOCK

On June 8, 2010, a coalition of over forty human rights and civil society organizations formed the Bety Cariño and Jyri Jaakkola Humanitarian Aid Caravan, in an attempt to break the paramilitary blockade holding the Autonomous Municipality of San Juan Copala hostage. This was the same Indigenous Triqui community, described in chapter 3, whose members found refuge at CASOTA after their eviction from their encampment in the zocalo. The encampment and humanitarian aid caravan were responses to the increasingly dire situation for the people of Copala. In January 2007, twenty Triqui communities in the district of Juxtlahuaca in the Mixtec region of Oaxaca declared themselves autonomous from the state and its political parties, thereby attempting to unify a politically divided and fragmented area that has been besieged with violence for generations (López Bárcenas 2009). This move was set in motion during the social movement of 2006, when several Triqui and Mixtec communities in the region took over the city hall in the county seat, Santiago Juxtlahuaca, and declared themselves a regional APPO organization (Stephen 2013).

The Triquis have been engulfed in a long, complicated history of organized resistance, internal division, displacement, and state and paramilitary violence.[3] The Autonomous Municipality of San Juan Copala emerges within this complex history. Some of its members previously belonged to the Movement for Triqui Unification and Struggle (MULT), which was originally formed as an independent leftist organization before years of conflict pushed them to make an alliance with the ruling PRI party, essentially turning the MULT into a paramilitary group (De Marinis 2016). The group that went on to form the autonomous municipality in 2007 had recently splintered from the MULT and formed the Independent Movement for Triqui Unification and Struggle (MULTI) in an attempt to realign themselves with the group's founding ideals and original independence from the state. Another PRI-backed paramilitary group, the Union for the Social Well-Being of the Triqui Region (UBISORT), was originally allied with MULTI before turning on the autonomous municipality in 2010 and forming the blockade in question (Stephen 2013).

VOCAL and CASOTA stood in solidarity with Copala from the moment they declared themselves autonomous. They supported the community in many ways, from fund-raising and physically reinforcing the Encampment of Displaced Women and Children of San Juan Copala to raising awareness of the situation the community faced for attempting to exercise their rights as Indigenous peoples to control their own political futures. According to town officials, these consequences included the murder of twenty-five people by paramilitary forces over a one-year period between 2009 and 2010, as well as the direct impacts of the blockade, which left residents cut off from food, clean water, and medical attention.[4] With the situation in Copala worsening, leaders from the community reached out to VOCAL, CASOTA, and other movement allies for support. In spring 2010, members of VOCAL and CASOTA, together with international human rights observers and other activists, organized a human rights caravan to San Juan Copala. The caravan was ambushed by paramilitaries on April 27, one day after UBISORT leader Rufino Juárez Hernández offered this thinly veiled threat at a press conference: "under absolutely no circumstances will we allow any kind of caravan to enter, and we cannot be held accountable if anything should happen to them" (Contralínea 2010).

Several members of VOCAL and CASOTA were shot during the attack, two of them went missing in the remote mountains for forty-eight hours, and Mixtec human rights activist Alberta ("Bety") Cariño Trujillo and Finnish activist Jyri Antero Jaakkola were murdered. Bety was the leader of CACTUS (Centro de Apoyo Comunitario Trabajando Unidos), an affinity group that was active in the 2006 social movement and regularly collaborated with VOCAL and CASOTA. Jyri was a longtime human rights activist and Zapatista sympathizer who was staying in the dormitory at CASOTA while he conducted research on Indigenous resistance to extractive development. After the ambush, their bodies were left in the middle of the road for eighteen hours, despite state police being in the area (Huerta 2016). An investigative report by Aristegui News revealed that the government of Ulises Ruiz Ortiz ordered police, who were in position to stop the ambush, not to intervene and instead to retreat to their barracks (Huerta 2016).

Instead of retreating themselves, activists organized a second, much larger caravan. On June 8, 2010, members of VOCAL and CASOTA were joined by around three hundred activists, including advisors from the APPO, members of Sección 22, alternative and mainstream media, and dozens of members of the Mexican Congress to form the Bety Cariño and Jyri Jaakkola Humanitarian Aid Caravan. In spite of the country's expanding military force and bloated security budget—thanks in large part to US aid—the government professed impotence in being able to assure safe passage for the caravan. In the face of the government's ongoing complicity in the paramilitary siege of San Juan Copala and the lack of political will to ensure the safety of human rights workers, various groups associated with the social movement of 2006 organized a series of direct actions to draw attention to the caravan and crisis in Copala. One of the more visible actions on June 8 was the occupation of Cinco Señores, one of the busiest intersections in the city and home to one of the most important and militantly independent barricades during 2006. Most CASOTA and VOCAL organizers that did not go on the second caravan participated in this action, though a few also formed part of the media team based at the Sección 22 radio station, Radio Plantón, which continued to serve a crucial function disseminating news the mainstream media ignored or glossed over.

The Cinco Señores intersection has long been an important landmark in urban Oaxaca. It sits east of the zocalo, just outside the city center, and is the confluence point where Federal Highway 175 connects the capital city with San Juan Bautista Tuxtepec to the north, Puerto Ángel to the south, as well as local roads leading to the nearby state university campus (UABJO) and various working-class colonias. As a result, Cinco Señores was a key barricade in 2006 for defending the movement installations located on the UABJO campus and blocking entrance by the federal police. These same characteristics made the intersection a logical and highly symbolic choice for the 2010 road block, placing the direct action within the cartography of the 2006 movement.

Shortly after seven o'clock in the morning of June 8, I walked the six blocks from CASOTA to the zocalo with about a dozen activists. We made our way through the occupied square, where the encampment of displaced women and children from Copala shared the plaza with the teachers' union's annual encampment. We wove through the intricate spiderweb of rope, tents, and rainbow-colored tarps suspended in the air, many at just the right height to make me duck my head to avoid being clotheslined. Once we arrived at the kiosk in the center of the plaza, I was able to straighten my neck and lift my gaze to see that there were about sixty activists from several organizations and groups already congregated there. Everyone came together near the kiosk for an assembly meeting to strategize that day's action. After a brief discussion, the decision was made to split up into two groups. One contingent was to walk the fifteen blocks southeastward to the Cinco Señores intersection, while the other was to commandeer buses to use to block the intersection. The plan of having a smaller, less-visible group commandeer the buses did not last long. In the time it took to walk the two blocks east to the nearest bus stop, the group had swelled to about 120. The group consisted mostly of young men, along with a couple of families, a handful of women of various ages, and a few older men.

Upon seeing the large group of people on the street corner, the first few bus drivers blew past their designated stops. Realizing this, several young men from an organization of street vendors walked up to a bus in the middle of the street, got onboard, and directed the driver to the nearest stop. There, they unloaded passengers in exchange for a contingent of activists. They commandeered three more buses this way and loaded everyone from the contingent onboard. Watching the process unfold quite smoothly, it was clear that this urban activist piracy of buses to reinforce barricades was a tool in activists' "repertoires of contention" (Tilly 1978) that they had sharpened during the self-defense campaigns of 2006. The buses were taken without violence or even raised voices. One of the drivers responded to the young men who commandeered his bus, "I agree with the movement, but I cannot afford to fix the bus if anything happens to it. All I ask is that you respect that and you will have no problems from me." The young men assured the driver that they had no intention of harming his bus. The driver then asked where they wanted to go and if they wanted the door open or closed.

One of the activist bus pirates explained, "this is only necessary because the government doesn't listen to *el pueblo* unless we make *un escándalo* (a scene)." Clearly, this pirate of buses understood the power of disruption (Rancière 2010). He understood that in order to engage in politics, people had to disrupt the normal order of things. In order to make themselves visible, they had to create *un escándalo*. To be heard, they had to translate their outrage over the injustices and human rights violations being committed against the people of San Juan Copala from noise into intelligible discourse through *disruption*.

Such performances of political power must be used sparingly, however, due to the Mexican government's history of repressing and incarcerating activists, in addition to the toll such actions take in the realm of public opinion—an issue I will return to at the end of the chapter. Along with the four city buses, several heavy trucks were commandeered to block the large intersection (figure 16). Once the intersection was blocked and the flow of morning traffic stopped, an assembly took place at the confluence of the five streets, where activists debated whether to perform a full or partial roadblock. The organizations present included the street vendors, VOCAL, CASOTA, Sección 22, an organization of Indigenous campesinos, and the Bloque Negro Libertario (Liberationist Black Bloc).[5] The diversity of organizations, as well as the horizontal decision-making process, followed the same organizing logic that allowed the counterspaces explored in chapter 1 to flourish and expand during the height of the 2006 movement. Consensus-driven decision making is not the quickest way to carry out actions, but it creates space for direct democratic organizing. In this case, it also kept the dynamic horizontalist political culture youth had experimented with in the counterspaces of 2006 alive and evolving.

After several minutes of discussion and debate, the assembly decided to begin that morning with a partial roadblock, allowing activists to distribute

FIGURE 16. Banner reading "Respect the Autonomy of San Juan Copala" is hung from a commandeered bus blocking the Cinco Señores intersection in 2010. Photo credit: the author.

flyers and news to drivers and passersby about the caravan and about Copala. They would then escalate to a total roadblock later in the morning, as a show of force to the government. Each group took responsibility for a portion of the intersection but coordinated their actions in concert. In addition to displaying horizontal organizing in action, the debate surrounding the road-block reinforces the notion that the disenfranchised, or political society to use Chatterjee's (2004) term, know that they must disrupt the normal order of things. They need to "make a scene" to be heard by the state, the media, and other sectors of society (locally and abroad). The epigraph I began this chapter with echoes activists' understanding of their actions. They literally transformed and refigured the street from a "space of circulation" where there was "nothing to see" into a space of politics, "a space for the appearance of a subject," in this case *el pueblo* (Rancière 2010). Activists clearly understood that day's action as a public performance of their collective power, although those in favor of the partial roadblock highlighted the opportunity to edu-cate their fellow residents about the injustices being perpetuated in San Juan Copala (table 1).

TABLE I. Reasons Offered by Activists for and against a Total Roadblock

Reasons in favor of a complete shutdown of the intersection (i.e., not allowing any vehicles to circulate)	Reasons in favor of a partial roadblock (i.e., slowing down traffic but still allowing intermittent circulation)
"That way we show Ulises [the governor] that we are not going to be ignored! All eyes are on Copala. We will paralyze the city if we must but we will have justice!" (man in his mid-thirties from the organization of street vendors)	"With a partial roadblock, people can still get to work and go about their business . . . but they will pass through the intersection and we will tell them of the assassination of Bety, of Jyri, of the ambush, and most importantly they will learn of Copala's struggle and all of their dead. . . . We will disseminate the news of Copala and show that we can still shut the city down if he [Ulises] and his assassins are not brought to justice and the autonomy of the brothers and sisters of Copala is not respected!" (young man in his late twenties from VOCAL)
A total roadblock would be a show of force and prevent *porros* (government-backed provocateurs) from infiltrating the action by inciting violence, as is common practice in many parts of Mexico. (young man from the Bloque Negro Libertario)	Others who agreed with the partial roadblock included a middle-aged man representing the group of Indigenous campesinos and a middle-aged woman from the organization of street vendors. Both of them spoke mainly about disseminating news of the human rights violations in Copala.

SOURCE: Author's field notes.

The loose network of activists did have some miscues that day. While they were coordinating the placement of buses and trucks, for example, one of the truck drivers drove off. The organizers quickly brushed it off, however, and adjusted the placement of the buses to compensate for the escaped truck. Mishaps like this are not surprising, perhaps, given the diversity of agendas and political cultures of the organizations they represented. Add to this the fact that they executed the direct action using horizontal organizing (i.e., no chain of command) and without predetermined plans. Given all of this, the execution of the partial roadblock was chaotic and uneven at first. The release of vehicles was coordinated through hand signals and whistling across the vast intersection. The activists managing the five points of the intersection were visibly not on the same page at first. After a few rounds of stopping and releasing vehicles that way, activists reconvened in the middle of the intersection and decided on an alternative, much smoother method of holding traffic. They decided to stop all vehicles through one entire cycle of the stoplights and then allow vehicles to circulate on the second green light. While traffic was stopped, organizers handed out pamphlets with information about Copala and the murder of Bety and Jyri. Ultimately, the collective experience of horizontal organizing among the groups prevailed, with a creative and effective response to logistical challenges.

Perhaps the greatest moment of tension during the roadblock did not come from angry motorists or even police. It came several hours into the action, around two o'clock, when a middle-aged male teacher arrived at the intersection and promptly proceeded to spray-paint "Fuera Ulises!" (Ulises get out!) on one of the buses. The bus driver was understandably upset, given the previous agreement to respect the buses. Having arrived late and without consulting any of the organizations, the teacher was not aware of the decision to leave the buses untouched. A VOCAL organizer called the teacher over and asked him if he had spray-painted the bus, to which the middle-aged man replied indignantly, "What does it matter?" After the young man filled the teacher in on the arrangement they had made with the drivers, the older man cussed at him and walked away dismissively.[6] The disconnect and tension between the organizing logics of 2006 Generation collectives like VOCAL (horizontal) and established ones like Sección 22 (vertical) often bubbled to the surface during mobilizations and direct actions. Although many rank-and-file teachers had great respect for the role that 2006 Generation activists played in the 2006 social movement, this teacher was clearly not keen on taking orders from them—even though the decision had actually been arrived at through consensus.[7]

The partial blockade was held for about an hour and a half before activists shut down the intersection completely. The timing was prompted in part by the arrival of transit police, who positioned themselves a few blocks away and began redirecting traffic away from the intersection. Eventually, reporters from local commercial and alternative media showed up for a press conference that organizers convened on the east side of the intersection. Representatives from the collectives and organizations took turns explaining their reasons for participating in the roadblock, educating the press on the Triquis' struggle for autonomy, the murders of Jyri and Bety, the death threats made against the caravan, and the government's complicity in it all.

Throughout the day, I received updates on the progress of the Bety Cariño and Jyri Jaakkola Humanitarian Aid Caravan via text message from a friend of mine, Abril, who is a teacher in the union. She participated in the second caravan because her daughter Mónica was shot during the UBISORT ambush that killed Bety and Jyri. Mónica was a member of CASOTA and my first contact with the collective. Abril joined the second caravan despite the possibility of another ambush, as a show of support for Mónica's activism. She also explained that as a teacher and member of the APPO, she wanted to demonstrate her solidarity for the community of San Juan Copala and their struggle for autonomy.

Abril and Mónica's activism suggests an interesting twist to theorizations of how activists are politicized. Previous studies have documented two common themes driving people to activism: (1) proximity to activism, usually through kin or social networks, and usually at a young age; and (2) a political opening—often an injustice that sparks collective action, like police brutality, for example (Auyero 2003; Brodkin 2007; McAdam 1999; Pulido 2006). Mónica, much like La Bruja, had developed a level of social consciousness at a young age, due in part to her mother's militancy in the teachers' union (proximity to activism). It was the extraordinary sociopolitical milieu of 2006, however, that pushed Mónica to put her emergent politics into practice through collective organizing (political opening). The interesting development with Mónica and Abril is that the daughter's increasingly radical activism functioned as a sort of reverb, reinforcing the mother's militancy and pushing her to deepen her own involvement. Knowing that her daughter risked her life by participating in the first caravan and ultimately was shot, Abril's already deep resolve and commitment to San Juan Copala's struggle for autonomy were deepened. This is an important, if subtle and understudied, dynamic to appreciate, because it highlights the multidirectionality of intergenerational activism and social change.

Once the organizers implemented the complete shutdown of the Cinco Señores intersection and the flow of traffic stopped, the scene was less chaotic and even tranquil. A street kid, who was maybe ten years old, played soccer in the intersection with young men from the Bloque Negro and the street vendors. The routinization of such direct actions in post-2006 Oaxaca was made even more apparent when a street vendor sold *raspados* to activists who were resting on the curb after a long morning of managing the roadblock. Such acts of entrepreneurial hustle are regularly on display during marches and other mobilizations, where street vendors often show up selling everything from water and refreshments to rain ponchos and umbrellas. The concluding section of this chapter discusses some of the implications of the routinization of mobilizations for popular politics in Oaxaca.

Around five o'clock, news reached the intersection that the caravan had entered the Mixteca region under the cloud of increasingly hostile threats from UBISORT. The police and military continued to refuse to guarantee the safety of the caravan. State officials repeatedly drew on racially coded language, suggesting that they could not control the deep-seated violence of the Triquis, who they claimed had been murdering each other for generations. The Secretary General of Oaxaca ended any question about who was in charge of the region when he declared at a press conference "Now is not the time to enter. . . . The conditions to enter do not exist, because that is what Ubisort has expressed" (Sánchez 2010). In response to the unequivocal threats of violence and signs of the government's complicity, the Autonomous Municipality of San Juan Copala asked the caravan's organizers to abandon their efforts. They could not bear the weight of any more martyrs. Upon learning the news, organizers of the Cinco Señores action reconvened in the middle of the intersection and discussed the next move. They decided to lift the blockade and march back to the zocalo, where they would join the larger encampments to discuss further actions. The impromptu decision to march back to the zocalo exposed a serious challenge for organizing such actions through temporary coalitions and horizontal decision making between disparate groups: ensuring security despite the fluidity of actions.

By this point in the afternoon, the group had swelled to about two hundred activists. We marched back to the zocalo in five contingents, representing the groups that took the lead in shutting down the five-way intersection. As activists relinquished control over the intersection, they took over the streets leading back to the main plaza, holding traffic as they passed and filling the air with chants: *"Oaxaca no es cuartel / fuera ejército de él! / Copala no es cuartel / fuera paramilitares de él!"* (Oaxaca is not a barracks / military get out! . . .) and *"Autonomía / autogestión / autodefensa para la revolución!"* (autonomy / *autogestión* / self-defense for the revolution!). Jyri and Bety's friends in the VOCAL/CASOTA contingent denounced the governor's complicity in their assassinations, *"Jyri no murió / Ulises lo mató! Bety no murió / Ulises la mató!"* (Jyri did not die / Ulises killed him! Bety did not die / Ulises killed her!"). With each cathartic chant, we walked farther away from an intersection freshly inscribed with similar messages. The graffiti and charred remnants of burned PRI campaign materials were left behind as testaments of that day's actions (figure 17).

FIGURE 17. Campaign ads being burned in the Cinco Señores intersection. The banner in the background reads "APPO: All Power to the People." Photo credit: the author.

About ten blocks into our return to the zocalo, our contingent noticed that the rear of the march was falling behind. People began yelling for them to catch up so that traffic would not split the march into smaller groups. The fear was that without the protection afforded by numbers, police or paramilitaries would start rounding up or picking off people who fell behind. The most vocal person from the rear was a middle-aged woman, who I recognized from her participation in the assemblies throughout the day and later learned was a teacher from Sección 22. The teacher was visibly upset and refused to continue toward the zocalo. She clutched her cell phone and yelled frantically that her daughter Yolanda was left alone at the intersection.[8] After several tense minutes of yelling back and forth, and of organizers from the front running back and forth conveying messages, the woman put an end to the debate when she yelled at her would-be persuaders, "You all can go wherever the fuck you want, but we are going back to Cinco Señores!" The march split into several smaller groups, with some toward the front having already left us behind, continuing toward the zocalo while the debate played itself out.

The coalition's actions that day were driven by a commitment to horizontality, which created space for intense debate, compromise, and when necessary independent action. The mid-march debate lasted for over five minutes—in the middle of a busy street, during rush hour, with lots of angry drivers displaying their displeasure at being kept on the road at the end of the workday, and some marchers visibly tired and upset from the long day and stress of worrying about being attacked by the police or paramilitary units. Horizontal organizing may not lead to the most streamlined actions, but it allows groups to maintain autonomy over their own decision making and take separate paths forward when consensus cannot be reached. The Cinco Señores roadblock, together with the various other actions that day, activist media coverage, and the caravan itself, speak to the power of having vertical and horizontal organizing logics operating simultaneously within a social movement. The political culture that emerged from the 2006 social movement combined the flexibility, creativity, and autonomy of horizontalist organizing with the ability to scale up actions that is afforded by organizing alongside better resourced and more experienced organizations like the teachers' union. This kind of organizing is one of the significant legacies of the 2006 social movement (Magaña 2014).

Upon arriving at the zocalo, we marched past the various encampments, weaving through the narrow corridors created by the rainbow of tents and tarps until we reached the kiosk at the center of the plaza. After the various groups reported back to their delegations, who had stayed to protect the larger encampment, Yolanda's mother arrived at the zocalo without her. She filled us all in on the details: Her daughter was safe but distraught after calling her from aboard a bus. She and a middle-aged man named Elias, who was a neighbor and supporter of CASOTA, stayed behind with audio equipment, waiting for a friend to pick them and the equipment up. Before their ride arrived, they were surrounded by two pickup trucks full of men, who immediately started beating Elias with what Yolanda described as clubs or metal pipes. They hit him in the head and swarmed on him once he hit the ground. They yelled, "You are fucking *appos*, aren't you? We don't want any fucking *appos* in Oaxaca!" One of them tried to grab Yolanda, but she managed to get away, though not before they struck her in the shoulder with a pipe or club. She ran toward the now flowing traffic and boarded a bus. She saw the men throw Elias into the bed of one of the pickup trucks. Yolanda eventually made it to the safety of the occupied zocalo and was soon sharing her story with a reporter.

Shortly after Yolanda's mother debriefed everyone about what had happened—and after many unsuccessful attempts at reaching Elias by phone—a large assembly broke out. Many details about the day's action were discussed and debated. At one point, a young man from VOCAL who is often outspoken at meetings got into a heated exchange with a middle-aged woman. She repeatedly claimed that the two activists were attacked because of poor planning by the organizers. The young man agreed but insisted on moving the discussion beyond finger pointing and toward solutions. The discussion looped back around multiple times, with the two of them repeating the same points in incrementally louder voices. Eventually, the young man began to dominate the discussion, silencing the woman by talking over her. This type of domineering performance by men in political spaces is likely familiar to anyone who has spent much time in such arenas (Stephen 2013; Zibechi 2014). These are the types of power plays that collectives like VOCAL and CASOTA consciously work to overcome in their social and political relationships. Recognizing this, a young woman from VOCAL intervened. She told her fellow organizer that he was being disrespectful by interrupting the woman. He conceded and deferred to the woman, but not without a frustrated shake of his head that slightly undermined his verbal concession. The middle-aged woman again repeated her disapproval of leaving Yolanda and Elias behind. Another young woman from VOCAL stepped in and attempted to move the discussion forward by asking the larger assembly if everyone agreed that no matter the circumstance, no one should ever be left behind after or during an action. Several people audibly agreed, people nodded their heads, and no one disagreed. Consensus was reached: no one should be left behind.

Several other moments when activists were vulnerable that day were identified by the assembly, solutions were debated, and some agreed upon. Other contentious issues that were discussed included the revelation that one of the groups involved in the roadblock solicited donations from drivers. The debate about this practice seemed to break pretty clearly along organizational lines, with groups that already had antagonistic relationships going back and forth.

Several groups, including CASOTA and VOCAL, argued that asking for donations during a roadblock was in poor form and could be misinterpreted as paying for passage. The other group argued that they needed the money to pay for the cost of printing the informational flyers that were handed out that day. No consensus could be reached as far as barring the practice. A compromise was reached, however, that donations would have to be collected in sealed containers and brought back to the assembly, where they could be distributed to organizations as needed to help cover action-related expenses, such as the printing of flyers. Ultimately, the assembly lasted well over an hour, but consensus was reached on several important issues and compromises on several others.

While the assembly was still going on, some organizers returned to CASOTA in case Elias showed up—which he did . . . eventually. After the beating, paramilitaries dumped him in the middle of a street in a colonia near downtown. A good Samaritan picked him up and took him to CASOTA. From there, a couple organizers took him to a nearby hospital, where he spent the night being treated for his injuries. After the assembly in the zocalo, organizers regrouped at CASOTA, made phone calls, sent text messages, listened to the radio, and checked the internet for news coverage on the caravan, as well as disseminating their own news about the day's events to allied media. Around 9:30 or 10 p.m., those still at the house convened a smaller meeting to recap the day's events, and they agreed to hold another meeting the next day to discuss further Copala-related actions after a good night's rest.

Remapping Social Movement Geographies

The Cinco Señores action is emblematic of how, through their organized resistance and spatial practices, social movements can transform urban space and remap social and political linkages. The Cinco Señores intersection has long been an important convergence point in urban Oaxaca. The area appears as a landmark in city maps dating back to at least 1910. With the erection of the Cinco Señores barricade in 2006 and subsequent actions like the roadblock in 2011, activists effectively *placed* the intersection within the already existing cartography of resistance in the city, and thus contributed a new layer to the palimpsest of urban Oaxaca. Cinco Señores is now connected to the zocalo, El Cerro del Fortín, and other key sites where horizontal organizing, radical direct action, and popular control of public space are practiced (figures 18 and 19). The appropriation of these sites by social movements is, of

FIGURE 18. Activist spray-painting "Copala Resists" with an anarchist symbol during the march in 2010. Photo credit: the author.

FIGURE 19. "Jyri and Beti Live" scrawled on the walls of the Palacio de Gobierno (Oaxacan State House) on the south side of the zocalo. Photo credit: the author.

course, momentary and uneven. The quotidian configuration of power and space is such that highly visible public spaces appear to be under state control, with resistance taking place in underground spaces like CASOTA. In this way, these first two vignettes from 2010 and 2011 provide windows into the temporal and spatial life of a social movement, highlighting the dynamic connections between the ephemeral spaces of direct action and the everyday spaces of organizing.

VIGNETTE III: REBEL AESTHETICS AND PALIMPSESTIC SPACE

The images on the previous page illuminate a fresh perspective on one of the main arguments in this book, that through the production and maintenance of counterspace, youth helped spatialize the power generated during the height of grassroots control of the city and helped incubate activism through the ebbs and flows that followed. The images of politically charged graffiti inscribed on walls in the colonial city center expose another layer of counterspace. In the first two vignettes, we saw how organizers networked counterspaces of direct actions with territorialized counterspaces like CASOTA. Vignette III illuminates how the visual interventions artists and activists inscribe into the city's walls and other highly visible spaces constitute important counterspaces that are integral parts of post-2006 constellations of resistance and creation. These interventions, whether utilitarian graffiti scrawled on the walls of the Oaxaca state house or elaborate murals, have the capacity to spark and inform dissident politics.

Through their public and often illicit art, artists challenge regimes of police surveillance, private property, and tourism-based development. Their art adds another layer to the palimpsest of Oaxaca's urban spaces and exposes another dimension to the physical and discursive battle over who has the right to shape and transform the city. This battle is another manifestation of the ongoing tension explored throughout this book between the state's authority to shape and intervene on the existing architecture of the city and the right of "inhabitants" and "users" to alter their environment. These struggles over the urban spaces of Oaxaca are often couched in the language of cultural patrimony and heritage politics that we saw play out in chapter 1. Grafiteros who paint in the city center, for example, are publicly derided for damaging the state's cultural patrimony and negatively impacting tourism, and hence the economy. The government is criticized for unpopular renovations of the historic city center that alter its "authenticity." Returning to Lefebvre's (1991) spatial triad—representations of space, representational spaces, and spatial practices—we can understand illicit artistic interventions as grassroots practices that reconfigure the images, symbols, and language of *representational space*. Through these reconfigurations, artists create counterspace.

Activists and artists give form to their social and political imaginations and sensibilities through collective practices I call *rebel aesthetics*. In the case of the 2006 Generation, rebel aesthetics include the practices that create utopian spaces like the Okupa and CASOTA, where alternative social and political relations are enacted. Rebel aesthetics also include artistic practices that open up space for the viewer to imagine their own utopian worlds and what they might look like in urban space. I think of rebel aesthetics as a bridge between what anthropologist Jessica Winegar refers to as aesthetics of protest and aesthetic ordering (2016). In her work on the Egyptian protest movement that brought down Hosni Mubarak, Winegar focuses on acts of "aesthetic ordering." She uses this concept to frame "collective action seeking to beautify public space and regulate behavior in it," which she juxtaposes with the "aesthetics of protest" that she argues is more traditionally covered by media and academics and that includes "chants, poetry, music, and anti-regime graffiti" (2016, 610). Rebel aesthetics include graffiti, which Winegar places in the latter category and which tends to contain more didactic messages scrawled on walls by protesters (i.e., not necessarily art by artists). Rebel aesthetics also include elaborate artistic interventions like murals, which are meant to beautify public space and shape behavior in it, consistent with Winegar's aesthetic ordering. In the case of 2006 Generation Oaxaca, these forms of interventions are not easily distinguished. The protest graffiti scrawled hastily on a wall during a march or in the middle of the night cannot be disconnected from the elegant mural offering a glimpse into a better, more just world. They both contain a clear invitation to imagine alternatives to the current spatial and social orders. Bridging these categories is important in the case of Oaxaca, because the diversity of visual interventions that many have come to associate with popular politics in the state since 2006 defies categorization as either protest art or art meant to beautify public space—it is often both, other times one or the other, and sometimes neither.

When looking for the most visible, highly trafficked spaces for their interventions, street artists are often drawn to the city center, whether their art is explicitly political in nature or not. They do so risking arrest, police and vigilante violence, and being accused of damaging Oaxaca's cultural patrimony and negatively effecting tourism, and hence the economy. Under these circumstances, street artists often deflect blame toward unpopular government remodels of the city center or omnipresent electoral campaign propaganda, which are often painted on the same walls that artists covet. One afternoon in the summer of 2010, I was helping a local street artist affiliated with Estación Cero and Arte Jaguar with an art installation he was invited to contribute at a community art space on the outskirts of the city. We were walking to the corner store to purchase some food for a quick lunch when we passed one of these political advertisements. He gestured to the wall, shook his head disapprovingly, and said:

> They call *us* vandals and criminalize our art, but at least our work beautifies our environment and makes people think. We challenge Oaxacan society to reflect and imagine a more just society, or at minimum we highlight the beauty of our people, of our diversity. These [political] parties fill the walls, our walls, the people's walls, with their electoral trash (*porquería*), which is full of empty promises aimed at getting votes, and the [art] work isn't even well done.

Clearly this artist had developed a political analysis of his own artwork and the cultural politics of public space. In arguing for the political and social significance of street art, I want to be careful not to imply a pedagogical reading of art, where the viewer is "induced" to the specific reading of the piece intended by the artist, and is then consequentially moved to a particular action as prescribed by the artist's intent (Rancière 2010, 136). I do, however, share this artist's analysis of the politics of aesthetics. He rightfully highlights the power of art to disrupt the dominant spatial logic and discourses, or the "distribution of the sensible" (Rancière 2010), by "making people think," "reflect," and "imagine a more just society."

Let us now consider two photographs that were taken in Oaxaca during the lead-up to the 2016 elections (figures 20 and 21). They are evidence of an ongoing and contentious battle over space. A battle over the materiality of space— as in who has the right to physically intervene on a public-facing wall—as well as a battle over the discursive production of space—as in who has the right to curate the messages that appear in that space. The public mural was produced by the Zapotec art collective, Los Tlacolulokos.[9] The mural was located on an outside-facing wall of a privately owned house adjacent to the entrance of the Zapotec archaeological site of Zaachila, which is roughly ten miles outside

FIGURE 20. Mural by collective Tlacolulokos in Zaachila, Oaxaca. Photo Credit: ZaanArte.

FIGURE 21. The same mural whitewashed by an electoral campaign advertisement for the longtime ruling party (PRI). Photo Credit: ZaanArte.

of Oaxaca City in the present-day town of the same name. Zaachila was the last capital of the Zapotec civilization and also conquered at one point by the Mixtecs. The mural by the Tlatolulokos depicts a young Indigenous woman in typical Zapotec dress of the Central Valley of Oaxaca, covered in tattoos, taking a selfie with a smartphone. The image is framed by Zapotec-style figures and geometric detail and the words "I am like this because of you." The mural, with its combination of signs—the women, tattoos, Zapotec dress and symbols, and the smartphone coupled with the text—is open to interpretation. The selfie could be interpreted as challenging the invisibility of Indigenous people in Mexican society and of young Indigenous women in particular. The woman in the mural is pronouncing that she is here. She is present. And with the combination of the smartphone and tattoos, the artists make clear that the young Indigenous woman is not stuck in time. With the placement of the mural at the entrance of an archaeological site, the artists could also be claiming the cultural patrimony of Zapotec civilization for present-day Zapotecs. According to the artists, the location "was an important part of the concept, we chose it because of the cultural, ancestral, and symbolic power" of the archaeological site. The idea was to "create a reflexive dialog" (pers. comm.) between artwork and location.

The message conveyed by the whitewashing of the mural by the ruling PRI party is a little more straightforward. The party is exerting its power and legitimacy to control public space and demonstrating its indifference or even hostility toward street art. I asked the artists for their interpretation of the PRI's action:

> The message is clear. The responsibility for a mural ultimately falls on the property owner, and they can easily change their mind for a few pesos. The culture pays the cost of social neglect. And to make matters worse, it was political propaganda. This also reflects the inevitable and ephemeral advertisements that contaminate our lives year in and year out.

Juxtaposing the images of the mural and the political propaganda reveals the competing meanings, ideas, and symbols layered throughout urban Oaxaca. We can see how 2006 Generation artists use street art to reclaim space and inscribe themselves and their communities into this palimpsest. We also see Zapotec artists contesting the ownership and importance of the archaeological site vis-à-vis its place in official histories, as a draw for tourism, and as an object of study for archaeologists. The Tlakolulokos reclaimed the site as the cultural patrimony of contemporary Indigenous peoples and as a place for them to

FIGURE 22. Wheatpaste art on cathedral wall depicting police as a fascist force, Oaxaca 2007. Photo credit: the author.

be seen and heard. With the political propaganda, we also see how the state actively works to silence counternarratives and exert its control over public space. The whitewashing of the mural in favor of an electoral advertisement is perhaps the clearest example of why the metaphor of the palimpsest works so well for understanding the politics of public space. The mural is layered on top of the archaeological site, and the propaganda is layered on top of both. In each instance, the *scriptio inferior* or "underwriting" is still visible. The mural is in clear dialog with the foundational level of the palimpsest, which is centuries of Indigenous (both Zapotec and later Mixtec) power, society, and culture. After the whitewashing, both of these layers of underwriting are still visible and present. Despite the power (political and economic) of the ruling PRI party to have their message seen, the previous messages and symbols are still visible. The competing and dialogic process also points not only to the physical and spatial dimensions of the palimpsest, but also to its temporal dimensions (Alexander 2005). If we follow the logic of the palimpsest, we can be certain that the 2016 electoral propaganda will not be the final inscription on the wall. The battle will continue and artists will not be silent.

Finally, I ask you to observe a series of three more photographs (figures 22–24). These were taken outside of the cathedral on the north side of the zocalo in 2007 and 2010. The first image shows a line of wheatpaste police depicted as a fascist force with the accompanying text, "Warning, fascism is

FIGURE 23. Whitewashing of wheatpaste art, Oaxaca 2007. Photo credit: the author.

FIGURE 24. Former governor depicted as a clown on the same cathedral wall, Oaxaca 2010. Photo credit: the author.

in our house ... GET OUT FECAL AND URO." URO refers to the former Governor Ulises Ruiz Ortiz, and fecal is an irreverent play on language which takes the acronym for former President Felipe Calderón's name and merges it with the word *fecal*, which incidentally has the same meaning and spelling in Spanish as it does in English. The fascist police force was created by a collective of artists that formed during 2006 and continues to produce street art and gallery art. In the first photograph, the wheatpaste police are the *scriptio superior*. They were placed over a series of flyers announcing a social movement mobilization that had already passed. The *scriptio inferior* of both the flyers and fascist police was the centuries of power and symbolism of the Catholic Church and Spanish colonialism as manifest in the architecture of the colonial era church. Soon after they were placed on the church, however, the fascist police and irreverent text were haphazardly covered up with nonmatching paint. As with the mural in Zaachila, the viewer could still see the underwriting.

The third image shows this same wall three years later. Former Governor Ruiz was again the subject of an illicit artistic intervention, this time portrayed as a clown and with the text URO Payaso Asesino (URO Assassin Clown). Following the logic of the palimpsest, we can be certain that the battle over the walls of the cathedral and surrounding zocalo will continue. While the first two vignettes demonstrated the importance of the zocalo as a central counterspace for direct actions, this last series of photographs illustrates how through their rebel aesthetics, movement artists contribute additional layers and dimensions to the ongoing production of the zocalo as counterspace. In doing so, they connect with counterspaces formed through direct actions and more permanent spaces, like CASOTA and Estación Cero, to form constellations of resistance and creation that have allowed activists to maintain an organized presence in the city since 2006, even with the dangers and limitations posed by neoliberal militarization. Moreover, through the collective practices and sensibilities of its members, the 2006 Generation continues to find creative ways of sparking the radical imagination of passersby.

CONCLUSION: CONCEPTUALIZING SOCIAL MOVEMENT NETWORKS, COUNTERSPACE AND CONSTELLATIONS OF RESISTANCE IN POST-2006 OAXACA

Mass mobilizations and encampments have long featured prominently in Oaxacan popular politics. As we saw in the first two vignettes, this kind of spatial disruption can be a highly effective way to unsettle the "normal" order of things, especially when those spaces of direct action are linked to more permanent spaces for everyday organizing. Since 2006, however, mass mobilizations and direct actions have become increasingly common, to the point of routinization and saturation. In 2009, for example, the municipal government of Oaxaca documented forty-four marches and seventy-nine roadblocks within the city limits of the capital city alone (Martínez 2010). Not surprisingly, this leaves many Oaxacans increasingly frustrated with the regular disruptions to their daily lives. Therefore, organizers must respond nimbly and intentionally with the kinds of spatial politics they employ. The growing hostility toward the disruption of urban life in Oaxaca is portrayed by an anonymous commenter, who left this response to an alternative media blog's coverage of the February 15, 2011, action described in the first vignette:

> Those of us who actually work are the people that are contributing something to our state, we are the ones that make Oaxaca prosper, we are not out being lazy in marches where the only thing that you do is degrade the image of the state, we DON'T damage the patrimony. The majority of us think that what you, the teachers, the so-called *appo*, call "STRUGGLE" is bullshit. . . . You block our way, we arrive late to work. Are you going to pay us the wages they take from our pay? I didn't think so, so please stop with your stupidity and bullshit. ("Reflexión de un joven" 2010)

The balance of public opinion is something that 2006 Generation collectives take into account as they work to come up with more targeted and creative ways of disrupting without alienating potential allies and sympathizers. An organizer with VOCAL reflected on this: "We need to find new strategies of protest that reach those in power, those that abuse, without harming or upsetting people who are just trying to work, humble people like us, struggling to make a living." As we saw in the third vignette, 2006 Generation artists contribute to this end by visually occupying and altering public space with their dissident cultural production.

Creative disruption of the spatial order is all the more important as groups in power, those proximate to them, and even organized crime adopt the direct-action tactics that have become staples for Mexican social movements. During 2010, for example, taxi drivers' unions affiliated with the ruling PRI party and supporters of the PRI candidate for governor of Oaxaca in that year's election organized marches and executed roadblocks. The same VOCAL organizer quoted earlier recounted how one evening as he arrived home to his colonia, a frustrated neighbor asked him, "Now what are you (plural: *ustedes*) after?" At first, he was confused about his neighbor's question, but soon realized that he was chiding him because of the roadblock that complicated his commute home that evening. He laughed as he recounted this story and asked rhetorically, "What good are roadblocks anymore when the PRI and the government use them?"

In addition to public opinion and appropriation, direct actions of this sort are difficult to sustain because of fatigue, repression, and the inverse relationship between routinization and impact. Maintaining a dissident presence in the city is even more difficult for youth who lack the economic capital of the local middle class, business class, and expats living in the city, or the political capital of Oaxaca's more powerful opposition groups. CASOTA, Estación Cero, and the dozens of other counterspaces opened since 2006 serve as more permanent and central bases for organizers to congregate, socialize, organize, and mobilize. Without centrally located counterspaces, responding to fluid events like those occurring during February 15, 2011, and June 8, 2010, would have been much less feasible.

While the zocalo has long served as *the* space for popular politics, it is now connected to a dynamic constellation of counterspaces. These spaces include the streets of Oaxaca, which once housed a city-wide network of barricades and are now covered in the rebel aesthetics created by street art and direct actions. The constellation also includes the sonic space produced by the proliferation of community radio stations, protest music, and the virtual space created by the online presence of alternative media collectives, as well as the physical, political, and social spaces created by the emergence of dozens of youth collectives formed out of the experience of the 2006 social movement. Chapter 5 builds on this chapter's analysis by examining in depth the role of cultural production and rebel aesthetics in the development of the 2006 Generation's politics and spatial practice. As we have seen throughout the book, 2006 Generation artists have been important makers of counterspace and visionaries of more dignified futures. In chapter 5, we get a better sense of the genealogies of their rebel aesthetics, including the significant role that migration has played in their development. I finish the book with a chapter focusing on artists and cultural production because, as I will expand upon, their futures are in many ways emblematic of the possibilities for urban, Indigenous, and youth politics in Mexico more broadly.

FIVE

Rebel Aesthetics

GIVING FORM TO THE 2006 GENERATION'S LIBERATIONIST IMAGINATION THROUGH STREET ART, PUNK, AND HIP-HOP

La calle esta gritando, esta diciendo cosas
Mire a tu alrededor, ¿qué es lo que ves? ¿son solo calles?
Eso parece porque no miras con detalle
Observa bien, cada muro encierra tu esencia
Dicen que las paredes todo escuchan y ellas cuentan, ellas resisten
. . .
Un movimiento que se escapa de la sombras
Que tiene mil matices y las calles las transforma
Que toma forma de la escritura en la paredes

(English translation)
The street is screaming, it's saying things
Look at your surroundings, what do you see? Are they only
    streets?
That is what it seems because you don't look closely
Pay attention, every wall contains your essence
They say the street hears all, they tell stories, they resist
. . .
A movement that escapes from the shadows
That has a thousand meanings and is transformed by the streets
That take shape in the writing on the walls

LYRICS FROM THE SONG "LA CALLE GRITA,"
BY MARE ADVERTENCIA LIRIKA

MARE'S LYRICS CAPTURE THE POWER of graffiti and visual street art to transform mundane public space into a terrain of popular politics, where the "screams" of the marginalized are given form and amplified. As we saw in chapter 4, rebel aesthetics—or the collective practices through which activists and artists give visual form to their utopian visions and sensibilities—have allowed the 2006 Generation to maintain a visible presence in the city center and public sphere in spite of increased militarization and surveillance. This chapter further illustrates how their rebel aesthetics disrupt politics and business as usual in the city by remaking highly transited spaces into open political terrains where youth have the power to engage fellow citizens, passersby, and the government. If politics can be reconceptualized as a form of daily imagination, as Susana Draper (2018) convincingly argues in her analysis of 1968 in Mexico, then the rebel aesthetics discussed here must be recognized as having the potential to impact politics by radically infusing that imaginary. The 2006 Generation artists regularly represent Indigenous people as contemporary agents of change, thus adding another layer to the disruption of Mexico's racial geographies described in previous chapters.

In addition to remaking public space, youth culture can create the structural mechanisms for collective action and foster politicized identities, discourses, and political cultures. Punks and *grafiteros* framed the emerging 2006 uprising as their chance to fight back against the police who had been harassing, beating, and arresting them for years. They took to the streets and barricades of Oaxaca as members of collectives that already had a history of organized struggle. This included, but was not limited to, resisting policing practices aimed at making them invisible in public space. Certain currents of the Oaxacan punk, graffiti, and hip-hop scenes were intimately interwoven with grassroots organizing networks that predate the 2006 social movement and that traverse and bridge geographic scales (local, national, transnational, and diasporic). For example, the independent hip-hop scene that Mare helped pioneer is part of horizontal, autonomist, migrant, Indigenous, and feminist organizing networks throughout the Americas. Anarcho-punk collectives are animated by their anarchist and liberationist politics and are part of global anarcho-punk networks. This chapter excavates these intertwined histories of youth culture and political organizing in Oaxaca, considering how their trajectory sheds light on possible futures for 2006 Generation collectives and organizers more broadly, especially as they relate to state and market forces in the context of neoliberal militarization.

A careful analysis of the 2006 Generation's rebel aesthetics reveals a rich cross-fertilization and overlap between punk and hip-hop cultures, which manifests most saliently in the aesthetic practices, style, and symbols found in street art. The influence of punk and hip-hop culture on the 2006 Generation's cultural politics pushes us to consider how the particularities of race, ethnicity, gender, migration, place, class, and histories of organized

FIGURE 25. Mural by member of Arte Jaguar, 2013. Photo credit: Aler Arte Jaguar.

struggle have produced politicized urban youth cultures in Mexico. These cultural histories complicate attempts to construct linear, "West–to–rest" genealogies of punk and hip-hop, or attempts to impose rigid boundaries around them. Punk studies scholarship, in particular, has been criticized for constructing an Anglocentric history of punk that privileges Whiteness and obscures the culture's globality and diversity (Nikpour 2012). Similarly, hip-hop studies and popular representations of hip-hop often erase the contributions of woman and queer people, as well as those of people and cultures outside of the United States (Clay 2008; Pabón-Colón 2018; Pough et al. 2007). Moreover, graffiti and street art culture are often conflated with hip-hop. While the two are intimately connected, conflating them misses the influence of other music and youth cultures on the continued development of both graffiti/street art and hip-hop (Bloch 2019; Pabón-Colón 2018). This chapter addresses these misrepresentations of hip-hop and punk cultures by examining how they influenced the development of politicized graffiti and street art in Oaxaca through the formation and work of two pioneering crews, Arte Jaguar and AK Crew (figure 25).

Interwoven throughout the chapter are short biographical vignettes of prominent Zapotec rapper, feminist, and activist Mare Advertencia Lirika (Lyrical Warning). Her story offers a glimpse into how art and activism intertwined in the lives of 2006 Generation youth, with special attention to the role that transnational and urban migration, uneven urbanization, gender and racial discrimination, and government surveillance and co-optation have played in the formation of politically engaged urban youth cultures in Oaxaca. Based on her experience as an urban migrant, pioneer within the local hip-hop scene, and intersectional feminist organizer, Mare's art and activism challenge one-dimensional tropes that represent Mexican return migrants, particularly youth influenced by hip-hop culture, as primarily responsible for "negative social remittances" (violence, drug use, gangs, etc.). Instead of focusing on these widely circulated narratives that paint Mexican youth as deviant and pathological, I have chosen to highlight the power of youth to create collective political visions and sociospatial practices that counter dominant systems of oppression.

This chapter focuses on artists because in many ways they represent the contradictory, fraught, but also hopeful futures of the 2006 Generation. Grafiteros and urban street artists find themselves simultaneously targeted by government technologies of surveillance and repression, but also of co-optation through financial support and other forms of state patronage. That this should be the case is not surprising, perhaps, if we consider the complicated relationship between the postrevolutionary Mexican state and artists such as José Guadalupe Posada and *los tres grandes*—José Clemente Orozco, Diego Rivera, and David Alfaro Siqueiros (Coffey 2002). Some Oaxacan artists have carved out a niche in the art and tourism market, capitalizing on the signature aesthetic of the 2006 movement by selling art, T-shirts, and other products to tourists and exhibiting their work internationally. Others have retreated from the city center back to their peripheral urban neighborhoods and rural communities, where most continue their political and artistic work. Understanding their trajectories can help us appreciate the possibilities and limits of autonomous and horizontal organizing in the era of neoliberal militarization.

URBAN YOUTH CULTURES AS SITES FOR COUNTERNARRATIVES, SELF-REALIZATION, AND GRASSROOTS ORGANIZING

To understand the contours and power of the 2006 Generation's rebel aesthetics, we must first contextualize its emergence within the era of neoliberal militarization. Youth in Mexico face greater rates of unemployment and criminalization than the general population (Saraví and Makowski 2011), and homicide is the leading cause of death for youth (Rocha 2011). In addition to violence and lack of educational opportunities, meaningful access to public space, and to the city center in particular, is heavily restricted for many youth in Oaxaca. This is especially true for the urban Indigenous, migrants, and working class, whose racialized and classed bodies are incongruous with the elite's vision for the city (Overmyer-Velásquez 2006). They tend to be pushed outside of the city center and into peripheral neighborhoods, which are often founded as squatter settlements. The precarity of life for communities on the fringes of urban life has the potential to foster oppositional identities and conceptions of citizenship (Holston 2008). It is in such contexts that youth in cities across the globe find a sense of belonging and spaces for participation through urban youth cultures such as hip-hop, graffiti, and punk (Baulch 2007; Fernandes 2011; Forman and Neal 2004; Valenzuela Arce 2009).

The radical economic liberalization and economic crisis of the 1980s and '90s in Mexico played a major role in accelerating and exacerbating the uneven urbanization that shaped the 2006 Generation's experience of Oaxaca City and its periurban neighborhoods (Pérez 2003). Mare's biography reflects the connection between neoliberal economic reforms and the rise of hip-hop and graffiti in Oaxaca. Her family moved from their Zapotec town in the Sierra Norte to a recently settled neighborhood in Oaxaca City after the murder of her father in the early 1990s. Her siblings developed health issues as a result of the trauma caused by their father's violent death, and their mother was forced to work long hours outside the home. Mare became the primary caretaker at home and thus was intimately aware of the economic difficulties her family faced. She also recognized her neighbors confronting many similar hurdles in their daily lives. Around this time, she began reciting poetry in primary school, which became her gateway to a new lyrical world:

> When I was in fourth grade, a girl who was in the sixth grade recited a poem that was an adaptation of "México, creo en ti" (Mexico, I Believe in You), which is a very popular poem in Mexico. But she recited an adaptation that was called "México, no creo en ti" (Mexico, I Do Not Believe in You). That poem was very critical—we are talking about 1995 more or less, during the (economic) crisis here in Mexico, and this poem criticized the inflation of prices, it was very critical of this campaign that was going on at the time of everyone being so proud of being Mexican, everyone united with Mexico,

together we will make Mexico grow and overcome the crisis, and blah blah blah. When I heard that adaptation I was studying in a public school, I lived in a new *colonia* where there weren't even basic services like water and electricity. The roads weren't paved, there was no transportation, there was no healthcare in the community. So that poem was telling my reality. It told my story and, like I said, I became my mother's right hand, so I knew how much everything cost, what the household expenses were, what we could afford and what we couldn't. I realized all of these things at a very early age, and it all made me see things in a different light . . . that there were reasons that my family was struggling. This poem contextualized a Mexico in crisis, and that is how it changed my life. It really did, that poem changed my life.

The critical poetry Mare heard as a fourth grader provided a counternarrative to the nationalism and empty promises being made by politicians trying to sell NAFTA. For Mare, recognizing her family's story and that of her neighbors articulated through poetry was a life-changing event. Her love of poetry was ultimately the catalyst for her highly successful career as an emcee. Around the same time that she was seeking out poetry that spoke to her reality, hip-hop culture was becoming an everyday presence in her colonia:

Oaxaca was experiencing its graffiti boom then [mid-1990s]. My first contact with hip-hop was through graffiti. Suddenly, it was what was different, what was in style, what was cool. At the same time, there was a lot of ignorance, because many people saw it as only painting, as something for cholos [gang members]. It carried with it that stigma of being something very radical, something bad, something rebellious, something that has to be done illegally. I began to see it because of migration, that is how it arrived to the colonia where I live. When we moved there eighteen years ago [1992] it was a new colonia. So that was part of it as well, people were coming from [rural] communities to live in the city, but they lived in the peripheries, in the new colonias. There were also a lot of people returning from *el norte*, and they came to reside in the city. They brought with them this idea of this being a barrio thing, of how it was in the United States . . . and then the music [rap] starts to seep into Oaxaca too. . . . So graffiti starts to arrive in Oaxaca and then a little bit of rap too, but when it arrives it is distorted and it becomes even more distorted because of the stigmas associated with it in the city.

Rapid urbanization during the 1980s and '90s helped fuel the spread of global hip-hop, making it one of the most popular forms of expression for urban youth from Mexico to Australia, Senegal, and the Philippines (Fernandes 2011; Fredericks 2014; Pérez Ruiz and Valladares de la Cruz 2014; Perillo 2013). Mare highlights this trend in the Mexican and Oaxacan context, where transnational circuits of migration and culture were shaped by the massive displacement of farmers from the countryside (Bacon 2004), and the US deportation regime that has forced millions of people to Mexico over the last decade (De Genova and Peutz 2010). Significant here is that these cultural exchanges are multidirectional and transnational, not one-way flows from the United States outward. Hip-hop in the United States, in fact, has always been shaped by global music and culture.[1]

2006 Generation hip-hop also challenges one-dimensional representations of Mexican migrant and Chicano youth, who are frequently depicted in popular and even scholarly accounts as bringing criminality and socially detrimental behavior to Mexican communities (i.e., "negative social remittances"). For example, in a recent study of transnational migration between Yalálag, Oaxaca, and Los Angeles, California, the researcher lamented the existence of "behaviors and cultural values remitted from violent, anti-social, and drug-related gang culture of inner-city neighborhoods in Los Angeles to the village community of Yalálag" (Cruz-Manjarrez 2013, 154). While these dynamics certainly exist, urban youth culture and migration in the lives of the 2006 Generation suggests that this trope is only part of the story. Unfortunately, when it comes to Mexican (and Central American) youth, the narratives most often heard are those that perpetuate fear around the transnationalization of gangs and the criminal flow of "bad hombres" (Cornejo 2017; Rosas 2012; Zilberg 2011).

At first glance, Mare's recounting of graffiti and rap's arrival to her colonia seems to reinforce tropes of delinquency and criminality. She discusses how hip-hop has been stigmatized as being very "radical," "rebellious," and "illegal." However, these are caricatures of migrant youth and hip-hop culture. Mare is acutely aware of this, what she refers to as a "distortion" of the culture. There are certainly segments of the Oaxacan hip-hop scene that more closely resemble the tropes mentioned above. The independent hip-hop scene in Oaxaca, which Mare helped pioneer and of which she is the biggest star and ambassador, actively works against multiple forms of violence and oppression prevalent under capitalist patriarchy in Mexico and beyond. The late Stuart Hall theorized Black popular culture as "where we discover and play with the identifications of ourselves, where we are imagined, where we are represented, not only to the audiences out there that do not get the message but to ourselves for the first time" (Hall 1993, 113). Rather than the violent, misogynist, materialistic tropes they are often saddled with, 2006 Generation hip-hop, punk, and graffiti are more often sites for self-discovery, realization, and politicization.[2] The visual lexicon developed by 2006 Generation artists offers a window into how this process of political identity making played out in Oaxaca.

REVOLUTIONARY PUNKS, URBAN INDIGENEITY, AND THE 2006 REBEL AESTHETIC

If there is one image that captures the cultural politics of the 2006 Generation, it is the one Oaxacan artists referred to as "El Juárez Punk." The image (figure 26) features Oaxaca's own Benito Juárez with a punk haircut, earrings, leather jacket and choker complete with metal spikes. The image was found throughout Oaxaca, stenciled on walls and silkscreened on T-shirts and stickers during and immediately after the social movement of 2006. I found something about this particular merging of nationalism, Indigenous history, and punk aesthetic especially captivating. I asked around about the genesis of El Juárez Punk and learned that the most likely creator of the popular image was Smek, of the pioneering graffiti crew Arte Jaguar and art space Estación Cero. Smek responded to my inquiry about the origins of the image:

> There is a very famous quote of his [Benito Juárez] that says "Peace is respecting the rights of others." I thought it would be cool to reclaim the image. . . . But every time when I would go out to paint, or when *we* would go out to paint, illegally or legally, the police always showed up to fuck with us. "You can't do that! What the hell do you think you are doing? What you are doing is bullshit! It's visual pollution!" And they would arrest us. But we would say, "We have the right to express what we feel, too." You know, like Juárez said about peace and respect. And I think the punk *cresta* "mohawk" has always had a connection to the rebelliousness of youth . . . so I thought it was cool to re-create the image, uniting Juárez and the punk *cresta*. I reclaimed that image, which I had actually first seen on a patch at a punk flea market in Mexico City. It was Benito Juárez with his punk *cresta*, and I thought "You have got to be kidding me. That is so fucking cool!" So I immediately bought that punk patch. And then later, I was looking through some books and I saw a photograph from the 1970s of a punk inside his bedroom, sitting on his bed with his *caguama* [thirty-two-ounce bottle of beer]. Behind him you see his records and there are drawings on the wall, and there it is, a drawing of El Juárez Punk. And this photo is from Ciudad Juárez [located along the US-Mexico border]! So I thought, "Damn this is bad ass! How from the North, all the way to here in the South, one can identify with that kind of symbol." So that's how it came about. For me, what's important is not

FIGURE 26. "Benito Juárez Punk," by Arte Jaguar. Photo credit: Susy Chávez Herrera.

necessarily originality, rather it's about producing images on the spot, when there is that need, when it's necessary, then you create it, and that's how it came about. I enjoyed it a lot.

In (re)creating the image of El Juárez Punk, Smek merged seemingly disparate visual vocabularies to create a unique and powerful symbol that invites the viewer to imagine alternate social realities, such as a world where young people are allowed to express their "rebelliousness" in public space without the fear of being arrested or worse. In "uniting" and "reclaiming" the image of Benito Juárez with hallmarks of the punk aesthetic, Smek (and countless other artists who have since reproduced and altered his reproduction) contributed to the palimpsest of urban Oaxaca. He inscribed images on the city's walls that cue over a century of Mexican history and traverse fourteen hundred miles of Mexican soil from Ciudad Juárez to Mexico City and all the way to Oaxaca—the home state of the northern city's namesake. This was all done while drawing on, and adding to, transnational circuits of youth culture—namely punk and graffiti. In so doing, artists reclaimed the extraordinary figure of Benito Juárez from his official role as national liberal reformer to Oaxaca's native son, who subverted the social hierarchies of his time to become the nation's first, and only, Indigenous president. As members of the 2006 Generation, artists like Smek and the rest of Arte Jaguar hone and experiment with a cultural politics whose contours were in large part shaped in the streets and counterspaces of the 2006 social movement, but also predated and exceeded them.

To create El Juárez Punk, Smek drew on multiple histories, temporalities, and symbols to produce a provocative palimpsest that indigenizes and "Oaxacanizes" punk, and vice versa. By superimposing symbols of punk youth rebelliousness (the *cresta* or "mowhawk" haircut, leather jacket, spikes, etc.) onto the image of Benito Juárez, artists offer the viewer a glimpse into the diverse political and cultural genealogies that animate the 2006 Generation's political imagination. This mix of influences is on display in the logo for CASOTA (see figure 10), which featured the profile of anarchist revolutionary Ricardo Flores Magón with a punk *cresta,* in a move similar to that which was used to create El Juárez Punk. Retro, an artist and organizer with CASOTA, explained what "El Magón Punk" meant to him: "Magón was a great revolutionary and anarchist from here in Oaxaca, and the punk *cresta* has always had a connotation of rebelliousness and of youth struggle, so 'Magón punk' is a way to bring them together in one image." El Magón Punk is an alternative to El Juárez Punk for those who find Benito Juárez's liberal politics too moderate and prefer the decolonial anarchism inspired by combining Magonismo and comunalidad.[3] Many of those same youth referred to their city as Oaxaca de Magón, instead of its official name of Oaxaca de Juárez, to signal their anarchist-inspired politics, while not letting go of their Oaxacan identity. The figure of Ricardo Magón—whether through El Magón Punk or Oaxaca de Magón—can be understood as animating alternative (decolonial) imagined pasts, presents, and futures for the 2006 Generation.

A deeper look at two prominent and pioneering street art crews offers another window into the genealogies of the 2006 Generation's cultural politics. Arte Jaguar and AK Crew were formed in the years just before the 2006 social movement and were among the most well-respected graffiti and street art crews in Oaxaca. These two crews helped form the visual vocabulary and techniques that came to be associated with the social movement. In fact, Arte Jaguar and AK Crew continue to evolve and push Oaxacan and Mexican street art forward. Smek and Cer were founding members of both crews and are brothers from a colonia located along the federal highway to Mexico City, about six miles outside the center of Oaxaca City. They first encountered graffiti when they were in middle school and high school, after a friend in the local punk scene brought back zines, photographs, and sketches of graffiti from Mexico City. A couple years later, Smek formed a collective with other youth from his colonia. They called the newly formed collective El Muro (The Wall). According to Smek, they painted in the streets and put together a punk fanzine where they reproduced articles, poetry, and other texts "related to social issues and politics." El Muro distributed their zines free of charge. This type of cultural production and distribution exemplifies the punk do-it-yourself (DIY) ethic, which has been a hallmark of anarcho-punk and liberationist collectives in Mexico for decades (Valenzuela Arce 2009). Zines allow collectives to horizontally disseminate information and participate in social and political dialogs via intergenerational and international networks (Greene 2016; Moore and Roberts 2009).

It is worth making the distinction here between subcultural resistance through consumption, à la Centre for Contemporary Cultural Studies, and resistance through the production of culture and knowledge that is intimately connected to grassroots organizing.[4] The latter is what we see with 2006 Generation artists and activists. Their primary mode of resisting dominant society is not through their "style" or consumption patterns—though this is certainly part of it. Rather, they build deep networks of grassroots organizing and dissemination of counterhegemonic knowledge through fanzines, graffiti, punk music embedded with social commentary, and in the case of 2006, programming on movement-run radio. This DIY ethic and means of distribution was also on display in Smek's explanation of how he came across the image of El Juárez Punk. He described its circulation—from a drawing in the bedroom of a punk youth in 1970s Ciudad Juárez, to a photograph of the image in a magazine that a friend brought from Mexico City in the 1990s, to the image's current life as an oft-reproduced stencil graffiti. Moreover, Smek made clear that the value of the image for him was not derived from its originality or proprietary authorship. For Smek, Benito Juárez Punk's value was derived from the function it served in the streets: "For me, what's important is not necessarily originality, rather it's about producing images on the spot, when there is that need, when it's necessary, then you create it, and that's how it came about."

Around the same time Smek and Cer were forming their various graffiti crews, two future members of Arte Jaguar named Vain and Aler were experimenting with stencil graffiti. Among the pioneers of the stencil in Oaxaca, they were respected for the quality and creativity of their work, as well as for not shying away from social and political content. In 2002, after several years of working with stencils and before the formation of Arte Jaguar, they formed a collective called Stencil Zone. Vain pointed specifically to the influence that punks had on his politically charged stencils:

> The technique was not very common at the time [late 1990s]. Back then it was more about bombs [pieces with fat, intricate lettering] and tags and that whole thing, but there wasn't much work being done with stencils. . . . The ones who would work with stencils, though, were the punks, the rockers, they were the ones who put stencils in the streets back then. . . . They did their anarchy letters, "October 2 is Never Forgotten," stuff like that, but they did them as stencils and it looked cool. They caught my attention, and that is how I started working with stencils.

In addition to being influenced by the aesthetic practices of anarcho-punk collectives, 2006 Generation street art crews and liberationist collectives also mirror their structure and politics in many ways. For example, 2006 Generation crews and collectives tend to be relatively small, fluid groups with overlapping memberships, an emphasis on horizontality, liberationist politics, autonomy and independence, DIY ethics, mutual aid, solidarity, and horizontal cultural exchange. This is not to say that the cultural politics of grafiteros and their collective projects are derivative of anarcho-punk collectives. Much like 2006 political collectives, they draw on a deep well of influences and experiences that include the 2006 social movement but also predate it. Arte Jaguar, for example, was formed in 2004 and itself grew out of previous street art crews that revindicated local Indigenous identities, made regular references to Zapatismo, and drew on their own experiences of migration, social inequality, and uneven urbanization. Cer explained some of the antecedents to Arte Jaguar and AK Crew:

> I remember I was really into painting Indigenous people in my graffiti. Other grafiteros criticized me for that because they were all into painting robots and shit like that. They were really influenced by el D.F. (Mexico City) and that whole egotistical vibe. We were never into that. We have always been about representing Oaxaca. Its people. Its struggle. Its culture. I remember one time Smek did this big piece with 3-D lettering, but it didn't even say his name, it said "Resistance." Sometimes we didn't even put our tags, just a word or message. Another time we put the name of our pueblo and I drew people from the community.
>
> In 2000, we formed a crew called RAIZ [which means "root" or "origin" in Spanish]—Resistencia Aborigen de Insurgencia Zapatista [Indigenous Resistance of Zapatista Insurgency]. We weren't so worried about the quality of the work like in other crews. This was about having everyone participate. We made decisions as a group. If someone was arrested or needed help, we would respond. It could be holding a cultural event where everyone came together [to raise funds]. We organized several fiestas that way. When the Zapatistas had their Zapatour that went all the way to el D.F. in 2001, the crew got together to put up some bombs to welcome them to Oaxaca. We were doing this illegally and the cops arrested us, so we didn't get to finish our pieces.

The public artwork that RAIZ artists created signaled their solidarity with the organized resistance of the Zapatistas and celebrated Oaxacan indigeneity rather than embracing the nationalist project of mestizaje (Chassen de López 2004; Lomintz 2001). By merging urban youth culture with affirming representations of Indigenous Oaxacans, their illicit artwork manifests an insurgent urban indigeneity that disrupts Mexico's racial geographies. In rendering Indigenous people visible in urban space, they subvert the dominant spatial and temporal ordering of "racial regions, cultural territories, and mestizo urban squares" (Poole 2009, 222). In this way, 2006 Generation street artists articulate a visual discourse of indigeneity that parallels the discourse of (urban) indigeneity articulated and mobilized by VOCAL, the group analyzed in chapter 2.

In a separate interview, Smek explained the multiple meanings and influences behind the name of their more famous street art crew, AK Crew. He explained that the "AK" in their name was originally a reference to the AK-47 assault rifle commonly used by Latin American guerrilla movements. Eventually, however, they decided that they needed to include names that reflected the urban environment that they lived and painted in, so they expanded the possible meanings of AK to include Arte Kallejero [Street Art], Arte Klandestino [Clandestine Art], and Amotinación Kallejera [Street Rebellion]. Through the multiple meanings in their crew's name, they bridged the urban and rural with the common thread of rebellion. Smek also pointed out that "the point of bringing grafiteros from all over the city together in these crews was to get a shitload of *banda* to participate." In essence, by forming these various crews that united banda from across the city to transform the streets, they were building decentralized networks that were later mobilized in 2006 and in subsequent battles over and in urban space in Oaxaca.

STREET ART AS DISRUPTION

The dialectic relationship between youth culture and the production of urban space has inspired a great deal of academic research. Hip-hop studies scholar Murray Forman, for example, has analyzed how marginalized communities in the United States forge collective identities rooted in urban places through the "spatial practices and spatial discourses underlying hip-hop culture" (2002, 3). Unfortunately, the relationship between hip-hop culture and urban life is often framed in much less nuanced ways. Instead, academic research, and urban ethnography in particular, often reinforce long-standing racial tropes that paint Black and Brown youth as pathological, nihilistic, dysfunctional, ahistorical human beings trapped in cultures of poverty (Kelley 2003; Romano 1968). In contrast, the case of the 2006 Generation suggests that urban youth culture has the potential to be a positive resource that can be harnessed for collective action.

For grafiteros, the streets and walls are their primary canvas and platform, which makes their relationship to urban space a foundational part of their identity and cultural practice. Serckas of AK Crew describes this relationship:

> In the streets you can walk past a bomb done by one of the pioneers of Oaxacan graffiti and right next to it you could see a bomb done by someone who just started [graffiti] that same day. So you see, the streets don't discriminate . . . not the quality of work, not the type of work, whether it is a piece, a portrait, or whatever. The street accepts all formats, which is very different from in a gallery, where there are always restrictions. The streets are not like that. The streets are free. The streets are not going to refuse your work.

Of course, banda will push you and demand that you keep getting better. Otherwise, what would the point be of doing this? But at the end of the day, you feel comfortable there [in the streets] because that is where you are from, that's where your people are, and that is where you have learned. It's like giving back a piece of yourself to the streets.

Serckas articulates a view of the streets as democratic, egalitarian, and accessible—a sort of public gallery and space for intervention. Their visual interventions in the streets also work in concert with direct actions such as the roadblocks, marches, and encampments to produce ephemeral counter-spaces that challenge the dominant spatial order and logic. In subverting the neoliberal militarized control of Oaxaca's streets, 2006 Generation artists and organizers add fresh layers to the palimpsest of resistance in Oaxaca.

Smek alluded to the disruption such interventions cause when describing his interpretation of a famous image by Mexican photographer Manuel Álvarez Bravo called *Obrero en huelga asesinado* (Striking Worker, Assassinated). The graffiti image portrays the bloody corpse of a striking worker with the message "Nos han asesinado sin dar explicaciones . . . por tener conciencia de dignidad y justicia! Esta es la verdad" (They have murdered us without offering explanations. . . . It is for having awareness of dignity and justice! This is the truth). He made the stenciled graffiti image as a response to a staged assassination attempt by then Governor José Murat. Smek understood this as an attempt to shift attention away from allegations of corruption and garner sympathy for the unpopular governor. He created the image of the murdered worker to highlight the actual violence perpetuated and condoned by the government, and he placed it where he thought it would make a meaningful impact:

> For me, the images we used were in the right place at the right time. For example, the Benito Juárez Punk or the stencil I did of the Manuel Álvarez Bravo photograph called *Obrero en huelga asesinado*. I put it right in front of the Law School in downtown and I really enjoyed the reaction it caused. A lot of people noticed it and liked it, since we used the wall and part of the sidewalk. I made that image because there are always events that in some way or another impact us, and as a creator, as a grafitero, as a person from the pueblo, from the barrio, these events have consequences for you. And these consequences are manifested in one form or another, painting, writing, singing, et cetera. And all the things that you hear about and see in the news, or when the banda tells you about what just happened, like "Damn did you hear what the governor did? He went too far!" Then immediately you have to do something to denounce it. It is our way of responding.

Artwork like the *Obrero en huelga asesinado* transform the streets, walls, and sidewalks, disrupt the dominant spatial order and are part of the political process through which grafiteros make themselves visible and heard. They take highly transited spaces and reshape them into open political terrains where grafiteros engage fellow citizens, passersby, and the government. This transformation is inherently a disruption, as Rancière (2001) reminds us, because the grafitero, or more often the crew—that is, a collective, not an individual—establishes the street not as a place of "moving along" where there is "nothing to see" but as a place where there *is* something to see, and dialog and politics to engage in.

SURVEILLANCE AND CO-OPTATION

In the process of perfecting their paint lines, grafiteros became accustomed to run-ins with law enforcement. The police, after all, do not sit idly by as grafiteros alter Oaxaca's carefully crafted spaces of tourism. One artist from Arte Jaguar who was active in his neighborhood barricade in 2006 connected his antagonistic relationship with the police and his involvement as a barricadero:

> In 2006, after the federal police were trying to take the university, which is not far from my neighborhood, my brother and I went to help fight them off. It was like revenge for all the times they beat us and put us in jail for painting. We threw rocks at them and reinforced the barricades.

His experience was echoed by other grafiteros who developed an antagonistic relationship with the state at an early age, foreshadowing later battles over Oaxaca's public spaces. Politicians fuel the attack on grafiteros by attempting to pass draconian zero-tolerance policies throughout Mexico, like one in the neighboring state of Puebla that demanded up to twelve years in prison for "any graffiti or paintings done in groups" (Hernández 2015). This heavy-handed proposal was couched as "an act of justice . . . against gangs." A deeper look into the context surrounding its development suggests that the anti-gang public safety discourse was a thinly veiled attack on political dissent. The proposed law came days after students disrupted a visit to a local university by then President Enrique Peña Nieto, and images of young protesters spray painting government buildings with anti-government slogans were widely circulated on social media.

Although many grafiteros do not view their painting in the streets as a political act, my interlocutors overwhelmingly do. Felix, an artist of Oaxacan descent living in Mexico City, explained his understanding of the political nature of graffiti and street art: "The very act of going out into the streets and appropriating them, is a political act. It has become much more difficult to paint in the streets because of police surveillance, so appropriating a wall and putting your message there is itself a political act." Artists like Felix understand police harassment as being meant to enforce the invisibility of working-class youth. Ironically, perhaps, this *invisibility* increasingly relies on a form of *hypervisibility* vis-à-vis a growing regime of surveillance in Oaxaca. A network of 230–400 surveillance cameras was installed throughout the city in 2012 and monitored in real time by dozens of police officers (Archibold 2012; Estes 2013). Like zero-tolerance laws, the rise of high-tech surveillance in Oaxaca was justified through the discourse of public safety. Several grafiteros shared stories of being arrested after being caught on camera painting in the streets. Despite the growing web of surveillance, violent crime, especially attacks against women, youth, journalists, and activists, frequently goes unprosecuted.

On the other hand, governments the world over have invested a great amount of energy into initiatives that attempt to use urban youth culture to shape young people into desirable citizens. These range from government initiatives in Brazilian cities that attempt to "construct a citizenship of the subaltern" through hip-hop (Yúdice 2003, 126) to the Cuban state's (ambivalent) embrace of local rap movements to foster political support (Fernandes 2011; Perry 2016). The US Agency for International Development and State Department have also sponsored hip-hop events and spaces in places like Palestine and Cuba in the hopes of sowing antigovernment discord (Maira 2013; Perry 2016). The US government has used popular culture as a medium for shaping youth's perceptions of its activities in Latin America dating at least as far back as the Office of the Coordinator of Inter-American Affairs' use of Hollywood films during World War II and the US Information Agency's use of rock music to target students and youth activists in the 1960s and '70s (Zolov 1999). The Mexican government, meanwhile, has long attempted to contain and manage youth culture while "not losing control over its disruptive, countercultural, wedge element" (Zolov 1999, 10). The struggle faced by Mexican youth today is how to resist and survive the repressive mechanisms of Mexican statecraft while also navigating attempts at management and censorship through co-optation.

FIGURE 27. Zapatista-inspired mural circa 2007 on walls previously used for IJO competitions. Photo credit: the author.

The Oaxacan government's principal mechanisms for managing youth expression in the years leading up to the 2006 uprising were the Institute of Oaxacan Youth (IJO for its initials in Spanish) and Espacio Multidisciplinario Juvenil (ESMUJ; Multidisciplinary Youth Space).[5] They sponsored cultural events and workshops that were well attended by youth. Some of the more popular events were their annual graffiti competitions that opened up walls adjacent to downtown for grafiteros (figure 27). The spaces created by IJO and ESMUJ were important in bringing youth who inhabited an otherwise fragmented urban landscape together in the center of the city. In fact, many grafiteros from different crews and neighborhoods met at these events, which inadvertently helped extend and fortify networks that were mobilized in the context of the social movement of 2006 and subsequent direct actions. For instance, Aler and Vain, then of Stencil Zone, were invited to join Arte Jaguar after other members noticed their work at the government-sponsored graffiti competitions.

IJO and ESMUJ sponsored events were some of the only spaces where grafiteros could practice their art in public without fear of being arrested or beaten by police. The government even hired an ex-grafitero as the director of ESMUJ and a local rapper to act as liaison with collectives and crews. Their events, however, were tightly controlled, and participants were required to register. Although IJO and ESMUJ events were very popular at the time, participants would later critique the level of censorship and surveillance that went unnoticed by many of them at the time. There was, however, also a movement to create a local hip-hop scene that was independent of the government. Mare was part of an all-woman hip-hop group known as Advertencia Lirika (Lyrical Warning) who were part of this movement. In fact, when I asked Mare about her participation in the 2006 social movement, she made clear that the struggle for independent hip-hop was an important antecedent to her subsequent activism:

> Before [2006] we already had a struggle with the IJO taking over all of the spaces that held together the whole hip-hop scene here. Collectively, we were trying to build an independent hip-hop scene, but they created a monopoly on hip-hop in Oaxaca. So eventually that became our struggle, because this institute wouldn't allow you to do things independently. They would block independent projects, and if you refused to perform at their events, they blacklisted you. If you put on an event, they would announce one for the same day. But they would bring in someone from outside of Oaxaca [to perform], and their event was free. They would try and manipulate us and divide us. They would say, "Look, they are only in it for the money. They are not your banda because they are charging you 20 pesos for tickets." And we didn't even make back the money we spent to organize the events, but it was very easy for a government institution to turn around and say, "They are charging you and we give it to you for free." But they had a budget for exactly that. They weren't doing anyone any favors, that was their job and that is what they created the organization for in the first place. So there was a whole generation of grafiteros that worked only with them because they had the money, they had the means to pay for cans [of spray paint] and to give cash prizes. All of a sudden, there were no independent events. So that became our struggle, to find the means to begin to put on independent events, to create spaces.

Government co-optation and regulation of hip-hop and graffiti was formative in shaping Mare and many of her peers' relationships with the government, as well as their determination to fight for the creation of meaningful space for banda. Their rejection of government patronage and commitment to creating independent spaces outside of government control proved prophetic. Many grafiteros and members of the hip-hop scene allege that the IJO and ESMUJ cooperated with police in 2006 by identifying youth they suspected were active in the social movement. IJO and ESMUJ staff were said to have identified the artists behind antigovernment/pro-movement graffiti and murals based on their familiarity with grafiteros' tags and styles. They are also said to have turned over their registration rolls to the police, which contained the legal names, addresses, and phone numbers of youth who participated in their events. Artists reported receiving phone calls threatening them and their families with violence and even murder for their assumed participation in the movement, and several were arrested and tortured.

Beto was one of those who was arrested and tortured in 2006 based on information believed to have come from the IJO and ESMUJ.[6] He is a contemporary of Mare and also a well-respected rapper in the Oaxacan hip-hop scene. Like Mare, Beto was also active in the post-2006 organization of spaces and collectives. He often emceed hip-hop events at CASOTA, where he introduced the next generation of artists. He would sometimes bless the crowd with a couple of verses, which always elicited loud applause, whistling, and hollers of approval from the audience and other emcees. Such receptions spoke to his standing in the hip-hop community. When he was behind the microphone, he painted a picture of a jovial, confident, and powerful steward of independent hip-hop, with his wide body and sharp wordplay. Shortly after meeting him for the first time in 2010, however, I found that behind his forceful voice, large personality, and even bigger smile, he hid serious trauma.

Beto was a migrant to the city from the Sierra Sur region of Oaxaca. He cherished the sense of family and community he found in the city's small but emerging hip-hop scene. Beto had worked closely with the IJO and ESMUJ in 2004–6 and was even on staff at one point. Like many victims of repression I spoke with, Beto did not go into details about what happened to him in 2006, nor did I prod. But he was adamant that his former employers gave his name to the police. National and international human rights organizations paint a disturbing picture of what he likely endured while in police custody. They have documented hundreds of cases of arbitrary incarceration in the aftermath of the 2006 takeover of Oaxaca City, and the Supreme Court of Mexico acknowledged that many of those arrested were tortured, mistreated, and denied their legal and human rights. Some of the common tactics used by Mexican police and military against suspected dissidents include rape, electrocution, sleep deprivation, being forced to stand naked for days with no food, water, or bathroom access, and countless other humiliating and dehumanizing tactics (CODIGO-DH 2014, 7–9). Moreover, youth as young as fifteen were sent to an adult prison in the state of Nayarit, nearly eight hundred miles to the north of Oaxaca (CCIODH 2007, 115).

The Mexican state systematically uses mass arrests and torture to combat dissent, which has wide-ranging effects on individuals, families, communities, and social movements (Hernández Castillo and Speed 2012). These impacts include: causing victims to withdraw socially and endure economic hardship, fomenting suspicion within movement,; and inhibiting political participation and engagement (CCIODH 2007, 183–85). The effects of torture are magnified when there is no justice for victims, nor even a glimmer of hope that the perpetrators will be held accountable (Antillón Najlis n.d.). With only 3 percent of the 1,230 human rights abuses reported to the National Human Rights Commission in 2008 resulting in a conviction, activists know that impunity is the most likely outcome (Corrales 2012, cited in Speed 2016, 9). Like countless other Oaxacans, Beto fled Oaxaca City in favor of his hometown in the Sierra Sur as a result of the widespread repression against presumed social movement activists. The retreat of activists or would-be activists from organizing was one of the consequences of the widespread repression that followed the uprising in 2006.

The targeted repression of youth associated with Oaxacan hip-hop and street art also resulted in an increase in artists identifying as "independent," which in this context means independent of the government and mirrors the antistatist politics of liberationist and anarcho-punk collectives.[7] Mare, and members of Arte Jaguar and AK Crew, all emphasized the impact that the ESMUJ/IJO betrayal had on their refusal to work with the government in any capacity. The extent to which independent artists were committed to such a politics of independence was seriously challenged, however, once a multiparty coalition led by the PRD and PAN won the governorship in 2010. The coalition was able to oust the PRI from its eighty-year control of the state in large part by riding the political momentum generated by the 2006 social movement. The coalition's political strategy included courting Local 22 leadership and others within the APPO—both during the electoral campaign and upon entering office. The administration of the new governor, Gabino Cué, also courted street/urban artists through grants and commissions for public murals and exhibits.[8] Although different administrations in Oaxaca and throughout Mexico have had a contentious relationship with graffiti, the Mexican state has a long history of harnessing public art for political purposes dating back at least to the era of postrevolutionary muralism (Coffey 2002).[9]

Since 2010, dozens of art spaces have opened throughout the city center, especially those featuring street/urban art and printmaking. In addition to state patronage, artists and collectives capitalized on a tourist market hungry for their revolutionary art. Artists have also gained access to international university, museum, and gallery circuits, where they exhibit and sell their art, offer workshops, and give talks. This absorption of "street" art into formal institutions and markets occurs alongside the fortification of the state's regime of surveillance and policing of street art. Artists are invited to create public murals emphasizing those aspects of Oaxacan culture that fit within the logic and marketing of neoliberal multiculturalism (Hale 2005; Poole 2011), like ethnic diversity or Día de los Muertos. Those same artists, however, face harsh consequences if they are caught producing political street art in the streets. These shifting dynamics, audiences, markets, and relationships with the state have amplified already existing fractures among 2006 Generation artists—a theme I will return to in the conclusion chapter.

NOT PLAYING (RESPECTABILITY) POLITICS

In contrast to the youth cultures that were deemed manageable, or perhaps worthy of management, by the Oaxacan government before 2006 (IJO/ESMUJ) and after 2010 (under Cué), the punk movement was not embraced in the same way. Many punks discussed being barred from organizing cultural events anywhere near the city center and of being subject to police violence and arrest if they broke the informal ban.[10] Instead, they often held events in abandoned lots in their colonias, which resulted in a unique set of challenges, such as a lack of electricity and remote locations, but was often a safer alternative. The censorship of punk is reminiscent of state censorship of rock music in Mexico dating back to the 1950s due to both its affront on prevailing social norms and perceptions of rock as US cultural imperialism (Zolov 1999). These attempts to control rock several decades ago also had the effect of forcing live music performances into working-class barrios, which helped fuel the politicization of the genre. Even today, punk has not received the kind of visibility in the city center as other 2006 Generation youth cultures, nor has the anarcho-punk movement matched the visibility of collectives like VOCAL and CASOTA. There are several reasons that might explain this disparity.

First, and perhaps most significant, the anarcho-punk movement has been around longer than collectives like VOCAL and CASOTA and even crews like Arte Jaguar or AK Crew. The fact that anarcho-punks were not part of an emergent movement might have changed the calculus of government officials looking to absorb and manage youth "subcultures." Punks in Mexico and Oaxaca, particularly anarcho-punks, have always operated on the margins of society and even of opposition politics. Their liberationist politics is

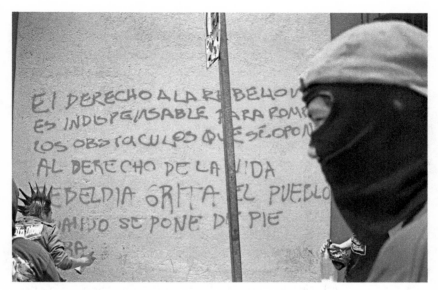

FIGURE 28. "El Derecho a la Rebelión" (The Right to Rebellion) 2006. Photo credit: Baldomero Robles Menéndez.

deep-rooted, unwavering, and autonomous from the state- and market-based economy. Government bureaucrats may have decided that investing in trying to co-opt the anarcho-punk movement was not worth their resources, given the perceived likelihood of failure. Perhaps anarcho-punks were just too radical, too far from the mainstream in their sensibilities, their lack of acquiescence to authority simply too offensive. Moreover, much like rock in 1950s Mexico, punks unapologetically challenge the social norms of *buenas costumbres* or middle-class Mexican values (Zolov 1999). With their hardcore music and in-your-face styles, perhaps punks wear their "Otherness" too proudly and in ways that are reinforce their "ungovernability" (Reguillo Cruz 2012).

Many of the same cultural and political characteristics that made the anarcho-punk movement ungovernable also made them unmanageable for traditional opposition groups. Like the liberationist politics of their 2006 Generation peers in CASOTA and VOCAL, anarcho-punks' vehement rejection of hierarchy and *protagonismo* did not translate well into spaces like the APPO and Local 22 assemblies. Moreover, punks were (and remain) heavily stigmatized and misunderstood within broader society, including among opposition groups (figure 28).[11] Mentes Liberadas described the punk movement's relationship to the teachers' union before 2006: "Society has always viewed the [punk] movement with bad eyes, like all we were was a bunch of potheads who were out in the streets. There was no recognition of what it is that we actually do. Like silk-screening and printing, for example."

We saw in chapter 1 how the social stigma aimed at punks gradually eroded within the extraordinary milieu of the 2006 social movement. The anarcho-punk movement as a whole, and particular collectives like CESOL, built what appear to be long-lasting relationships with other sectors of civil society as a result of the coproduction of counterspaces like Okupa, the barricades, and occupied radio. It is also true, however, that certain experiences in 2006, and in the months that followed, further reinforced a distrust of, and distaste for, traditional opposition politics among many horizontalist and liberationist youth. For example, the stipulations placed on political prisoners to make them eligible for legal help from APPO lawyers left many anarcho-punks to fend for themselves. Anarcho-punks have not forgotten the experience of watching fellow political prisoners get released while they remained in jail indefinitely.

An interaction I witnessed with La Bruja during a march in 2010 offers another window into the complicated nature of the relationship between the teachers' union and some of the more militant members of the 2006 Generation. It bears reminding that her father is a teacher, an active member in the union, and a very influential person in her life. It would be inaccurate to say that she didn't respect Sección 22 teachers. However, like many of her fellow youth organizers, she had a contentious relationship with the leadership and would-be *protagonistas*. During this particular march, La Bruja got into a loud argument with a group of teachers. She yelled at them so passionately that she shook with rage. The teachers had been chiding a group of young marchers who had their faces covered with bandannas. The teachers demanded that they show their faces and not "go around looking like criminals." La Bruja came to their defense. She placed her body in between the youth and the teachers, saying:

So now you don't want us here? Now you don't want us youth around at your marches, but in 2006 during the attacks we were more than welcome, weren't we? We cover our faces because we don't have a union behind us for protection! Covering our faces *is* our protection! And we aren't going anywhere! This is our movement too!

La Bruja's defense of youth covering their faces during marches for safety reasons resonates with stories I heard from youth of being targeted by police and vigilantes after marches. To be fair, members of the teachers' union attempting to assert control over marches should be understood in the context of media coverage and government campaigns aimed at capitalizing on the fatigue that many Oaxacans felt over repeated mobilizations and road-blocks (see chapter 4) to turn public perception against Sección 22. Consider for example, the coverage of an October 2, 2014, march where teachers and anarcho-punks mobilized to commemorate the Tlatelolco Massacre:

> Under the protection and cover of Sección 22 of the CNTE, anarcho-punk youth from the so-called black block commemorated October 2, 1968, by damaging banks, private businesses, and the Governor's Palace. . . . Later on in the march and under the cover of Sección 22 they started painting graffiti on commercial establishments, and they burned sawdust on the *periférico* [beltway], which caused fear among motorists. They also broke windows with rocks at the offices of the Federal Electricity Commission. [Later in the march] they set off fireworks, which upset the contingent of teachers who were marching alongside the youth. (García 2014)

Tensions around covered faces, graffiti, and other forms of property damage in the context of mass mobilizations and social movements are not new or unique to Oaxaca. Similarly, scholars and activists have examined the role of respectability politics in the civil rights movement (White 2010) and immigrant rights movements in the United States (Dominguez 2014),[12] to show how "respectability" has been used to police the boundaries of movement communities.[13] Similarly, anthropologist Jessica Winegar (2016) examined how the Egyptian Revolution was shaped through the practices of activists who reproduced middle-class sensibilities through "aesthetic ordering," such as beautifying public space through collective clean-ups and creating respectable spaces through the policing of bodies. Anarcho-punks and many other 2006 Generation collectives refuse to be managed or have their participation within the movement policed. Indeed, the tension around what constitutes acceptable protest and who legitimate actors are within the post-2006 social movement highlights some of the social and political differences that continue to fracture coalitions that emerged in 2006.

THE POWER OF ART FOR ORGANIZING
AND PRODUCING COUNTERSPACE

This chapter excavated the intertwined histories of urban youth culture and political organizing in Oaxaca. We saw some of the ways that the sociospatial practices involved in cultural production created the structural mechanisms for collective action, helping to foster politicized identities, discourses, and political cultures for young people. Punk, hip-hop, and graffiti/street art collectives already had histories of organizing that predated the social movement of 2006, so they were ready to pounce when the opening was created in June 2006. Spatial confinement to their underresourced neighborhoods, the criminalization of their cultural practices, and lack of access to meaningful public space fueled the politicization of youth cultures and their spatial practices.

Artists used youth culture to transform urban space and sustain social movement energy. For example, artists created counterspace throughout the city by visually and symbolically taking over space. Visual counterspace played a crucial role in allowing the 2006 Generation to maintain a visible dissident presence in the city and surrounding colonias, despite the dangers posed by militarization and surveillance in Oaxaca City. Through their artistic interventions in urban space, artists disrupt the dominant spatial order, often destabilizing Mexico's racial geographies, denouncing state violence, and challenging the political and economic elite's control over public space and public life. While youth culture provided powerful and meaningful forms of expression and activism, we also saw how state and market forces incorporate and manage certain artists and artwork, while repressing and excluding others. This book's conclusion considers how artists' have remade the urban landscape of Heritage Oaxaca through the proliferation of art spaces that have opened in recent years. The conclusion also places the trajectories of artists in relation to possibilities for the future of urban, Indigenous, and horizontal politics in Mexico, especially as they relate to state and market forces in the context of neoliberal militarization.

Conclusion

SHIFTING CARTOGRAPHIES
OF (YOUTH) RESISTANCE

POST-2010 DISPERSAL/REORGANIZATION

What some call *dispersión* [dispersal] in reality is a reflection of
the fact that many spaces have reorganized in their own places
and territories. A new stage [of the movement] is coming, but no
one can predict what it will look like.

—VOCAL

Between 2007 and 2011, I witnessed a phase of political activity in Oaxaca
City characterized by the emergence and networking of youth collectives and
youth-run counterspaces concentrated in and around the center of the city.
These collectives and spaces, including CASOTA, VOCAL, and Estación
Cero, built on the extraordinary experiences that movement youth shared
during the six months of grassroots control of the city. Together they formed
dynamic constellations of resistance and creation that allowed residents of
peripheral *colonias* and rural communities to have a foothold in the historic
city center, so dominated by tourists, government, and business. As this chapter's epigraph alludes to, however, this concentration of political activity by
social movement youth in the city center was not permanent.

Much of the power of networked social movements comes from their
fluidity, dynamism, and difficulty targeting them for co-optation and repression due to their decentralized structure. One of the challenges for such fluid
movements is maintaining coherence and momentum based on those same
characteristics.[1] The horizontalist initiatives that emerged from the 2006
social movement reflect these dynamics, with some groups dissolving, others
growing, and new ones emerging. Following the historic election of Gabino
Cué as governor in 2010, his administration courted and incorporated

activists and artists in various ways, including through cabinet positions (Stephen 2013) and state support for the arts.

Some currents within the street/urban art scene thrived in this new landscape. They opened art spaces in the city center, received state support for public works, and tapped into the tourism market. Indeed, in the time it takes to drink a cup of locally sourced coffee from one of Oaxaca's many coffeeshops, you can visit a dozen of these art spaces sprinkled throughout the city center. Most of the 2006 Generation projects I researched for this book, however, no longer have spaces downtown.[2] This is due in part to their shared ethos of independence and autonomy, which led them to refuse state support, putting them at a relative disadvantage to groups who accepted such patronage. There were also other reasons for the retreat from the city center. Estación Cero, for example, closed in 2013 and merged with a community space Cer and Smek operated from a family lot in their colonia. Cer explained the decision to close Estación Cero and focus on the community space as being in large part because "Our people also deserve to see art, yet many of them don't have enough money to come to the center. There are elders that have never even been to the center." Eventually, the benefits of having a space in the historic city center were outweighed by financial constraints and the pull of returning to work in their colonias and towns.

I discussed the shifting landscape for street/urban artists with members of Arte Jaguar. Aler criticized opportunists who he claimed only started working with stencils and graffiti after they saw the market demand for it and who remained "stuck in 2006" (in terms of images and style). Cer echoed Aler's critique and expanded on the delicate matter of balancing the important legacy of the 2006 social movement with the artistic and personal imperative of growth and transformation:

> I really like what Aler just said. . . . 2006 was great, politically, and with everything that was achieved, but then what? We can't just stay there [in 2006]; we are still moving, and we will always be moving. We have to take the necessary steps for what's next, and I believe what's next is to reclaim more spaces for the people and not just downtown. 2006 brought a bunch of change and consequences, and Estación Cero was one of those consequences. [Names another art space] was one, and CASOTA was another.[3] But we also can't stay stuck. . . . We keep remembering the people and the images of 2006, or even 1968—they were historic, but we also have to keep creating new images and create other things. It's like in a march—you can't just stay on the same corner. You have to keep protesting, maybe in

a different way, but you have to keep moving until you get where you are going. . . . We stay connected to 2006, but we keep moving forward and who knows how far we will get. When the opportunities are there to support other people and collective projects, we will continue to support, because that is where we are from and we feel the pain. I think that the things we have seen, what we have lived through, have impacted us a whole fucking lot, and they always will. These were historic events and they have marked us, they have touched our families, but we keep moving forward.

Cer highlights how the social movement and government repression marked his generation and their collective projects in ways that push temporal, spatial, and aesthetic boundaries placed on movements. Part of the progression Cer and Aler allude to with not "being stuck in 2006" boils down to the idea of artistic growth. Arte Jaguar and AK Crew were important protagonists in the first big wave of Oaxacan graffiti and street art, but the individual artists have all continued to experiment with different art genres and mediums, such as wood carving, installation art, sculpture, and other studio arts.[4] While individual artists keep experimenting with different forms of cultural expression, they have stayed true to Cer's proclamation that they would continue to support other collectives and communities. One clear example of this came with the infamous case of the forty-three missing students (and the three who were found dead at the scene) from Ayotzinapa Rural Teachers' College in Iguala, Guerrero. The 2006 Generation artists and organizers were active in solidarity efforts, including holding actions in Oaxaca to keep pressure on the government to solve the crime and hosting parents of the missing students as they toured the country demanding justice for their children. During a global day of action in September 2016 that marked the second anniversary of the attack in Iguala, artists from various collectives, including Arte Jaguar and AK Crew, painted portraits of some of the missing students along the main tourist promenade in the city center, including an homage to Christian Tomás Colón Garnica who was from the Zapotec town of Tlacolula de Matamoros, Oaxaca (figure 29).

In the post-2010 period of reorganization, members of Arte Jaguar and AK Crew demonstrated a renewed emphasis on fostering intergenerational exchanges with residents of working-class colonias, rural Indigenous communities, and provincial cities throughout Mexico and other Latin American countries. They visited communities and exhibited their work, contributed public murals, and held free workshops for children and youth on creating

FIGURE 29. Portraits of missing students from Ayotzinapa Rural Teachers' College in the historic city center, circa 2016. Photo credit: the author.

graffiti stencils, calligraphy, murals, and Día de los Muertos masks. The 2006 Generation artists and organizers did not retreat from the city center, however. It would be more accurate to say that they *decentered* the city center in their constellations of resistance and creation by bolstering their presence in the working-class periphery of the city, in rural communities, and outside the state, while still having a presence downtown. Artists from Arte Jaguar and AK Crew, for example, participate in new spaces that have opened downtown such as collective art studios, and they continue to contribute art for social movement actions like the Ayotzinapa march in 2016.

The anarcho-punk movement, meanwhile, opened various spaces after they abandoned the Okupa in late 2006. Members of the liberationist collective CESOL, for example, opened a bookstore named Mompracem Libros in the city center in 2010. The bookstore specialized in used books and hard to find political writings—especially anarchist, liberationist, and feminist texts—as well as literature, including science fiction in Spanish. In early 2018 they relocated to a smaller space but remained in the city center and added a gallery space. In addition to selling books and displaying and selling art, they use their space to host book exchanges, political discussions, readings, and art workshops. Along with Estación Cero and CASOTA, they hosted the national hacktivism and freeware meeting "Hackmitin" when it was in Oaxaca in 2010. Anarcho-punks also opened other counterspaces, including a gallery located in a working-class colonia near the main public market (Central de Abastos) that offered art and photography to Oaxacans outside of the tourist-dominated city

FIGURE 30. Members of the anarchist delegation demanding justice for Salvador Olmos García in the Guelaguetza Popular *calenda*, July 24, 2016. Photo credit: the author.

center. Anarcho-punks have also opened social centers and communal houses that tend to be squats and thus emerge and disappear sporadically.

Mentes Liberadas and fellow punk activists organized free workshops for urban and rural communities on how to build bicycle-powered machines like water pumps, blenders, and washing machines. The appropriation of technology, self-sufficiency, and free exchange of knowledge and skills are hallmarks of the punk DIY ethic and the desire to live with as little reliance on the state and dominant markets as possible. Passing their knowledge on through free workshops also allowed activists to nurture intergenerational relationships made in 2006 and foster new connections beyond the anarcho-punk movement, while also circumventing traditional opposition politics organizations. They did activate social movement networks when needed, however. One example came in 2016, when they sent a delegation to the Guelaguetza Popular *calenda* (procession) to join other anarchist collectives in demanding justice for Salvador Olmos García (figure 30). He was a beloved anarchist activist and community radio journalist who had been killed by police in the town of Huajuapan de León a month prior. For the most part, however, the anarcho-punk movement did not participate in the post-2006 period of creating counterspaces in the city center as did other 2006 Generation groups like CASOTA, VOCAL, and street/urban artists. Instead, anarcho-punks retreated back to their colonias and towns immediately following the loss of popular control of the city in late 2006, returning to the city center mostly for sporadic mobilizations and actions like the 2016 *calenda* or the annual October 2 marches. In this way, the spatial politics and general invisibility and marginalization of anarcho-punks in Oaxacan society did not shift the way it did for other groups, like street artists.

CASOTA, meanwhile, shut its doors in 2011 after rents became unsustainable. Members of the collective believed that the landlord, who had been sympathetic to their cause, was pressured to raise the rent as a means of forcing them out. Soon after they moved out, a corrugated metal fence was placed around the property, and the house was demolished. As of July 2020, rubble, overgrown vegetation, garbage, and the metal fence are the only physical remnants found at the former site of CASOTA, the most active and visible youth counterspace I observed in Oaxaca City from 2008 to 2011.[5] With the loss of the house, CASOTA as a collective effectively ceased to exist. VOCAL continues to exist in principle but has been less active since the loss of CASOTA. It would be a mistake, however, to conclude that this meant the end of the political projects advanced by the two collectives. Instead, VOCAL and CASOTA organizers took the loss of the house as an opportunity to reorganize and concentrate more deeply on initiatives in their own communities and colonias, while expanding and fortifying networks of solidarity.

Many of their projects were intentionally intergenerational, emphasized bridging urban and rural communities, and were tied to autonomy projects and defense of communities threatened by the confluence of neoliberal militarization. This included strengthening already existing ties with Indigenous communities like San Juan Copala and San José del Progreso, as well as continuing to seek justice and accountability for activists killed by the state and paramilitaries over the years. For example, 2006 Generation organizers continue to participate in an international campaign to pressure the Mexican government to prosecute the UBISORT gunman responsible for the murders of Alberta (Bety) Cariño Trujillo and Jyri Antero Jaakkola on April 27, 2010. Those responsible for the ambush and killing have been identified and arrest warrants issued. Despite diplomatic pressure from the United Nations and European Union, several of the accused gunmen remain free. As discussed in chapters 4 and 5, the widespread impunity for human rights violations and violence against activists and journalists is a continual challenge for social movements and attempts by civil society to hold those in power accountable.

Solidarity initiatives tied to autonomy and the defense of territory have been effective in allowing 2006 Generation organizers to establish new connections with communities in struggle. For example, organizers participated in solidarity work with Huave and Zapotec communities who were affected by a devastating series of earthquakes and thousands of aftershocks in the Isthmus of Tehuantepec in 2017. Over eight hundred thousand people were affected by the natural disasters, more than seventy people lost their lives, and at least eighty thousand homes were damaged (Briseño et al. 2017). The federal government's response was slow, with responders taking five days to arrive after the initial earthquake (Poole and Renique 2017) and failing to reach the people most in need. As is tradition in Mexico, civil society stepped up in the face of natural disaster and government failure. CNTE, for example, delivered more than two hundred tons of food and aid to a million people within a week of the first quake (Poole and Renique 2017). Several activists whom I first met during their time with VOCAL and CASOTA helped organize grassroots brigades from Oaxaca City to deliver aid and supplies to communities who were ignored or forgotten by the state.

The brigades to the isthmus delivered not "only" urgent emergency aid and supplies. They also brought 2006 Generation organizers to new communities, where they shared space, conviviality, and knowledge with residents. One of the exchanges that was most meaningful to Silvia and Mare, for example, was their opportunity to share knowledge of how to make and use nontoxic, reusable menstrual cups and pads with women in the isthmus. In addition to being ecofriendly and more affordable than disposable pads or tampons, these practices are part of a decolonial feminist praxis of corporeal education and hygiene. They were able to share this knowledge with dozens of women and girls of all ages. It is also significant that among the 2006 Generation organizers and artists I spoke to, it was mostly women who participated in these brigades. The prominent role of women in connecting with and helping affected communities can be partly explained by their embrace and mobilizing of *feminismo comunitario* (communitarian feminism). This strand of feminism is inspired by Bolivian theorist and activist Julieta Paredes's (2008) work and that of her grassroots group Mujeres Creando Comunidad, which grounds feminism through an intersectional, decolonial, and collective politics and analysis.

In Oaxaca, communitarian feminism brought together women (for the most part) across difference and generation. It provided a shared vocabulary and praxis for exchange and solidarity with women across the Americas where similar epidemics of violence against women and gender-based discrimination were—and continue to be—widespread. *Feminismo comunitario* resonated with organizers like Silvia, Mare, and Mónica for many reasons, some particular to their own biographies and other common to their shared experience of organizing in the social movement as young women. The emergence of *feminismo comunitario* as a major organizing force in Oaxaca also dovetailed with a burgeoning woman-led movement against feminicides and gender-based violence in the state, nation, and region. A critical, collective, and decolonial feminist praxis is a necessary response to the unspeakable violence that women, especially poor and racialized women, face in Mexico in the era of neoliberal militarization (Hernández Castillo and Speed 2012). Such a feminist politics is both a site of great hope and potential for the 2006 Generation, as well as a potential fault line if more men do not join the women who are leading the way toward a more just and dignified future.

Another challenge faced by the 2006 Generation moving forward, as well as for horizontalist and urban autonomy projects in general, is sustaining them while staying true to their ethos and ethics. That many of the spaces opened by horizontalist, autonomous, and independent collectives in the center of the city have closed speaks to this challenge, as well as to the durability and ubiquity of the exclusionary forces keeping *banda* from the city center that organizers sought to challenge through their network of post-2006 counterspaces. I would like to suggest, however, that these challenges are not insurmountable. While they might signal a shift in organizing efforts, they do not signal the end of the activism that emerged from the 2006 social movement. As I have argued throughout this book, that energy may transform, but it does not disappear. Emerging politics and identities, such as *feminismo comunitario*, urban indigeneity, and decolonial anarchism, are some of the ways that the cultural politics honed and incubated in the counterspaces examined in this book live on, even after those spaces have closed. The images and narratives articulated through the rebel aesthetics of artists represent another dimension of how the radical imagination of the 2006 Generation will continue to be articulated to challenge the status quo. Moreover, the shift in this generation of organizers' sense of ownership of the city appears to be more durable than many of the spaces themselves. This too, is an important part of the legacy of the social movement of 2006.

SPACE, RACE, AND GENERATION IN THE OAXACAN SOCIAL MOVEMENT OF 2006

Let us return to the original query driving this book: What happens when social movements are not (visibly) moving? This is the question I grappled with when I returned to Oaxaca in 2009 to conduct long-term fieldwork on the social movement. The mass mobilizations, encampments, and other obvious signs of organized resistance I had become accustomed to seeing on previous visits were no longer visible. As we have seen throughout the pages of *Cartographies of Youth Resistance*, movements move in many different ways—most of which are not as easily perceptible as a march through the zocalo. In an attempt to make the everyday engagements that sustain social movements through the ebb and flow of mobilizations visible, I analyzed how youth organizers and artists networked counterspaces before, during, and after the height of social movement activity.

Once we move beyond a view of social movements as discrete units with a clear beginning and end, an important part of the story becomes the layering of histories of activism and competing regimes of space making. I used the metaphor of the palimpsest to demonstrate how youth carve out space for themselves to be seen and heard in urban space, while not losing sight of the fact that they do so in a terrain shaped by centuries of colonial and state control, capitalist influence, and Indigenous and grassroots organizing and resistance. We saw myriad manifestations of the palimpsest, including battles over the meanings, use, and ownership of public space in the highly symbolic historic city center. The 2006 Generation organizers participated in these battles, in part, through direct actions that disrupted the carefully crafted image of Heritage Oaxaca. By reclaiming public space via militant actions, organizers created counterspace and inscribed themselves into the social and political life and history of the city, shifting its racial and spatial landscape in the process.

Given the realities of neoliberal militarization, however, direct actions are exceedingly dangerous for activists, especially those with little political or economic capital, such as the youth in this study. *Cartographies of Youth Resistance* has demonstrated how, in militarized and neoliberal Oaxaca, the 2006 Generation has been able to maintain a visible dissident presence in the city and surrounding colonias through the cultural work of movement youth. We saw, for example, how artists disrupted the dominant spatial order with their visual interventions on the façade of the Catholic Church denouncing state violence. Through their art, 2006 Generation artists engage the city and visually reclaim urban space for marginalized populations. In the process, they create counterspace that offers radical, autonomist, decolonial visions of the city "otherwise."[6] Visual counterspace, then, connects with the ephemeral counterspace produced through direct actions and more territorialized counterspaces such as social centers and cultural venues to produce constellations of resistance and possibility in the militarized tourist city. We also saw the writing and overwriting characteristic of the palimpsest play out in the back-and-forth between artists and the whitewashing of their interventions. Viewing resistance and space making through the lens of the palimpsest allows us to see them as continual, fluid processes, while not losing sight of the various histories, interests, and forces involved.

This book has also highlighted some of the ways in which activists reimagine and articulate leftist and Indigenous politics and identities in post-NAFTA, post-immigration Mexico. Through the politics practiced by 2006 Generation collectives, we witnessed how Indigenous repertoires of organizing and visions of autonomy and self-determination travel from pueblos to the city, where they exist alongside and enmeshed with politicized youth cultures and other leftist organizing traditions. For different collectives of organizers and artists that came of political age during the 2006 social movement, this unique blend of influences helped form a politics of horizontalism, urban autonomy, and what I call *decolonial anarchism*. In the process of creating emergent politics and counterspace, organizers and artists not only sustained the social movement, they also created emergent identities. In the process, the 2006 Generation reshaped the racial, cultural, and political landscape of the city and the horizons of the radical imagination.

The case of the 2006 Generation also highlights the necessity for scholars and observers to reimagine what social movements look like in the twenty-first century. This is an urgent task considering the proliferation of militarized policing and zero-tolerance approaches to dissent globally. From Ferguson, Missouri, and Managua, Nicaragua, to the Gaza Strip and Oaxaca, governments in supposedly democratic countries increasingly deploy military and/or militarized police forces to squash protests, often relying on the sheer disproportionality of force as a deterrent against nonviolent dissent. In this context, we cannot expect that activists will be able to sustain mobilizations and direct actions in the same way that some of their counterparts of previous eras have. We must, therefore, be able to recognize and analyze social movement activity that manifests through forms and norms that are sometimes unfamiliar or unexpected. Doing so involves being attentive to space-making practices without fetishizing the materiality of space.

An exchange I had with Silvia speaks to the nuance needed in recognizing the importance of counterspace in sustaining social movements and the energy they produce, while not fetishizing the material. On a Friday afternoon

FIGURE 31. Memorial tribute to Alberta (Bety) Cariño Trujillo and Jyri Antero Jaakkola. Photo credit: Susy Chávez Herrera.

in February 2011 I sat down with Silvia in the courtyard of CASOTA, where she was living at the time. I asked her how long she planned on participating in the space, and she answered:

> However long the project lasts. It's a rented house, but we can't just think about the material. Instead, we have to think about what it is that has been achieved. . . . For example, the barricades are no longer in the streets, but the barricades weren't just the physical space. They are also the deep transformation that they produced, the social relations, the everyday interactions. These things will be in my heart, whether I am here in the house, or in another space, that spirit doesn't die. It's alive. I mean that, truly alive.

Silvia captures quite eloquently that which social movement scholars have difficulty explaining—the cultural, subjective, and embodied impacts that social movements can have over time and space. If we take her words seriously, our task becomes to develop frameworks and vocabularies for understanding and tracking that spirit of resistance and creation across time and space.

In addition to expanding how we think about social movements, the case of the 2006 Generation organizers and artists offers a counternarrative to widely circulating tropes that criminalize and disparage Mexican youth. They are commonly depicted in popular discourse, mainstream media, political rhetoric, and academic scholarship as gang members, drug smugglers, and drug users. *Cartographies of Youth Resistance* offers another reality: Mexican youth as agents of social change, creators of more just social, political, and economic relations, and dreamers of liberatory and dignified futures. I hope that this book contributes to the social history of the social movement that has been called "the first insurrection of the twenty-first century" (Osorno 2007) by placing young people at the center of the story. This is an especially urgent corrective, given that poor and racialized Mexican youth are often the invisible faces and disposable bodies that bear much of the brunt of racism, economic restructuring, drug policy, and militarization in Mexico and the United States.

NOTES

INTRODUCTION

1. Here I am also drawing on the work of sociologist Fran Tonkiss (2005), who reinterprets Lefebvre's work. Sociologist Francesca Polletta (1999) coins a related and useful concept: "prefigurative spaces." She defines them as follows. "Explicitly political and oppositional (although their definition of politics may encompass issues usually dismissed as cultural, personal, or private), they are formed in order to prefigure the society the movement is seeking to build by modeling relationships that differ from those characterizing mainstream society" (Polletta 1999, 11).

2. Performance artist and theorist Kai Barrow first suggested that I engage the concept of palimpsest to frame the layered nature of space in my work. Many thanks to them and to Joo Ok Kim, Christopher Perreira, and Magalí Rabasa, who organized the symposium at the University of Kansas that brought Kai and me together with other activist media producers and scholars.

3. The other Mexican state with majority Indigenous population is Yucatán.

4. The Mesoamerican Integration and Development Project replaces Plan Puebla Panamá (PPP), which the Mexican government repeatedly tried and failed to implement in the early 2000s. PPP was to connect Central and Southern Mexico, including Oaxaca, with Central America in order to create a "development corridor," but the plan was met with vigorous organized resistance from those concerned about the continued syphoning of wealth from the region and degradation of the environment.

5. The government's complicity in the violence has been laid bare through the courageous work of journalists, human rights organizations, and survivors. This includes the disappearance of the forty-three students and murder of six people from Ayotzinapa Rural Teacher's College in the state of Guerrero in 2014, the continual discovery of mass graves throughout the country where the bodies of thousands of murdered migrants are discarded, and the unprosecuted murder of thousands of women annually in Mexico, at a rate of six every day. See the investigation into the Ayotzinapa case by the Forensic Architecture team (2017) for a groundbreaking

visual narrative of the murders and disappearances that took place on the night of September 26–27, 2014, in Iguala, Guerrero. See also the work of journalists Anabel Hernández (2017) and of John Gibler (2017), whose investigations inform the former. See Ioan Grillo (2017) for coverage of Mexico's mass graves, Rubio-Goldsmith et al. (2016) for migrant deaths along the US-Mexico border, and Fregoso and Bejarano (2010) for analysis of feminicides in Mexico and across the Americas.

6. See Kency Cornejo (2017) for a decolonial analysis of how Central American artists challenge similar rhetorics and visual tactics of coloniality that render Central American youth as public enemies.

7. All translations are my own unless otherwise noted.

8. Here the work of Maylei Blackwell (2017) on "geographies of indigeneity" and María Josefina Saldaña-Portillo's (2017) work on critical Latinx indigeneities are especially useful for thinking about how the mobility—often forced—of Indigenous and Afro-Indigenous communities unsettles static notions of Indigenous peoples as bound to a particular place.

9. By referring to the network of youth activists in this book as the "2006 Generation," I highlight the fact that their shared experiences of organizing during the height of mass mobilizations and peak movement activity in late 2006 played a significant role in shaping their political imaginations, subjectivities, and organizing practices. I do not, however, mean to limit their activism or politics to the year 2006, or even to the social movement of 2006. I also do not want to imply that the 2006 Generation shares a homogenous politics or experience. What united them in the first instance was the collective experience of mobilizing as youth during the popular takeover of Oaxaca City in 2006. This was also a key year because it marked a significant intensification in the ongoing crisis of militarization and the criminalization of dissent in Mexico. Indeed, seeking to live dignified lives under the specter of neoliberal militarization has also significantly shaped this generation of youth and their politics. Therefore, the political organizing of the 2006 Generation is an important site for understanding authoritarianism in the twenty-first century, as well as the social movements driving the creation and imagination of alternative presents, futures, and possibilities. See Cole and Durham (2006) for more on youth and generation as an analytic framework for studying social reproduction and change.

10. Liberationist politics refers to a leftist, nonhierarchical, antiauthoritarian politics, and reflects my translation of the organizers' own self-identification as *libertari@s*. They often use this term interchangeably with anarchist. Special thanks to Ed McCaughan, who helped me decide on the best translation.

11. Horizontalism refers to a nonhierarchical form of organizing and sociality. See Sitrin (2006) for more on horizontalism and social movements.

12. Fanzines or zines are magazines produced informally, usually through a process of cut and paste, collage, and photocopying. Although not exclusive to punk culture, they exemplify its do-it-yourself (DIY) ethic. The content of punk zines is often a combination of essays, poems, short stories, social and political commentary and manifesto, visual art, and news.

13. Traditionally hip-hop has been thought to consist of four elements: emceeing (rapping), deejaying, graffiti, and b-boying (Schloss 2009), though some practitioners like Zulu Nation founder Afrika Bambataa include a fifth element: knowledge (Gosa 2015).

14. The punk scene in Mexico City is especially strong and has been prominent since the 1970s (Hernandez 2011), but the southern states of Oaxaca and Guerrero also have rich histories of politically active punk movements (García Leyva 2005).

15. Mimi Thi Nguyen credits San Francisco-based queer punk art band Sta-Prest with coining the term *multisubculturalism* (2012, 221).

16. I chose not to translate grafiteros into the English "graffiti writers," because I feel that *grafitero* captures their multidisciplinarity in a way that the English translation does not and also respects the artists' self-ascribed identities.

CHAPTER ONE

1. Mentes Liberadas (Liberated Minds) is a pseudonym chosen by the subject.

2. *Banda* is a word used repeatedly by many of the youth in this book. This word is sometimes translated as "gang," but that is not the usage here. In this context, *banda* tends to refer to youth from popular neighborhoods or specifically to the speaker's group of friends. I chose to retain the original *banda* in my translations of interviews because of the messiness of translation. Unless otherwise noted, these excerpts come from my interviews, and all translations are my own.

3. In this study, as explained in the introduction, the term *liberationist* reflects the activists' own identification as *libertarios/as*; I use liberationist instead of the literal translation "libertarian" to emphasize the distinction from the libertarianism found in the Libertarian Party or certain sectors of the Tea Party movement in the United States, which emphasize the rights of the individual and fiscal conservatism. Rather, liberationists in this study are more in line with a libertarian-socialism; in some cases they use the labels *libertari@* and *anarquista* (anarchist) interchangeably. Thanks again to Edward McCaughan for helping me find the translation that best captures its spirit.

4. "Historic Centre of Oaxaca and Archaeological Site of Monte Albán." UNESCO. https://whc.unesco.org/en/list/415/.

5. *Horizontalidad,* translated as horizontalism or horizontality, is both the goal and tool for social movements that attempt to construct the horizontal social relations they seek in the present. Horizontalism "involves—or at least intentionally strives towards—non-hierarchical and anti-authoritarian creation rather than reaction. It is a break with vertical (hierarchical) ways of organizing and relating" (Sitrin 2006, 3). Importantly, horizontalism is a dynamic process and not a static outcome to be achieved, celebrated, and then abandoned.

6. Institutional Revolutionary Party (PRI) candidate Roberto Madrazo was a distant third in polls and in the final vote count.

7. I gave everyone who participated in this research the option of using pseudonyms to protect their identities. Some, including "Doña Inés," opted to use a pseudonym, while others chose to have only their first name used for security reasons.

8. Originally the *pueblos* (peoples) in APPO's name was the singular *pueblo*, but the name was soon changed to reflect the plurality of Oaxaca's people and of the movement.

9. One notable exception was youth organizer and APPO council member David Venegas, who was one of the founders of the collective VOCAL. I introduce David and VOCAL later in this chapter.

10. An activist from the youth collective VOCAL, to be discussed in great detail in chapter 2, helped repair the radio equipment to get Radio Universidad back on the air.

11. Aristeo López Martínez was later executed in the middle of the day in downtown Oaxaca in January 2009. At the time of his death he was a protected witness of the Procuraduría General de la República (Office of the General Prosecutor) in the investigation against allegations that police forces participated in paramilitary operations against the social movement in 2006.

12. See Poole (2007) and Stephen (2013) for more on the radio takeover in Oaxaca.

13. Although often remembered for his ethnographic fieldwork in small-scale societies, Turner, like any good anthropologist, attempted to connect the on-the-ground realities from his fieldwork to larger, more general phenomena. In the foreword to *The Ritual Process: Structure and Anti-Structure* (1969), for example, he responds to critiques that his work often overgeneralized concepts like liminality and communitas by taking them out of the context of "preliterate societies" to "describe or account for social and cultural processes and phenomena found in preliterate societies, but have limited use in explaining sociocultural systems of much greater scale and complexity" (vi).

14. The use of the @ symbol is meant to challenge the *de facto* masculine designation of the -*o* ending by including the feminine -*a*. It is a political statement that many youth are making throughout Latin America and the United States. Other alternatives are to substitute the @ with an *x* or with an *A* inside of an *O*, which is also the common symbol for anarchy.

CHAPTER TWO

1. Guelatao is home to a famous Indigenous community radio station, XEGLO Radio Guelatao: La Voz de la Sierra, which broadcasts in Zapotec, Mixe, and Chinantec languages. See Erica Cusi Wortham (2013) for a detailed analysis of Radio Guelatao and the regional Indigenous autonomy movement.

2. Less known outside of Mexico than the Tlatelolco massacre, the Halconazo was another massacre of student protesters in Mexico City. The Halconazo massacre was committed by paramilitaries or *porros*. See Zolov (1999) for more. This event was captured in the 2018 film *Roma* directed by Alfonso Cuarón.

3. See Laura Castellanos's (2007) canonical study of Mexico's twentieth-century guerilla movements, *México Armado, 1943–1981*.

4. Zapotec intellectual Jaime Martínez Luna and Ayuujk (Mixe) intellectual Floriberto Díaz are key figures in developing the concept in their theorizing of Indigenous communal life, identity and epistemology. Jaime Luna, from La Bruja's hometown of Guelatao, is the founder of Fundación Comunalidad A.C. See Jaime Martínez Luna (2010) andSofia Robles Hernández and Rafael Cardoso Jiménez (2007) for more on comunalidad.

5. In my analysis of Oaxacan youth organizing, I want to be clear that I am not suggesting that there exists a homogenous, static, "authentic" Indigenous communal life. Equally important, however, I want to be clear that I do believe it important to take *youth's own understanding* of their politics seriously. It is easy, after all, for even well-meaning anthropologists to continue the discipline's colonial legacy by questioning the authenticity of other's claims of indigeneity.

6. Two of the founders of the house were solidarity activists from the United States and England. They eventually moved out of the house but stayed connected to the project.

7. How this trend shifts or doesn't in Mexico since the 2018 election of the nation's first leftist president in nearly a century, Andrés Manuel López Obrador, will be fascinating to observe.

8. In 1995 the Zapatistas and the Mexican federal government began a process of negotiation in the town of San Andrés Larráinzar, Chiapas. During the first round of talks on constitutional reforms, the two parties came to an agreement to recognize the autonomy and rights of Indigenous communities. The Zapatistas broke off negotiations during the second round of talks in 1996, due to a perceived lack of concrete actions and mechanisms for accountability on the part of the government. The Congress of the Union eventually passed a watered-down version of the accords in 2001, after unilaterally removing some of the San Andrés agreements. See Speed, Hernández Castillo, and Stephen (2006), and González (2016) for more on the juridical and political details of how this process played out.

9. See Speed (2008) and Stone (2019) for more on *protagonismo* in Mexican social movements.

10. As a reminder, 2006 was a presidential election year. La Otra Campaña was planned as an alternative to the spectacle of those elections. National-level politics also factored greatly into creating the vacuum at the state level that the Oaxacan social movement filled, as well as the eventual decision to send the Federal Preventative Police to repress the movement.

11. Also relevant in understanding his interpretation of 2006 Generation politics is that this media activist was from a very different social location than these youth. In addition to generational difference, this man was also a middle-class mestizo from Mexico City.

12. The use of the word *Regeneración* in the name of the caravan is a deliberate way to connect it to the Mexican Revolution—but even more specifically to Magonismo and the Magonista publication *Regeneración*. This brand of anarchism,

rooted in Oaxaca in many complex ways, will be discussed later in this chapter and book. See Benjamín Maldonado (2000), Beas and Ballesteros (2010), Bufe and Verter (2005), Gómez (2016).

13. Here Rosalía is referring to the eight regions of Oaxaca: the central valley, the isthmus, the coast, the Mixteca, the Sierra Norte, the Cañada, the Sierra Sur, and the Papaloapan.

14. Silvia and two fellow VOCAL organizers wrote an unpublished article discussing the future of the movement circa 2008–9, which offered a concise understanding of the articulation between comunalidad and autonomy. After quoting Floriberto Díaz and Jaime Luna at length, they conclude that "comunalidad has been linked to autonomy since its inception." Autonomy, understood here as the power to self-govern, is derived "precisely from comunalidad, which is what constitutes and makes possible the conditions necessary for self-government." Comunalidad, for them, is not primarily about being recognized by the state, rather it is "the disposition to act critically and collectively against imposition, intolerance and electoral politics that seek only to recreate systems of domination." I do not offer the citation here for safety reasons, to conceal their full names.

15. The slogan most often associated with the original Zapatistas, *Tierra y Libertad*, was in fact first used by the PLM. An editorial in the Mexican newspaper *La Jornada* (April 8, 2008) explained the connection thus: "In our collective imagination, *Tierra y Libertad* is the link between Flores Magón and Zapata." More recently, the (neo)-Zapatistas named one of their autonomous governments after the Oaxacan anarchist and revolutionary.

CHAPTER THREE

1. See López Bárcenas (2009) for a detailed history and analysis of the situation in San Juan Copala.

2. When translating CASOTA into English I use *self-managed* for *autogestivo* because it is referring to the kind of *trabajo* or work they do, so "self-managed work" makes sense. When *autogestión* is used to refer to an organizing principle, however, I do not translate it, because I do not feel that any one word in English captures the multifaceted meanings it carries in the context of Latin American social movements, where it refers to processes related to autonomy: self-management, self-sufficiency, and self-organizing.

3. Stated in a video uploaded to YouTube (https://www.youtube.com/watch?v=rpROxKFiNZo) by the Oaxaca Secretaria de Turismo. Emphasis added.

4. During that week alone, at least 192 people were taken prisoner by the PFP, many of them shipped to a maximum security prison in the northern state of Nayarit (Stephen 2007b, 108), where many report being electrocuted, beaten, and sexually assaulted.

5. Trinidad Sampablo Cervantes, Lorenzo's sister, is a close ally of VOCAL and CASOTA youth and frequently attends their events. The youth participate in

annual commemorations of his murder and hold political events calling attention to the fact that his murder remains unpunished.

6. This is one way CASOTA and VOCAL participate in a national network that advocates for political prisoners, given the increasing criminalization of dissent in Mexico. Several youth organizers in Oaxaca, including David and Silvia of VOCAL, have been arrested for their association with the social movement.

7. Oaxacan artist Ruben Leyva published a book with hundreds of photographs and essays of the social movement, *Memorial de Agravios: Oaxaca, México 2006*, which sells on Amazon for 89.95 US$. Leyva donated copies of the book to families of those murdered in 2006, including the family of Lorenzo Sampablo Cervantes. The family had grown very close to CASOTA and VOCAL youth over the years so they asked them to sell their copies in the store for them- which is where I purchased my copy.

8. For more on the rich history of books and their circulation in autonomous movements in Latin America, see Rabasa (2019).

9. This room was originally an office for VOCAL, but members decided to convert the space into dormitories, since there was a sense that the project of CASOTA was losing its identity and being absorbed by VOCAL. Although there was a great deal of agreement in the two collectives' politics and some overlap in membership, there were points of difference that youth felt were necessary to preserve. One member of CASOTA recalled:

> A lot of times there arise conflicts based on ideologies or politics or difference in objective or proposals between groups, and that sometimes leads to them not working together based on these differences. We wanted CASOTA to be a space for the social movement of Oaxaca, where different people and groups with different political orientations could come together. We felt that some of these conflicts were carrying over to CASOTA because *banda* were thinking it was the house of VOCAL. That is why we decided: yes, VOCAL has an important place here in this project, *banda* from VOCAL are part of CASOTA, but we needed to establish this as a space for everyone from the social movement to come.

10. Estela Ríos González was active in human rights and women's rights organizing, helping to form the Oaxacan Women's Coordinating Committee (COMO) of the APPO and later the collective Mujer Nueva. Estela died after a long battle with cancer in 2008. She was survived by her partner (Demetrio) and two daughters (Erendira and Itza), who remain active in Oaxacan popular politics and arts.

11. Again, this is not to suggest that all the individual activists identify as urban Indigenous. Rather, it is to take seriously their mobilizing a collective politics of urban indigeneity (see the VOCAL manifesto quoted in chapter 2).

12. See Lynn Stephen (2013) for more on how transborder Oaxacan communities participated in the 2006 social movement.

13. Interestingly enough, very few of the activists I interviewed for this study had personal Twitter accounts. This platform was used more by collectives, especially alternative media collectives. This is likely due to security concerns, given the more public nature of tweets, which can be viewed by anyone.

1. When Jacques Rancière theorizes about the police in this chapter's epigraph, he is not referring to the institution of law enforcement or its agents. For Rancière, the police is "a symbolic constitution of the social," whose essence lies in partitioning and distributing the sensible, in dividing community (and the world) into countable and uncountable segments (i.e. the rich, poor, workers, citizens, immigrants, etc.) (2010, 36). Rancière positions the police in contrast with politics, which consists of counting the uncountable, challenging the police logic of division, making visible and audible those which the police would silence and make invisible.

2. Chapter 5 and the conclusion talk more about this distinction between post-2006 art spaces.

3. See López Bárcenas (2009) for a detailed history.

4. The Autonomía, Paz y Dignidad blog (https://autonomiaencopala.wordpress .com/) published and archived communiqués, calls to action, and human rights reports from and about the autonomous municipality from March 2010 through June 2011.

5. Despite sharing a liberationist politics in name, this organization had a contentious relationship with VOCAL and CASOTA. Members of the groups had previously organized together under a single organization before splitting, due to what was described to me as "irreconcilable differences in how to organize and relate to the state." Despite this fact, the groups still came together to carry out actions when their interests overlapped, as was the case in showing solidarity with Copala and demanding justice for those murdered, including Bety and Jyri most recently but also the dozens of Triquis killed by paramilitaries in recent years.

6. The VOCAL organizer apologized to the driver and assured him that they would remove the paint from his bus.

7. Chapter 5 offers another discussion about this tension between organizations, their political cultures, and generations.

8. Yolanda is a pseudonym.

9. The name of the collective, Tlatolulokos, is a play on the name of their town, Tlacolula, and the word *locos* (crazies).

CHAPTER FIVE

1. Mare's account also destabilizes the common narratives about hip-hop culture that privilege the music over the other pillars. Mare's history of hip-hop in Oaxaca starts with graffiti. See Jessica Nydia Pabón-Colón's *Graffiti Grrlz: Performing Feminism in the Hip Hop Diaspora* (2018) for more on reclaiming graffiti's place in hip-hop, as well as highlighting the role of diaspora within hip-hop.

2. There were credible accusations of sexual assault leveled against a member of a collective that I did not work with, in part due to my unease with what I observed of the collective's gender politics. Beyond the accusations against the artist, the

response by his collective and others in their network was troubling, essentially boiling down to blaming the victim. I did not feel comfortable amplifying the collective's work or name by giving them space in my book in the first place and will not do so even to call them out here. People close to the movement and arts scene in Oaxaca know who the person and collective are.

3. "Decolonial anarchism" is described in detail in chapter 2.

4. This distinction is not to deny or downplay the contributions to the study of subcultures and cultural studies made by the Centre for Contemporary Cultural Studies (CCCS, located at the University of Birmingham, England, during 1964–2002). CCCS moved the study of working-class youth away from a focus on deviance and pathology to instead highlighting their agency and resistance to subordination in the "Golden Age of Capitalism." The issue here is that CCCS theorists did not go far enough in appreciating the impact of working-class youth resistance and the diversity of youth actors (i.e., in terms of gender, race, religion, etc.). They framed subcultural resistance as largely symbolic and without a future. This can be partially explained by the lack of ethnographic grounding in the majority of their works—with the clear exception of Paul Willis's (1977) work.

5. The IJO was the predecessor to the current INJEO (Institute of Youth from the State of Oaxaca), which was created in 2013 and operates under the Secretary of Social and Human Development.

6. Beto is a pseudonym.

7. Interestingly, the meaning behind *independence* in Oaxacan hip-hop is quite different from what is considered independent hip-hop in the United States. In the latter case, independence is defined in relation to the major institutions for the distribution of music and management of talent (i.e. major record labels, play on mainstream media, etc).

8. I use "street/urban art" here for two reasons: (1) to signal a broadening of genres and mediums and (2) to recognize the contradiction in categorizing art that is featured in galleries as "street" art.

9. Public art in Mexico actually predates the formation of the Mexican nation-state, of course. Murals, sculptures, and other art have been found in countless archaeological sites through the country—from the Temple of Murals in the Mayan site of Bonampak to the danzantes of Monte Albán.

10. Kelley Tatro (2018) documents similar police violence targeting punks in Mexico City.

11. Chicano reporter Daniel Hernandez documented similar misunderstandings about punks on the outskirts of Mexico City, where punks' shaved heads are often mistaken for fascist skinheads, which causes added tension for them going about their everyday routines (Hernandez 2011).

12. It is no coincidence that some of the most important contemporary movements that are pushing back against this form of intramovement and intracommunity policing in the United States are led by queer youth, women, and young people of color whose dignity and humanity are regularly attacked by those both outside of and within their own communities. The Movement for Black Lives and

Undocumented Youth movements, in particular, have refused to apologize for their tactics or sanitize their messaging to appease moderate would-be allies or conservative critics.

13. Another area that requires more attention is the common discursive move conflating property damage and violence in the context of mobilizations, a conflation that happens both within movements and from the outside by the media, politicians, and researchers. We need to be more precise with our language and theorizing of violence. Otherwise, we risk being complicit in state violence when we fail to accurately address the immense gulf between police and juridical repression on the one hand, and broken windows and protest graffiti on the other. There are critiques to be made about property destruction during protests, to be sure, but we lose sight of those when we repeat narratives that draw dangerous moral equivalencies by not being more precise when we refer to actions as "violent."

CONCLUSION

1. See Castells (1996), Escobar (2008), Juris (2008), and Melucci (1996) for more on the transformation of networked social movements.

2. Some artists from Arte Jaguar and AK Crew participated in newer downtown spaces as individuals or as part of other collectives. Aler from Arte Jaguar, for example, started a collective called Jaguar Print that had a visible presence in the city center as of 2018.

3. The other art space Cer named was the one most closely associated with the allegations of sexual assault by an artist, discussed but not named in the notes to chapter 5.

4. Smek, for example, went on to earn a fine arts degree from the prestigious art college La Esmeralda in Mexico City. He exhibits his work nationally and internationally. Cer, meanwhile, took some architecture courses at the local public university and while he never earned a degree, the architecture training has clearly influenced his growing studio work. Serckas of AK Crew studied graphic design and is now a public school teacher and part of Local 22.

5. Given the prime location of the property, the fact that it remains unused seven years later is odd, to say the least.

6. See McTighe and Raschig (2019) for more on the anthropological possibilities of engaging the "otherwise."

WORKS CITED

Abu-Lughod, Lila. 1990. "The Romance of Resistance: Tracing Transformations of Power through Bedouin Women." *American Ethnologist* 17 (February): 41–55.

Ahmed, Azam, and Nicole Perlroth. 2018. "Using Texts as Lures, Government Spyware Targets Mexican Journalists and Their Families." *The New York Times*, February 23, 2018. https://www.nytimes.com/2017/06/19/world/americas/mexico-spyware-anticrime.html.

Alexander, M. Jacqui. 2005. *Pedagogies of Crossing: Meditations on Feminism, Sexual Politics, Memory, and the Sacred*. Durham, NC: Duke University Press.

Altamirano, Genaro. 2002. "Encabeza Toledo tamaliza contra McDonald's." *El Universal*, August 19, 2002. https://archivo.eluniversal.com.mx/estados/46782.html.

Amnesty International. 2017. "Mexico 2016/2017." https://www.amnesty.org/en/countries/americas/mexico/report-mexico/.

Antillón Najlis, Ximena. n.d. *Yo sólo quería que amaneciera: impactos psicosociales del caso Ayotzinapa*. Mexico City: Fundar, Centro de Análisis e Investigación A.C.

Aquino-Moreschi, Alejandra, and Isis Contreras-Pastrana. 2016. "Comunidad, jóvenes y generación: disputando subjetividades en la Sierra Norte de Oaxaca." *Revista Latinoamericana de Ciencias Sociales, Niñez y Juventud* 14 (1): 463–75.

Archibold, Randal C. 2012. "Deaf Officers Keep Watch over Crime in Oaxaca." *The New York Times*, December 18, 2012. https://www.nytimes.com/2012/12/19/world/americas/deaf-officers-keep-watch-over-crime-in-oaxaca.html.

Arellano Chávez, Daniel. 2010. "México: a 3 años de la ocupación de Oaxaca, a 10 años de la creación de la Policía Federal Preventiva (PFP)." http://old.kaosenlared.net/noticia/mexico-3-anos-ocupacion-oaxaca-10-anos-creacion-policia-federal-preven.

Auyero, Javier. 2003. *Contentious Lives: Two Argentine Women, Two Protests, and the Quest for Recognition*. Durham, NC: Duke University Press.

Babb, Florence. 2010. *The Tourism Encounter: Fashioning Latin American Nations and Histories*. Stanford, CA: Stanford University Press.

Bacon, David. 2004. *The Children of NAFTA: Labor Wars on the U.S./Mexico Border*. Berkeley: University of California Press.

———. 2012. "Blood on the Silver: The High Cost of Mining Concessions in Oaxaca." *NACLA*, November 8, 2012. https://nacla.org/news/2012/11/9/blood-silver-high-cost-mining-concessions-oaxaca.

Barkin, David. 2002. "The Reconstruction of a Modern Mexican Peasantry." *Journal of Peasant Studies* 3 (1): 73–90.

Baronnet, Bruno, Mariana Mora Bayo, and Richard Stahler-Sholk. 2011. *Luchas "muy otras": zapatismo y autonomía en las comunidades indígenas de Chiapas.* Mexico City: Centro de Investigaciones y Estudios Superiores en Antropología Social, Universidad Autónoma Metropolitana Xochimilco, and Universidad Autónoma de Chiapas.

Baulch, Emma. 2007. *Making Scenes: Reggae, Punk, and Death Metal in 1990s Bali.* Durham, NC: Duke University Press.

Beas, Juan Carlos, and Manuel Ballesteros. 2010. *Magonismo y movimiento indígena en México.* 6th ed. Mexico City: Ediciones Yope Power.

Blackwell, Maylei. 2011. *¡Chicana Power!: Contested Histories of Feminism in the Chicano Movement.* Austin: University of Texas Press.

———. 2017. "Geographies of Indigeneity: Indigenous Migrant Women's Organizing and Translocal Politics of Place." *Latino Studies* 15 (2): 156–81.

Bloch, Stefano. 2019. *Going All City: Struggle and Survival in LA's Graffiti Subculture.* Chicago: University of Chicago Press.

Bonilla, Yarimar, and Jonathan Rosa. 2015. "#Ferguson: Digital Protest, Hashtag Ethnography, and the Racial Politics of Social Media in the United States." *American Ethnologist* 42 (1): 4–17.

Bonilla-Silva, Eduardo. 2013 *Racism without Racists: Color-Blind Racism and the Persistence of Racial Inequality in America.* 4th ed. Lanham: Rowman & Littlefield Publishers.

Booth, William. 2012. "Mexico Is Now a Top Producer of Engineers, but Where Are Jobs?" *Washington Post*, October 28, 2012. https://www.washingtonpost.com/world/the_americas/mexico-is-now-a-top-producer-of-engineers-but-where-are-jobs/2012/10/28/902db93a-1e47-11e2-8817-41b9a7aaabc7_story.html.

Briseño, Patricia, Gaspar Romero, Fabiola Xicoténcatl, Rolando Aguilar, and Emmanuel Rincón. 2017. "Sismo dañó 80 mil casas; no habrá clases en todas las escuelas de Chiapas y Oaxaca." *Excélsior*, September 11, 2017. http://www.excelsior.com.mx/nacional/2017/09/11/1187530.

Brodkin, Karen. 2007. *Making Democracy Matter: Identity and Activism in Los Angeles.* New Brunswick, NJ: Rutgers University Press.

Browne, Simone. 2015. *Dark Matters.* Durham, NC: Duke University Press.

Bufe, Chaz, and Mitchell Cowen Verter. 2005. *Dreams of Freedom: A Ricardo Flores Magón Reader.* Oakland: AK Press.

CASOTA (Casa Autónoma Solidaria Oaxaqueña de Trabajo Autogestivo), Colectivo Libertario Magonista, and Voces Oaxaqueñas Construyendo Autonomia y Libertad (VOCAL). 2008. "En defenza de nuestro espacio Casota." La Haine, November 8, 2008, uploaded December 9, 2008. https://www.lahaine.org/mm_ss_mundo.php/atacada-la-casa-autonoma-solidaria-oaxaq.

Castellanos, Laura. 2007. *Mexico armado, 1943–1981*. Mexico City: Ediciones ERA.

Castellanos, M. Bianet. 2010. *A Return to Servitude: Maya Migration and the Tourist Trade in Cancún*. Minneapolis: University of Minnesota Press.

Castells, Manuel. 1996. *The Rise of the Network Society*. Malden, MA: Blackwell.

CCIODH (Comisión Civil Internaciónal de Observación por los Derechos Humanos). 2007. *Informe sobre los hechos de Oaxaca: 5ª visita*. Barcelona: Gráficas Lunas.

Chassen de López, Francie R. 2004. *From Liberal to Revolutionary Oaxaca: The View from the South: Mexico, 1867–1911*. University Park: Pennsylvania State University Press.

Chatterjee, Partha. 2004. *The Politics of the Governed: Reflections on Popular Politics in Most of the World*. New York: Columbia University Press.

Clay, Andreana. 2008. "'Like an Old Soul Record': Black Feminism, Queer Sexuality, and the Hip-Hop Generation." *Meridians* 8 (1): 53–73.

CMDPDH (Comisión Mexicana de Defensa y Promoción de Los Derechos Humanos). 2015. "En México 281 mil 418 personas son víctimas del desplazamiento interno forzado por la violencia." February 26, 2015. http://cmdpdh.org/2015/02/en-mexico-281-mil-418-personas-son-victimas-del-desplazamiento-interno-forzado-por-la-violencia/.

CODIGO-DH (Comité de Defensa Integral de Derechos Humanos Gobixha). 2014. *Rostros de la impunidad en Oaxaca: perspectivas desde la defensa integral de los derechos humanos*. Oaxaca, Mexico. https://codigodh.org/wp-content/uploads/2019/12/2014-Rostros-Informe-DDHH.pdf.

Coffey, Mary Katherine. 2002. "Muralism and the People: Culture, Popular Citizenship, and Government in Post-Revolutionary Mexico." *The Communication Review* 5 (1): 7–38.

Cole, Jennifer, and Deborah Durham, eds. 2006. *Generations and Globalization: Youth, Age, and Family in the New World Economy*. Bloomington: Indiana University Press.

Contralínea. 2010. "Seguimiento emboscada San Juan Copala," April 27, 2010. https://www.contralinea.com.mx/archivo-revista/2010/04/27/grupo-armado-ataca-caravana-de-paz-en-oaxaca/.

Cook, Maria Lorena.1996. *Organizing Dissent: Unions, the State, and the Democratic Teachers' Movement in Mexico*. University Park: Pennsylvania State University Press.

Cornejo, Kency. 2017. "Visual Counter Narratives: Central American Art on Migration and Criminality." *Journal of Commonwealth and Postcolonial Studies* 5 (1): 63–82.

Coulthard, Glen Sean. 2014. *Red Skin, White Masks: Rejecting the Colonial Politics of Recognition*. Minneapolis: University of Minnesota Press.

Cruz-Manjarrez, Adriana. 2013. *Zapotecs on the Move: Cultural, Social, and Political Processes in Transnational Perspective*. New Brunswick, NJ: Rutgers University Press.

De Genova, Nicholas, and Nathalie Peutz, eds. 2010. *The Deportation Regime: Sovereignty, Space, and the Freedom of Movement*. Durham, NC: Duke University Press.

De la Cadena, Marisol, and Orin Starn, eds. 2007. *Indigenous Experience Today*. Oxford: Berg Publishers.

De Landa, Manuel. 1997. *A Thousand Years of Nonlinear History*. New York: Zone Books.

De Marinis, Natalia. 2016. "Mujeres indígenas ante los escenarios del miedo en México: (In)seguridad y resistencias en la región triqui de San Juan Copala, Oaxaca." *Estudios Latinoamericanos*, no. 37, 65–86.

Denham, Diane and C.A.S.A. Collective. 2008. *Teaching Rebellion: Stories from the Grassroots Mobilization in Oaxaca*. Oakland, CA: PM Press.

Díaz Montes, Fausto. 2009. "Elecciones y protesta social en Oaxaca." In *La APPO: ¿rebelión o movimiento social? Nuevas formas de expresión ante la crisis*, edited by Víctor Raúl Martínez Vásquez, 247–73. Oaxaca: Universidad Autónoma Benito Juárez de Oaxaca.

Díaz-Polanco, Héctor, and Consuelo Sánchez. 2002. *México diverso: el debate por la autonomía*. Mexico City: Siglo XXI.

Dominguez, Neidi. 2014. "Our Vision Is More Than a DREAM: What's Next for Immigrant Youth?" Truthout, February 21, 2014. https://truthout.org/articles/our-vision-is-more-than-a-dream-whats-next-for-immigrant-youth/.

Draper, Susana. 2018. *1968 Mexico: Constellations of Freedom and Democracy*. Durham, NC: Duke University Press.

Dunlap, Alexander. 2017. "Wind Energy: Toward a 'Sustainable Violence' in Oaxaca." *NACLA Report on the Americas* 49 (4): 483–88. https://doi.org/10.1080/10714839.2017.1409378.

Durham, Deborah, and Jennifer Cole. 2006 *Generations and Globalization*. Indiana University Press.

Dzenovska, Dace, and Iván Arenas. 2012. "Don't Fence Me In: Barricade Sociality and Political Struggles in Mexico and Latvia." *Comparative Studies in Society and History* 54 (3): 644–78.

Escobar, Arturo. 2008. *Territories of Difference: Place, Movements, Life, Redes*. Durham, NC: Duke University Press.

Espinoza, Dionne. 2001. "'Revolutionary Sisters': Women's Solidarity and Collective Identification among Chicana Brown Berets in East Los Angeles, 1967–1970." *Aztlán* 26 (1): 17–58.

Estes, Adam Clark. 2013. "An Army of the Deaf Watches Surveillance Cameras in Mexico." Gizmodo, November 22, 2013. https://gizmodo.com/an-army-of-the-deaf-watch-surveillance-cameras-in-mexic-1469815334.

Esteva, Gustavo. 2010. "The Oaxaca Commune and Mexico's Coming Insurrection." *Antipode* 42 (4): 978–93.

Esteva, Gustavo, Rubén Valencia and David Venegas, eds. 2008. *Cuando hasta las piedras se levantan: Oaxaca, México 2006*. Buenos Aires: Antropofagia.

Fanon, Frantz. (1967) 2005. *The Wretched of the Earth*. Translated by Richard Philcox. Reprint, New York: Grove Press.

Faudree, Paja. 2013. *Singing for the Dead: The Politics of Indigenous Revival in Mexico*. Durham, NC: Duke University Press.

Feixa, Carles. 1999. *De jóvenes, bandas y tribus*. Barcelona: Editorial Ariel.

Fernandes, Sujatha. 2010. *Who Can Stop the Drums? Urban Social Movements in Chávez's Venezuela*. Durham, NC: Duke University Press.

———. 2011. *Close to the Edge: In Search of the Global Hip Hop Generation*. London: Verso.

Fitting, Elizabeth. 2006. "Exporting Corn, Importing Labor: The Neoliberal Corn Regime, GMO's and the Erosion of Mexican Biodiversity." *Agriculture and Human Values* 23:15–26.

Flores, Jerry. 2016. *Caught Up: Girls, Surveillance, and Wraparound Incarceration*. Oakland: University of California Press.

Forensic Architecture. 2017. "The Enforced Disappearance of the Ayotzinapa Students." Forensic Architecture, September 26, 2017. https://forensic-architecture .org/investigation/the-enforced-disappearance-of-the-ayotzinapa-students.

Forman, Murray. 2002. The 'Hood Comes First: Race, Space, and Place in Rap and Hip-Hop. Middletown, CT: Wesleyan University Press.

Forman, Murray, and Mark Anthony Neal, eds. 2004. *That's the Joint!: The Hip-Hop Studies Reader*. 1st ed. New York: Routledge.

Fortun, Kim, Mike Fortun, and Steven Rubenstein. 2010. Editors' introduction to "Emergent Indigeneities." *Cultural Anthropology* 25 (2): 222–34.

Foucault, Michel. 1990. *The History of Sexuality*. New York: Vintage Books.

Fox, Jonathan. 1994. "The Difficult Transition from Clientelism to Citizenship: Lessons from Mexico." *World Politics* 46 (2): 151–84.

Franco Ortiz, Itandehui. 2014. "El sur nunca muere: desplazamientos del graffiti en la ciudad de Oaxaca." Master's thesis, UNAM (Universidad Nacional Autónoma de Mexico), Mexico City.

Fredericks, Rosalind. 2014. "'The Old Man Is Dead': Hip Hop and the Arts of Citizenship of Senegalese Youth." *Antipode* 46 (1): 130–48. https://doi.org/10.1111/anti .12036.

Fregoso, Rosa-Linda, and Cynthia Bejarano, eds. 2010. *Terrorizing Women: Feminicide in the Americas*. Durham, NC: Duke University Press.

Gálvez, Alyshia. 2018. *Eating NAFTA: Trade, Food Policies, and the Destruction of Mexico*. Oakland: University of California Press.

García, Ángel. 2014. "2 de Octubre en Oaxaca: de la conmemoración al vandalismo desenfrenado." E-Consulta.com, October 2, 2014. http://e-oaxaca.com/nota/2014 -10-02/seguridad/2-de-octubre-en-oaxaca-de-la-conmemoracion-al-vandalismo -desenfrenado.

García Leyva, Jaime. 2005. *Radiografía del Rock en Guerrero*. Mexico City: La Cuadrilla de la Langosta.

Gasparello, Giovanna, and Jaime Quintana Guerrero. 2009. *Otras geografías: Experiencias de autonomías indígenas en México*. Mexico City: Universidad Autónoma Metropolitana, Unidad Iztapalapa.

Gibler, John. 2009. *Mexico Unconquered: Chronicles of Power and Revolt*. San Francisco: City Lights.

———. 2017. *I Couldn't Even Imagine that They Would Kill Us: An Oral History of the Attacks against the Students of Ayotzinapa*. San Francisco: City Lights.

Goeman, Mishuana. 2013. *Mark My Words: Native Women Mapping Our Nations*. Minneapolis: University of Minnesota Press.

Gómez, Alan Eladio. 2016. *The Revolutionary Imaginations of Greater Mexico: Chicana/o Radicalism, Solidarity Politics, and Latin American Social Movements.* Austin: University of Texas Press.

Gómez-Barris, Macarena. 2017. *The Extractive Zone: Social Ecologies and Decolonial Perspectives.* Durham, NC: Duke University Press.

Gonzales, Patrisia. 2003. *The Mud People: Chronicles, Testimonios & Remembrances.* San José, CA: Chusma House.

González, Miguel. 2015. "Indigenous Territorial Autonomy in Latin America: An Overview." *Latin American and Caribbean Ethnic Studies* 10 (1): 10–36. https://doi.org/10.1080/17442222.2015.1034438.

González, Pablo. 2011. "Autonomy Road : The Cultural Politics of Chicana/o Autonomous Organizing in Los Angeles, California." PhD diss., Austin: University of Texas.

González Castillo, Eduardo, and Patricia M. Martin. 2015. "Cultural Activism, Hegemony, and the Search for Urban Autonomy in the City of Puebla, Mexico." *Environment and Planning D: Society and Space* 33 (1): 52–66.

Gosa, Travis L. 2015. "The Fifth Element: Knowledge." In *The Cambridge Companion to Hip-Hop,* edited by Justin A. Williams, 56–70. Cambridge Companions to Music. Cambridge: Cambridge University Press. https://doi.org/10.1017/CCO9781139775298.007.

Greene, Shane. 2016. *Punk and Revolution: Seven More Interpretations of Peruvian Reality.* Durham, NC: Duke University Press.

Grillo, Ioan. 2017. "The Paradox of Mexico's Mass Graves." *New York Times,* July 19, 2017. https://www.nytimes.com/2017/07/19/opinion/mexico-mass-grave-drug-cartel.html.

Grosfoguel, Ramón. 2007. "The Epistemic Decolonial Turn." *Cultural Studies* 21 (2–3): 211–23. https://doi.org/10.1080/09502380601162514.

Guerrero, Jaime. 2017. "85.4% de la juventud en la informalidad en Oaxaca: INEGI." *Página3 - Noticias desde Oaxaca con perspectiva de género y responsabilidad social* (blog). May 2, 2017. http://pagina3.mx/2017/05/85-4-de-la-juventud-en-la-informalidad-en-oaxaca-inegi/.

Hale, Charles R. 2005. "Neoliberal Multiculturalism." *PoLAR: Political and Legal Anthropology Review* 28 (1): 10–19.

Hall, Stuart. 1993. "What Is This 'Black' in Black Popular Culture?" Social Justice 20 (1/2): 104–14.

Hall, Stuart, and Tony Jefferson, eds. 2006. *Resistance through Rituals: Youth Subcultures in Post-War Britain.* 2nd ed. London: Routledge.

Harrison, Faye V., ed. 1997. *Decolonizing Anthropology: Moving Further toward an Anthropology for Liberation.* 2nd ed. Arlington, VA: American Anthropological Association.

Hebdige, Dick. 1979. *Subculture: The Meaning of Style.* 1st ed. London: Routledge.

Hernández, Anabel. 2017. *La verdadera noche de Iguala: La historia que el gobierno quiso ocultar.* New York: Vintage Español.

Hernandez, Daniel. 2011. *Down and Delirious in Mexico City: The Aztec Metropolis in the Twenty-First Century.* New York: Scribner.

Hernández, Gabriela. 2015. "Propone el PAN poblano hasta 12 años de cárcel para grafiteros." *Proceso Portal de Noticias,* January 29, 2015. https://www.proceso.com .mx/394459/propone-el-pan-poblano-hasta-12-anos-de-carcel-para-grafiteros.

Hernández Castillo, Rosalva Aída, and Shannon Speed. 2012. "Mujeres indígenas presas en México y Estados Unidos: Un desafío hemisférico para los estudios indígenas." *LASA Forum* 43 (1): 17–20.

Hernández Navarro, Luis. 2013. "Las mentiras sobre la reforma educativa." *La Jornada,* January 15, 2013. http://www.jornada.unam.mx/2013/01/15/opinion /017a1pol.

Holston, James. 2008. *Insurgent Citizenship: Disjunctions of Democracy and Modernity in Brazil.* Princeton, NJ: Princeton University Press.

Huerta, Irving. 2010. "Permitió Gobierno de Oaxaca ataque a caravana humanitaria en 2010 (investigación especial)." *Aristegui Noticias,* May 12, 2010. https:// aristeguinoticias.com/1205/mexico/permitio-gobierno-de-oaxaca-ataque-a -caravana-humanitaria-en-2010/.

Human Rights Watch. 2017. "Mexico." https://www.hrw.org/worldreport/2017 /country-chapters/mexico.

INEGI (Instituto Nacional de Estadística y Geografía). 2010. "Lengua indígena." Censos y conteos. Población y Vivienda. https://www.inegi.org.mx/temas /lengua/.

Jackson, Jean E., and Kay B. Warren. 2005. "Indigenous Movements in Latin America, 1992–2004: Controversies, Ironies, New Directions." *Annual Review of Anthropology* 34 (1): 549–73. https://doi.org/10.1146/annurev.anthro.34.081804.120529.

Jagger, Bianca. 2017. "Stop the Murder of Environmental Defenders in Latin America." *HuffPost* (blog). May 10, 2017. Last modified September 11, 2017. https://www.huffpost.com/entry/stop-the-murder-of-environmental-defenders -in-latin-america_b_591345c4e4b0e3bb894d5caf.

Johnson, Gaye Theresa. 2013. *Spaces of Conflict, Sounds of Solidarity: Music, Race, and Spatial Entitlement in Los Angeles.* Berkeley: University of California Press.

Johnson, Reed. 2003. "McDonald's Loses a Round to Oaxacan Cultural Pride." *Los Angeles Times,* January 5, 2003. http://articles.latimes.com/2003/jan/05 /entertainment/ca-johnson5, accessed October 2, 2014

Juris, Jeffrey S. 2008. *Networking Futures: The Movements against Corporate Globalization.* Experimental Futures Series. Durham, NC: Duke University Press.

———. 2012. "Reflections on #Occupy Everywhere: Social Media, Public Space, and Emerging Logics of Aggregation." *American Ethnologist* 39 (2): 259–79.

Juris, Jeffrey S., and Alex Khasnabish. 2013. *Insurgent Encounters: Transnational Activism, Ethnography, and the Political.* Durham, NC: Duke University Press.

Juris, Jeffrey S. and Geoffrey H. Pleyers. 2009. Alter-activism: emerging cultures of participation among young global justice activists. *Journal of Youth Studies* 12 (1): 57–75.

Kelley, Robin D. G. 1996. *Race Rebels: Culture, Politics, and the Black Working Class*. New York: Free Press.

———. 2003. *Freedom Dreams: The Black Radical Imagination*. Rev. ed. Boston: Beacon Press.

Khasnabish, Alex. 2008. *Zapatismo beyond Borders: New Imaginations of Political Possibility*. Toronto: University of Toronto Press.

Lee, Brianna, and Danielle Renwick. 2017. "Mexico's Drug War." Council on Foreign Relations. https://www.cfr.org/backgrounder/mexicos-drug-war.

Lefebvre, Henri. 1968. *Le droit à la ville*. Paris: Anthropos.

———. 1991. *The Production of Space*. Oxford: Blackwell.

Lomnitz, Claudio. 2001. *Deep Mexico, Silent Mexico: An Anthropology of Nationalism*. Minneapolis: University of Minnesota Press.

López Bárcenas, Francisco. 2009. *San Juan Copala: dominación política y resistencia popular. De las rebeliones de Hilarión a la formación del municipio autónomo*. 2nd ed. Mexico City: Universidad Autónoma Metropolitana.

López Dávila, Alfonso. 2018. "Oaxaca, con Murat al frente, se vuelve el más violento contra activistas y derechos indígenas." Sin Embargo, February 17, 2018. http://www.sinembargo.mx/17-02-2018/3386014.

Low, Setha M. 2000. *On the Plaza: The Politics of Public Space and Culture*. Austin: University of Texas Press.

Magaña, Maurice Rafael. 2010. "Analyzing the Meshwork as an Emerging Social Movement Formation: An Ethnographic Account of the Popular Assembly of the Peoples of Oaxaca (APPO)." *Journal of Contemporary Anthropology* 1 (1), article 5: 72–87.

———. 2014. "Building Horizontal Political Cultures: Youth Activism and the Legacy of the Oaxacan Social Movement of 2006." In *Rethinking Latin American Social Movements: Radical Action from Below*, edited by Richard Stahler-Sholk, Harry E. Vanden and Marc Becker, 67–83. Boulder, CO: Rowman & Littlefield.

———. 2015. "From the Barrio to the Barricades: Grafiteros, Punks and the Remapping of Urban Space." In "New Dimensions in the Study and Practice of Mexican and Chicano Social Movements." Special issue, *Social Justice* 42 (1): 170–83.

Maira, Sunaina. 2013. *Jil Oslo: Palestinian Hip Hop, Youth Culture, and the Youth Movement*. Washington, DC: Tadween Publishing.

Maldonado, Benjamín. 2000. "El indio y lo indio en el anarquismo magonista." *Cuadernos del Sur* 6 (15): 115–38.

Maldonado-Torres, Nelson. 2007. "On the Coloniality of Being: Contributions to the Development of a Concept." *Cultural Studies* 21 (2–3): 240–70. https://doi.org/10.1080/09502380601162548.

Martínez Luna, Jaime. 2010. *Eso que llaman comunalidad*. Oaxaca: Conaculta.

Martínez Vásquez, Victor Raul. 2007. *Autoritarismo, movimiento popular y crisis política: Oaxaca 2006*. Oaxaca: Universidad Autónoma Benito Juárez de Oaxaca.

Massey, Doreen B. 1994. *Space, Place, and Gender*. Minneapolis: University of Minnesota Press.

Matías Rendón, Ana. 2015. "Los Jamás Conquistados / Ayuuk ja'ay." *Revista Sinfín* (blog). January 11, 2015. http://www.revistasinfin.com/articulos/los-jamas-conquistados-ayuuk-jaay/.

McAdam, Doug. 1999. *Political Process and the Development of Black Insurgency, 1930–1970.* Chicago: University of Chicago Press.

McCaughan, Edward J. 2012. *Art and Social Movements: Cultural Politics in Mexico and Aztlán.* Durham, NC: Duke University Press.

McTighe, Laura, and Megan Raschig. 2019. "An Otherwise Anthropology." Society for Cultural Anthropology, Theorizing the Contemporary, *Fieldsites* Series. July 31, 2019. https://culanth.org/fieldsights/series/an-otherwise-anthropology.

Melucci. Alberto. 1996. *Challenging Codes.* Rev. ed. Cambridge: Cambridge University Press.

Meyer, David S. and Nancy Whittier. 1994. "Social Movement Spillover." *Social Problems* 41 (2): 277–98.

Mignolo, Walter D. 2000. *Local Histories/Global Designs.* Princeton, N.J: Princeton University Press.

Milan, Stefania. 2015. "When Algorithms Shape Collective Action: Social Media and the Dynamics of Cloud Protesting." *Social Media + Society* (July). https://journals.sagepub.com/doi/full/10.1177/2056305115622481.

Mittermaier, Amira. 2014. "Bread, Freedom, Social Justice: The Egyptian Uprising and a Sufi Khidma." *Cultural Anthropology* 29 (1): 54–79.

Moore, Ryan, and Michael Roberts. 2009. "Do-It-Yourself Mobilization: Punk and Social Movements." *Mobilization: An International Quarterly* 14 (3): 273–91.

Mora, Mariana. 2017. "Ayotzinapa and the Criminalization of Racialized Poverty in La Montaña, Guerrero, Mexico." *PoLAR: Political and Legal Anthropology Review* 40 (1): 67–85.

————. 2018. *Kuxlejal Politics: Indigenous Autonomy, Race, and Decolonizing Research in Zapatista Communities.* Austin: University of Texas Press.

Morris, Nancy. 2014. "New Song in Chile: Half a Century of Musical Activism." In *The Militant Song Movement in Latin America: Chile, Uruguay, and Argentina,* edited by P. Vila, 19–44. Lanham, MD: Lexington Books.

Narro, Victor, Kent Wong, and Janna Shadduck-Hernández. 2007. "The 2006 Immigrant Uprising: Origins and Future." *New Labor Forum* 16 (1): 49–56.

Negrín, Diana. 2019. *Racial Alterity, Wixarika Youth Activism, and the Right to the Mexican City.* Tucson: University of Arizona Press.

Nguyen, Mimi Thi. 2012. Afterword in *Punkademics: The Basement Show in the Ivory Tower,* edited by Zack Furness, 217–23. New York: Minor Compositions/Autonomedia.

Nikpour, Golnar. 2012. "'White Riot' Another Failure. . . ." *Maximum Rocknroll* (blog). January 17, 2012. http://www.maximumrocknroll.com/white-riot-another-failure/.

Norget, Kristin. 2010. "A Cacophony of Autochthony: Representing Indigeneity in Oaxacan Popular Mobilization." *Journal of Latin American and Caribbean Anthropology* 15 (1): 116–43.

Organization of American States (OAS). 2017. "IACHR Condemns Murders of Human Rights Defenders in the Region." February 7, 2017. http://www.oas.org /en/iachr/media_center/preleases/2017/011.asp.

Osorno, Diego. 2007. *Oaxaca sitiada: La primera insurrección del siglo XXI*. Mexico City: Random House Mondadori.

Overmyer-Velázquez, Mark. 2006. *Visions of the Emerald City: Modernity, Tradition, and the Formation of Porfirian Oaxaca, Mexico*. Durham, NC: Duke University Press.

Pabón-Colón, Jessica Nydia. 2018. *Graffiti Grrlz: Performing Feminism in the Hip Hop Diaspora*. New York: NYU Press.

Paredes, Julieta. 2008. *Hilando fino: desde el feminismo comunitario*. La Paz, Bolivia: CEDEC and Comunidad Mujeres Creando Comunidad.

Pérez Alfonso, Jorge A. 2016. "Justifica Cué el uso de la fuerza: La PF reconoce que utilizó armas de fuego." *La Jornada*, June 20, 2016. http://www.jornada.unam .mx/2016/06/20/politica/003n2pol.

Pérez, Ramona. 2003. "From Ejido to Colonia: Reforms to Article 27 and the Formation of an Urban Landscape in Oaxaca." *Urban Anthropology and Studies of Cultural Systems and World Economic Development* 32 (3): 343–75.

Pérez-Ruiz, Maya Lorena, and Laura R. Valladares de la Cruz. 2014. *Juventudes indígenas de hip hop y protesta social en América Latina*. Mexico City: Instituto Nacional de Antropología e Historia.

Perillo, J. Lorenzo. 2013. "Theorising Hip-Hop and Street Dance in the Philippines." *International Journal of Asia Pacific Studies* 9 (1): 69–96.

Perry, Marc D. 2016. *Negro Soy Yo: Hip Hop and Raced Citizenship in Neoliberal Cuba*. Refiguring American Music series. Durham, NC: Duke University Press.

Polletta, Francesca. 1999 "'Free Spaces' in Collective Action." *Theory and Society* 28 (1): 1–38.

Poma, Alice, and Tommaso Gravante. 2016. "'Fallas del sistema': análisis desde abajo del movimiento anarcopunk en México." *Revista Mexicana de Sociología* 78 (3): 437–67.

Poniatowska, Elena. 2002. "Toledo versus McDonald's." *La Jornada*, November 13, 2002. https://www.jornada.com.mx/2002/11/13/017a1pol.php?origen=index.html.

Poole, Deborah. 2007. "The Right to Be Heard." *Socialism and Democracy* 21:113–16.

———. 2009. "Affective Distinctions: Race and Place in Oaxaca." In *Contested Histories of Public Space: Memory, Race and Nation*, edited by D. Walkowitz and L. Knauer, 197–225. Durham, NC: Duke University Press.

———. 2011. "Mestizaje, Distinction, and Cultural Presence: The View from Oaxaca." In *Histories of Race and Racism*, edited by Laura Gotkowitz, 179–203. Durham, NC: Duke University Press.

Poole, Deborah, and Gerardo Rénique. 2017. "Cashing in on the Quakes." *NACLA Report on the Americas* 49 (4): 387–90. https://doi.org/10.1080/10714839.2017 .1409004.

Postero, Nancy. 2017. *The Indigenous State: Race, Politics, and Performance in Plurinational Bolivia*. Oakland: University of California Press.

Pough, Gwendolyn D., Elaine Richardson, Aisha Durham, and Rachel Raimist, eds. 2007. *Home Girls Make Some Noise!: Hip-Hop Feminism Anthology*. 1st ed. Mira Loma, CA: Parker Publishing.

Pulido, Laura. 2006. *Black, Brown, Yellow, and Left: Radical Activism in Los Angeles*. 1st ed. Berkeley: University of California Press.

Quijano, Anibal. 2000. "Coloniality of Power, Eurocentrism, and Latin America." *Nepantla: Views from South* 1 (3): 533–80.

Quijano, Jesús. 2006. *La Guelaguetza en Oaxaca: fiesta, relaciones interétnicas y procesos de construcción simbólica en el contexto urbano*. Mexico City: CIESAS.

Rabasa, Magalí. 2019. *The Book in Movement: Autonomous Politics and the Lettered City Underground*. Pittsburgh: University of Pittsburgh Press.

Ramirez, Renya K. 2007. *Native Hubs: Culture, Community and Belonging in Silicon Valley and Beyond*. Durham, NC: Duke University Press.

Rancière, Jacques. 2010. *Dissensus: On Politics and Aesthetics*. London: Bloomsbury.

Redmond, Shana L. 2013. *Anthem: Social Movements and the Sound of Solidarity in the African Diaspora*. New York: NYU Press.

Reed, T. V. 2005. *The Art of Protest: Culture and Activism from the Civil Rights Movement to the Streets of Seattle*. Minneapolis: University of Minnesota Press.

"Reflexion de un joven estudiante libertario respeto a los acontecimientos en Oaxaca." 2011. *Radio Tepache* (blog), February 16, 2011. http://tepacheradio.blogspot.com/2011/02/reflexion-de-un-joven-estudiante.html.

Reguillo Cruz, Rossana. 2012. *Culturas juveniles: formas políticas del desencanto*. Rev. ed. Buenos Aires: Siglo Veintiuno Editores.

Ribando Seelke, Clare, and Kristin Finklea. 2010. "US-Mexican Security Cooperation: The Mérida Initiative and Beyond." Congressional Research Service Report R41349, updated June 29, 2017. https://crsreports.congress.gov/product/pdf/R/R41349.

Rios, Victor M. 2017. *Human Targets: Schools, Police, and the Criminalization of Latino Youth*. Chicago: University of Chicago Press.

Rivera Cusicanqui, Silvia. 1986. *Oprimidos pero no vencidos: luchas del campesinado aymara y qhechwa de Bolivia, 1900–1980*. Geneva: United Nations Research Institute for Social Development.

———. 2012. "Ch'ixinakax Utxiwa: A Reflection on the Practices and Discourses of Decolonization." *South Atlantic Quarterly* 111 (1): 95–109.

Rivera-Salgado, Gaspar. 1999. "Mixtec Activism in Oaxacalifornia: Transborder Grassroots Political Strategies." *American Behavioral Scientist* 42 (9): 1439–58.

Robles Hernández, Sofía and Rafael Cardoso Jiménez, eds. 2007. *Floriberto Díaz escrito: Comunalidad, energía viva del pensamiento mixe*. Vol. 14. Mexico City: Universidad Nacional Autónoma de México.

Rocha, Ricardo. 2011. "'Juvenicidio' masivo." *El Universal*, September 21, 2011. http://www.eluniversal.com.mx/editoriales/54790.html.

Rodríguez, Roberto Cintli. 2014. *Our Sacred Maíz Is Our Mother: Indigeneity and Belonging in the Americas*. Tucson: University of Arizona Press.

Romano, Octavio. 1968. "The Anthropology and Sociology of the Mexican-Americans: The Distortion of Mexican-American History." *El Grito* 2 (1): 13–26.

Rosaldo, Renato and William V. Flores. 1997. "Identity, Conflict, and Evolving Latino Communities: Cultural Citizenship in San Jose, California." In *Latino Cultural Citizenship: Claiming Identity, Space, and Rights*, edited by William V. Flores and Rina Benmayor, 57–96. Boston: Beacon Press.

Rosas, Gilberto. 2012. *Barrio Libre: Criminalizing States and Delinquent Refusals of the New Frontier*. Durham, NC: Duke University Press.

Rubin, Jeffrey W. 1997. *Decentering the Regime: Ethnicity, Radicalism, and Democracy in Juchitán, Mexico*. Durham, NC: Duke University Press.

Rubio-Goldsmith, Raquel, Celestino Fernández, Jessie K. Finch, and Araceli Masterson-Algar, eds. 2016. *Migrant Deaths in the Arizona Desert: La Vida No Vale Nada*. Tucson: University of Arizona Press.

Saldaña-Portillo, María Josefina. 2003. *The Revolutionary Imagination in the Americas and the Age of Development*. Durham, NC: Duke University Press.

———. 2016. *Indian Given: Racial Geographies across Mexico and the United States*. Durham, NC: Duke University Press.

———. 2017. "Critical Latinx Indigeneities: A Paradigm Drift." *Latino Studies* 15 (2): 138–55.

Sánchez, Julián. 2010. "Caravana parte a San Juan Copala." *El Universal*, June 8, 2010. https://archivo.eluniversal.com.mx/estados/76319.html.

Sánchez-López, Luis. 2017. "Learning from the Paisanos: Coming to Consciousness in Zapotec LA." *Latino Studies* 15 (2): 242–46.

Saraví, Gonzalo A., and Sara Makowski. 2011. "Social Exclusion and Subjectivity: Youth Expressions in Latin America." *Journal of Latin American and Caribbean Anthropology* 16 (2): 315–34.

Schloss, Joseph Glenn. 2009. *Foundation: B-Boys, B-Girls, and Hip-Hop Culture in New York*. Oxford: Oxford University Press.

Scott, James C. 1990. *Domination and the Arts of Resistance: Hidden Transcripts*. New Haven, CT: Yale University Press.

Sieder, Rachel, ed. 2002. *Multiculturalism in Latin America: Indigenous Rights, Diversity and Democracy*. Houndmills, Basingstoke, UK: Palgrave Macmillan.

Simpson, Audra. 2014. *Mohawk Interruptus: Political Life across the Borders of Settler States*. Durham, NC: Duke University Press.

Sitrin, Marina. 2006. *Horizontalism: Voices of Popular Power in Argentina*. Edinburgh: AK Press.

———. 2014. "Definitions of Horizontalism and Autonomy." *NACLA Report on the Americas* 47 (3): 44–45. https://doi.org/10.1080/10714839.2014.11721832.

Smith, Christen A. 2016. *Afro-Paradise: Blackness, Violence, and Performance in Brazil*. Urbana: University of Illinois Press.

Smith, Linda Tuhiwai. 1999. *Decolonizing Methodologies: Research and Indigenous Peoples*. London: Zed Books.

Sojoyner, Damien M. 2016. *First Strike: Educational Enclosures in Black Los Angeles*. Minneapolis: University of Minnesota Press.

Solano, Laura Poy. 2013. "La privatización educativa corre paralela en México y EU: expertos." *La Jornada*, January 5, 2013. http://www.jornada.unam.mx/2013/01/05/sociedad/025n1soc.

Sotelo Marbán, José. 2008. *Oaxaca: Insurgencia civil y terrorismo de estado*. Mexico City: Ediciones Era.

Speed, Shannon. 2008. *Rights in Rebellion: Indigenous Struggle and Human Rights in Chiapas*. Stanford, CA: Stanford University Press.

———. 2016. "States of Violence: Indigenous Women Migrants in the Era of Neoliberal Multicriminalism." *Critique of Anthropology* 36 (3): 280–301.

Speed, Shannon, R. Aída Hernández Castillo, and Lynn M. Stephen, eds. 2006. *Dissident Women: Gender and Cultural Politics in Chiapas*. Austin: University of Texas Press.

Stephen, Lynn. 1999. "The Construction of Indigenous Suspects: Militarization and the Gendered and Ethnic Dynamics of Human Rights Abuses in Southern Mexico." *American Ethnologist* 26 (4): 822–42. https://doi.org/10.1525/ae.1999.26.4.822.

———. 2002. *Zapata Lives!: Histories and Cultural Politics in Southern Mexico*. Berkeley: University of California Press.

———. 2007. *Transborder Lives: Indigenous Oaxacans in Mexico, California, and Oregon*. Durham, NC: Duke University Press.

———. 2013. *We Are the Face of Oaxaca: Testimony and Social Movements*. Durham, NC: Duke University Press.

Stone, Livia K. 2019. "Compañeros and Protagonismo: The Ethics of Anti-Neoliberal Activism and the Frente de Pueblos en Defensa de la Tierra (FPDT) of Atenco, Mexico." *Journal of Latin American and Caribbean Anthropology* 24 (3): 709–26. https://doi.org/10.1111/jlca.12415.

TallBear, Kim. 2014. "Standing with and Speaking as Faith: A Feminist-Indigenous Approach to Inquiry." Research note. *Journal of Research Practice* 10 (2), article N17. http://jrp.icaap.org/index.php/jrp/article/view/405/371.

Tarrow, Sidney G. 1998. *Power in Movement: Social Movements and Contentious Politics*. Cambridge: Cambridge University Press.

Tatro, Kelley. 2018. "Performing Hardness: Punk and Self-Defense in Mexico City." *International Journal of Cultural Studies* 21 (3): 242–56. https://doi.org/10.1177/1367877916688503.

Tilly, Charles. 1978. *From Mobilization to Revolution*. Reading, MA: Addison-Wesley.

———. 1986. *The Contentious French*. Cambridge, MA: Belknap Press.

Tonkiss, Fran. 2005. *Space, the City and Social Theory: Social Relations and Urban Forms*. Cambridge, MA: Polity.

Tuckman, Jo. 2015. "Thousands Displaced by Mexico's Drug Wars: Government Is 'Deaf and Blind' to Our Plight." *Guardian*, April 3, 2015. https://www.theguardian.com/world/2015/apr/03/mexico-drug-wars-thousan ds-displaced-from-homes.

Turner, Victor W. 1969. *The Ritual Process: Structure and Anti-Structure*. Chicago: Aldine Publishing.

Urteaga, Maritza. 2011. *La construcción juvenil de la realidad: Jóvenes mexicanos contemporáneos*. Mexico City: UAM, Unidad Iztapalapa J. Pablos.

Valenzuela Arce, José Manuel. 2009. *El futuro ya fue: socioantropología de l@s jóvenes en la modernidad*. Tijuana: El Colegio de la Frontera Norte.

———. 2015. *Juvenicidio: Ayotzinapa y las vidas precarias en América Latina y España*. Barcelona: NED ediciones.

VOCAL. 2007a. "Participacion de VOCAL en el segundo congreso de la APPO." http://www.rojoynegro.info/articulo/sections/participacion-vocal-el-segundo-congreso-la-appo-0.

———. 2007b. "VOCAL Manifiesto." Kaos en la red, March 9, 2007. https://kaosenlared.net/manifiesto-de-vocal/.

Walsh, Catherine. 2007. "Shifting the Geopolitics of Critical Knowledge." *Cultural Studies* 21 (2–3): 224–39. https://doi.org/10.1080/09502380601162530.

Warren, Kay B., and Jean E. Jackson. 2002. Indigenous movements, self-representation, and the state in Latin America. Austin: University of Texas Press.

White, E. Frances. 2010. *Dark Continent of Our Bodies: Black Feminism & Politics of Respectability*. Philadelphia: Temple University Press.

Willis, Paul. 1977. *Learning to Labour: How Working Class Kids Get Working Class Jobs*. Westmead, Farnborough: Saxon House.

Winegar, Jessica. 2016. "A Civilized Revolution: Aesthetics and Political Action in Egypt." *American Ethnologist* 43 (4): 609–22.

Wood, William Warner. 2008. *Made in Mexico: Zapotec Weavers and the Global Ethnic Art Market*. Bloomington: Indiana University Press.

Wortham, Erica Cusi. 2013. *Indigenous Media in Mexico: Culture, Community, and the State*. Durham, NC: Duke University Press.

Yúdice, George. 2004. *The Expediency of Culture: Uses of Culture in the Global Era*. Durham, NC: Duke University Press.

Zibechi, Raúl. 2010. *Dispersing Power: Social Movements as Anti-State Forces*. Translated by Ramor Ryan. Oakland, CA: AK Press.

Zilberg, Elana. 2011. *Space of Detention: The Making of a Transnational Gang Crisis between Los Angeles and San Salvador*. Durham, NC: Duke University Press.

Zires, Margarita. 2009. "Estrategias de comunicación y acción política: movimiento social de la APPO 2006." In *La APPO: ¿Rebelión o movimiento social? (nuevas formas de expresión ante la crisis)*, edited by Víctor Raúl Martínez Vásquez, 161–95. Oaxaca: Universidad Autónoma Benito Juárez de Oaxaca.

Zolov, Eric. 1999. *Refried Elvis: The Rise of the Mexican Counterculture*. Berkeley: University of California Press.

INDEX

insurgency, 9, 14, 56, 83, 147; and
indigeneity, 10–17, 70–73, 87
International Comunalidad
Conferences, 67
Iván Illich Center for Documentation, 100

Jackson, Jean, 72
jamás conquistados, los. *See* Ayuukjä'äy
Johnson, Gaye Theresa, 32
Jornada, La (newspaper), 92, 178n15
José (interviewee), 24
Juárez, Benito, 56, 142, 144
Juárez Hernández, Rufino, 111
Juárez Punk, El, 142–47, 149
Jueves de Café y Trova, 89
Juntas de Buen Gobierno (Good Gover-
nance Councils), 61
juvenicidios, 10

Kahnawà:ke Mohawk, 5
Kaos en la Red, 101
Kelley, Robin D. G., 15, 49, 83, 102

Latin America, 22, 25, 48, 61, 86; and
Indigenous people, 5, 69, 76–78, 82, 99,
163; and social movements, 48, 61, 89,
96, 147, 178n2; and the United States,
151, 176n14. *See also* Central America;
individual countries and regions
Lefebvre, Henri, 2, 18, 23, 31, 126, 173n1
liberationists, 14, 21, 30, 47, 58, 145–46,
174n10; and 2006 generation politics,
75–79, 107, 110, 136, 155–58; in solidarity
with the teacher's union, 38–39, 44;
and youth collectives, 57, 62, 89–91,
97*fig.*, 164, 180n5
Liberationist Social Center (CESOL), 20,
38, 49, 53, 75, 158, 164
López Martínez, Aristeo, 34, 176n11
López Obrador, Andrés Manuel, 26, 177n7
Lorenzo Sampablo Cervantes Community
Store, 94

Magonismo, 75–79, 144, 177n12
Magón Punk, 75–77*fig.*, 144–45
Maldonado, Benjamín, 75, 100
Maldonado-Torres, Nelson, 12
maquiladoras, 13

Marcha de las Cacerolas, La, 32. *See also*
Channel 9 (COR–TV); Radio Cacerola
March of the Pots and Pans, the. *See*
Marcha de las Cacerolas, La
Mare Advertencia Lirika (interviewee),
87–88, 99, 135–41, 153–55, 167, 180n1
Maribel (interviewee), 32
Martínez Luna, Jaime, 11, 64, 71, 78, 177n4
Marxism, 78, 100
Marxist-Leninist, 61
Massey, Doreen, 106
Maya, 13, 181n9
McDonald's, 23–24
media collectives, 66, 100–101, 134, 179n13.
See also global Indymedia collectives;
Kaos en la Red; Rojo y Negro
Mentes Liberadas, 20–21, 28, 38–43, 49–52,
75, 157, 165
Mérida Initiative, 8
Mesoamerica Integration and Development
Project, 5, 69, 173n4
mestizaje, 70, 147
mestizos, 12, 72, 147, 177n11
metal music, 15
metal prehispánico, 15
methodology of the book, 2, 13, 15, 17, 103.
See also anthropology; ethnography
Mexica. *See* Aztecs
Mexican army, 4, 104, 130. *See also* military
Mexican Commission on Defense and
Promotion of Human Rights, 9
Mexican Liberal Party (PLM), 76, 178n15
Mexican national census, 11, 70
Mexican state, the, 4–5, 8, 66, 154–55;
postrevolutionary, 25, 138
Mexico: Cancún, 13; Chiapas, 56, 65, 67,
177n8; Guerrero, 62, 163, 173–74n5,
175n14; Isthmus of Tehuantepec, 43, 73,
167; Michoacán, 96; Nayarit, 13, 154,
178n4; post-NAFTA, 18, 170; Puebla,
67, 150; San Salvador Atenco, 27;
Sonora, 62; southern, xviii, 6–7, 72, 81,
173n4. *See also* Indigenous Mexico;
Mexico City; Oaxaca
Mexico City, xvii, 11, 27, 64, 69, 90, 105;
and punk culture, 16, 142–47, 151,
181n11, 182n4; student movement in, 56,
176n2

Olivera, Omar, 100
Olmos García, Salvador, 165
organizing, 1–4, 6, 21, 99–103, 163–66,
169–71, 178n2, 179n6; and art, 159–60;
and barricades, 35–36, 44–45; being
prevented from, 155–56; and counterspaces, 37–40, 60, 83, 86–93, 96, 106–
19, 134–38; everyday, 125, 133; and *feminismo comunitario*, 167–68; grassroots,
139–42, 145; horizontal, xviii, 10, 19,
121–23, 136–38, 174n11, 175n5; and
indigeneity, 11–17, 55–58, 62–72, 76,
79–80; and radio, 31–34; vertical, 25, 30,
53; youth, 9–10, 23, 174n9, 177n5
Otra Campaña, La, 26–27, 62, 65, 68
Overmyer-Velásquez, Mark, 23

palimpsest, 78, 123, 149, 173n2; as metaphor,
3–4, 107, 169–70; and space, 125–32; and
time, 57, 72, 144
paramilitary, 6, 34, 39, 56, 69, 110–11, 121,
176n11; repression by, xiv, 14, 89, 103
Paredes, Julieta, 167
Party of Democratic Revolution (PRD), 26,
61, 155
Path of the Jaguar for the Regeneration of
Our Memory, The. *See* Sendero del
Jaguar por la Regeneración de Nuestra
Memoria, El
patriarchy, 63, 141
People's Front in Defense of the Land
(Frente del Pueblo en Defensa de la
Tierra), 27, 67
Plan Puebla Panamá, 33, 173
Plaza de la Danza, 91
police, 3, 31, 62, 112–13, 130*fig.*, 156, 180n1,
181n12; of bodies, 7, 22, 86, 159; militarized, xiv–xvii, 14, 95, 109, 170, 176n11;
and punks, 46–49, 142. *See also* Federal
Preventative Police (PFP); military, and
police; police surveillance; police violence; teachers' union encampment,
police disruption of
police surveillance, 2, 86–89, 104–5, 125–
26, 150–56
police violence, 20–21, 27–29, 37–40, 56,
92, 104–6, 126–27, 136; and punks,
154–56, 158, 165, 181n10

political dissent, 9, 30, 104, 150
political prisoners, 49, 60, 94, 158, 179n6.
See also prisons
political solidarities, 60
Popular Revolutionary Front (FPR), 61
popular security force, xiv, 37–42
poverty, 7, 33, 86, 148
prisons, 114, 150, 154, 178n4; carceral state, 8
protagonismo, 63, 157, 177n9
public transcripts, 2–3. *See also* hidden
transcripts
pueblos originarios, 71
punk movement, xiv, 11, 14–15, 57, 63,
174n12, 175n15, 181n10; anarcho-, 155–58,
164–66; and counterspaces, 82, 89, 159;
and graffiti crews, 18, 159; and indigeneity, 22, 55, 70, 74–79; and Okupa,
46–53; and political participation, xviii,
10, 175n14; as popular security force,
37–44; and rebel aesthetics, 135–47;
supporting the teacher's union, 20, 28.
See also Juárez Punk, El; Magón Punk;
Okupa

Quijano, Aníbal, 11–12

race, 8, 181n4; and access to the space, 23,
33, 168–72; and indigeneity, 72, 136. *See
also* racial geographies; racialization;
racism
racial geographies, 5, 8, 44, 70, 86, 136, 147,
160
racialization, xviii, 10–11, 72, 172; of bodies,
139; of space, 4–8; of women, 168
racism, 12, 42, 172
radical hope, xviii, 10
radical politics, 2, 18, 54, 78–79
Radio Cacerola, 32–34. *See also* Channel 9
(COR–TV); Marcha de las Cacerolas,
La (the March of the Pots and Pans)
Radio Plantón, 27, 29, 31, 112
Radio Universidad, 29, 32, 39, 42, 176n10
Ramirez, Renya, 13
Rancière, Jacques, 107, 150, 180n1
rapping. *See* emceeing
rebel aesthetics: definition of, 15, 18, 135;
and the imaginary, 136, 138, 142–48,
168; politics of, 125–32, 134

Founded in 1893,
UNIVERSITY OF CALIFORNIA PRESS
publishes bold, progressive books and journals
on topics in the arts, humanities, social sciences,
and natural sciences—with a focus on social
justice issues—that inspire thought and action
among readers worldwide.

The UC PRESS FOUNDATION
raises funds to uphold the press's vital role
as an independent, nonprofit publisher, and
receives philanthropic support from a wide
range of individuals and institutions—and from
committed readers like you. To learn more, visit
ucpress.edu/supportus.